JAZZOLOGY

The Encyclopedia of
JAZZ THEORY
for All Musicians

by
ROBERT RAWLINS

and
NOR EDDINE BAHHA

Edited by Barrett Tagliarino

ISBN 978-0-634-08678-6

7777 W. BLUEMOUND RD. P.O. BOX 13819 MILWAUKEE, WI 53213

In Australia Contact:
Hal Leonard Australia Pty. Ltd.
4 Lentara Court
Cheltenham, Victoria, 3192 Australia
Email: ausadmin@halleonard.com

Visit Hal Leonard Online at
www.halleonard.com

PREFACE

Jelly Roll Morton once claimed to have invented jazz in 1902. Aside from being one of the most brazen remarks ever made by a musician, the statement approximates the truth in two regards: Jelly Roll certainly was one of the significant pioneers of jazz, and 1902 seems as good a year as any for identifying the birth of the genre. Perhaps a reasonable conclusion is that jazz is just over one hundred years old and Jelly Roll was one of its most colorful characters.

The first century of jazz has been a tremendously active one. Spawning a host of substyles and a plethora of creative giants, jazz moved through many high points in terms of geographic or regional activity. A brief chronological list would include Storyville in the 1910s, Chicago in the 1920s, the "Golden Age" of jazz recording in the late 1920s, Kansas City in the 1930s, 52nd street in the 1940s, and the classic jazz LPs of the 1950s and 60s.

But if I were to choose the optimum time to be a jazz musician, that time would be now. For just as popular culture began to lose interest in jazz, the larger musical and educational establishment began to embrace it. During the past several decades thousands of dedicated jazz scholars and musicians have been hard at work creating, preserving, studying, and exploring the music. Jazz is now a viable course of study in most universities, and more young musicians are being trained in this style than ever before. Interest in jazz is greater and more widespread today than at any time in its history. This is borne out by the collaborative effort that resulted in *Jazzology*: that of an American college professor and an African jazz musician, united by our deep dedication to this great art form. The jazz age is here.

Fifty years ago, no one would have thought of "jazz theory" as a separate entity. Certainly there were devices and procedures in jazz that were not easily explained by traditional theory, but no separate discipline had been devised to account for the differences. Gradually, over the years, the creative activities of jazz musicians began to receive labels and explanations. Slowly but surely, a separate realm of jazz theory began to develop. In recent years a myriad of methods, details, devices, procedures, and explanations have appeared in print, in lectures, or sometimes only in conversation, to add to the discipline. This book is an attempt to assimilate, organize, and explain those phenomena as understood by the authors.

This book differs from others of its type in several ways. First of all, the authors themselves have completely different backgrounds that are likely to reflect the diverse audiences for which this book is intended. One is a keyboard player and composer, self-taught, with a deep knowledge of jazz literature and vast experience with several genres of non-Western music. The other is a saxophonist, college professor, with a Ph.D. in musicology, and extensive experience as a jazz and theater musician in the United States. Our backgrounds are as different as can be. Our understanding of the music is as one.

This book also differs from others in its pedagogical view. The authors have presented the material in the order that seemed best for assimilation. While explanations are given in encyclopedic fashion for use as ready reference, it has been borne in mind that many will wish to work through the book methodically. Moreover, a classroom setting was always envisioned. Thus ample exercises are provided that will not only give students practice with the material, but also provide teachers with a way of judging students' understanding and progress.

Finally, wherever possible, theoretical explanations are given for the concepts presented. In our view, it is not enough to provide practical instructions for the working musician. Describing what jazz musicians do without attempting to understand why those procedures work can lead to a formulaic approach to jazz. The student will have no alternative except to extract and insert devices exactly as he or she learned them, without alteration or creative input. On the other hand, understanding the theoretical reasons behind musical decisions opens up vast realms for experimentation and creativity. Instead of "copping that lick" from a favorite musician, a student will be able to invent an original one that works the same way. And that is what jazz is all about.

The authors welcome any discussion or comments pertaining to this book. They can be reached at: **jazzology@gmail.com**.

CONTENTS

INTERVALS

To understand any melodic or harmonic discussion, one must understand intervals. An interval measures the space between two pitches. The smallest interval in Western music is the semitone or half step (either name may be used). This is the distance from one key to the next on the piano, for instance from C to C♯.

The next-to-smallest interval is the **tone**, or **whole step**. This is the distance between notes that are two keys apart on the piano. For instance, from C to D is a whole step. The semitone and tone form the basis for measurement of larger intervals.

Interval measurements have two parts: **quantity** and **quality**. The quantity, or numeric value, is determined by the musical alphabet: C D E F G A B. For example, the interval formed by the notes C and G will always be some type of 5th, regardless of the quality of C or G (flat or sharp).

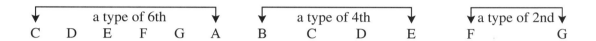

Major and Perfect Intervals

The *quality* of an interval is determined by comparison with the intervals found in the **major scale**. When compared with a major scale, a whole step is found to be equal to the distance from the first to the second note, giving us yet another name for it: the **major second**.

It should be committed to memory that any major scale contains half steps (h) between scale degrees 3–4 and 7–8, and whole steps (W) between all other pairs of notes. The half steps in any scale can be indicated with a wedge-shaped mark, or caret symbol (^). Here's the major scale in the key of C.

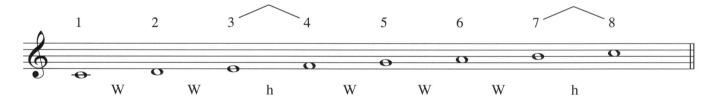

The distance from the root to the various pitches in the major scale form the basic intervals against which all others are measured. These eight intervals are divided into two basic types, **perfect** or **major**.

- **Perfect**: unisons, 4ths, 5ths, octaves
- **Major**: 2nds, 3rds, 6ths, 7ths

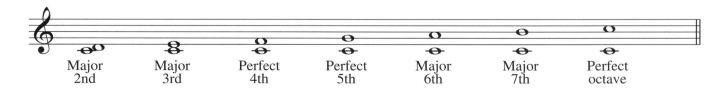

Minor, Diminished, and Augmented Intervals

A **chromatic half step** is a half step written as the same note twice with different accidentals (i.e., G–G♯), while a **diatonic half step** is a half step that uses two different note names (i.e., G♯–A). The appearance on the staff may be different, but the interval is the same.

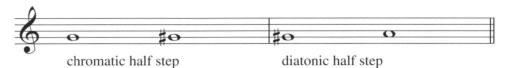

Major and perfect intervals may be **augmented** (increased in size) or **diminished** (reduced in size) by either type of half step to change their qualities.

Major and **perfect** intervals become **augmented** when the upper note is raised by a half step, or the lower note is lowered by a half step. The process may be referred to as **augmentation**.

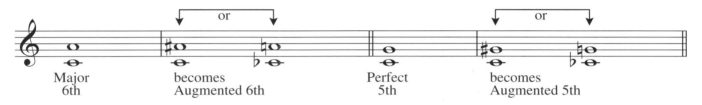

Intervals can be made larger by placing a ♯ before the upper note or a ♭ before the lower note.

An **augmented** interval becomes **doubly augmented** when the upper note is raised by a half step, or the lower note is lowered by a half step.

When a **major** interval is diminished by a half step it becomes **minor**.

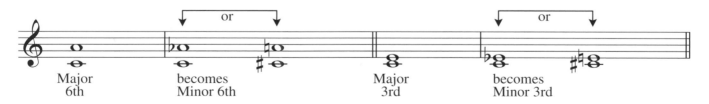

Intervals can be made smaller by placing a ♭ before the upper note or a ♯ before the lower note.

Through **diminution, minor** and **perfect** intervals become **diminished**.

A **diminished** interval becomes **doubly diminished** when the upper note is lowered by a half step or the lower note is raised by a half step.

This illustration will help you remember the order of changing interval qualities. Notice that perfect intervals jump directly to diminished; there is no such interval as a minor 5th!

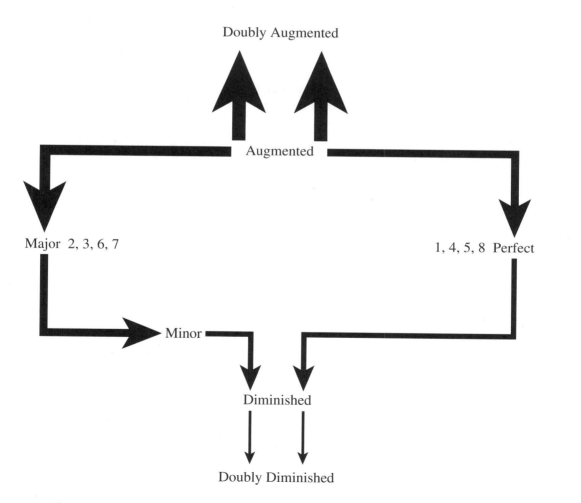

It is possible for notes and intervals to have different names in spite of containing the same number of half steps and producing the same sound. For instance, an augmented 2nd above C is D♯, and a minor 3rd above C is E♭. Both intervals contain three half steps, but occur in different situations. These intervals (as well as the notes D♯ and E♭) are referred to as **enharmonic equivalents**.

When an interval is **inverted** (the order of the notes is changed, i.e. C to D becomes D to C) you'll find its complementary partner. For instance, an inverted major 2nd is equal to a minor 7th, an inverted major 3rd is a minor 6th, and so on. Notice that inverted major intervals are minor (and vice versa) while inverted perfect intervals are still perfect. These interval pairs should also be memorized, to facilitate further study.

Inversions of Major Scale Intervals

| Minor 7th | Minor 6th | Perfect 5th | Perfect 4th | Minor 3rd | Minor 2nd | Perfect unison |

Interval Abbreviations

Intervals are used so often in describing chords and scales that they are sometimes named in an extremely abbreviated way. Learn to recognize these variations in interval names.

- Perfect and major intervals are implied by no mention of their quality at all: 5 for P5 (perfect 5th), 7 for M7 (major 7th), etc.
- The word "sharp," or the sharp symbol (♯) is often used instead of "augmented" (or its abbreviations, "**aug**" or "**+**").
- The word "flat" or the flat symbol (♭) is often used instead of "**min**" or "**m.**"
- When a perfect interval (1, 4, 5, or 8) becomes diminished, it may be written with one flat (♭) instead of **dim** or **d**, or the diminished symbol ("**°**").
- When a major interval (2, 3, 6, 7) becomes minor, it too is often written with a ♭ instead of **min** or **m**, for instance, ♭2 instead of **m2**.
- When a major interval becomes diminished, it can be written with two flats (♭♭) instead of **dim** or **d**, for instance ♭♭7 instead of **dim7** or **d7**.

This all boils down to exclusive use of the ♭, ♯, or no symbol to accomplish shorthand (though precise) naming of any interval. You should, however, still know that a ♭3 is **minor**, while a ♭5 is **diminished**.

When naming intervals, place the symbol before the number, not after: ♯4, ♭7, etc. (When naming **notes**, place the symbol after: F♯, B♭.)

The augmented 4th/diminished 5th intervals are also called the **tritone**, abbreviated **TT**. A tritone equals three whole steps.

The charts below list all the intervals up to the 13th, as they are most commonly named in the jazz idiom. (Not all possible augmented and diminished names are listed.)

Intervals smaller than an octave are called **simple intervals**.

Semitones	Interval	Abbreviations
0	Unison	
1	Min 2nd	m2, ♭2
2	Maj 2nd	M2, 2
3	Min 3rd/Aug 2nd	m3, ♭3, ♯2, +2
4	Maj 3rd	M3, 3
5	Perfect 4th	P4, 4
6	Dim 5th /Aug 4th	♭5, ♯4, +4
7	Perfect 5th	P5, 5
8	Min 6th/Aug 5th	m6, ♭6, ♯5, +5
9	Maj 6th/Dim 7th	M6, 6, ♭♭7, d7, °7
10	Min 7th	m7, ♭7
11	Maj 7th	M7, 7
12	Octave	P8, 8

Intervals larger than an octave are called **compound intervals**. They may be analyzed as a simple interval raised by an octave.

Semitones	Interval	Abbreviations	Simple Equivalent
13	Min 9th	m9, ♭9	♭2 + octave
14	Maj 9th	M9, 9	2 + octave
15	Aug 9th/Min 10th	♯9, ♭10	♭3 + octave
16	Maj 10th	M10, 10	3 + octave
17	Perfect 11th	P11, 11	4 + octave
18	Aug 11th	♯11, +11	♯4 + octave
19	Perfect 12th	P12, 12	5 + octave
20	Min 13th	m13, ♭13	♭6 + octave
21	Maj 13th	M13, 13	6th + octave

Consonant Intervals and Dissonant Intervals

A **harmonic** interval results if the notes are played at the same time, while a **melodic** interval occurs when the notes are played successively. The method of measuring intervals is the same for both harmonic and melodic intervals.

Harmonic intervals may be either **consonant** or **dissonant**.

- Consonant intervals occur when two pitches that are sounded together produce an agreeable sound. Consonance gives the impression of unity, cohesion, and stability.

- Dissonant intervals, on the other hand, occur when two pitches that are sounded together produce a sound that seems to require modification or resolution. Dissonance gives the impression of instability, tension, and the need to resolve to a consonance.

Consonant intervals are subdivided into three types:

PERFECT CONSONANCE	IMPERFECT CONSONANCE	VARIABLE CONSONANCE
Perfect Octave: P8 Perfect Fifth: P5	Major Third: M3 Minor Third: m3 Major Sixth: M6 Minor Sixth: m6	Perfect Fourth: P4

All the other intervals are dissonant.

Enharmonically equivalent intervals usually appear in different contexts and thus should not be considered the same as their counterparts, i.e. while a minor 3rd is consonant, an augmented 2nd is dissonant.

The consonance or dissonance of the perfect 4th interval also depends on the context in which it occurs. If it stands alone on the root of a key center, it is dissonant. It may be consonant if it occurs over other notes as part of a chord.

This is a simplification of the traditional rules of consonance and dissonance that were established during the Renaissance. Although the descriptions may not apply to the way modern ears hear these intervals, the principles still form the basis for Western harmonic practice, including jazz harmony.

Chapter 1 Exercises

1. Identify the following intervals.

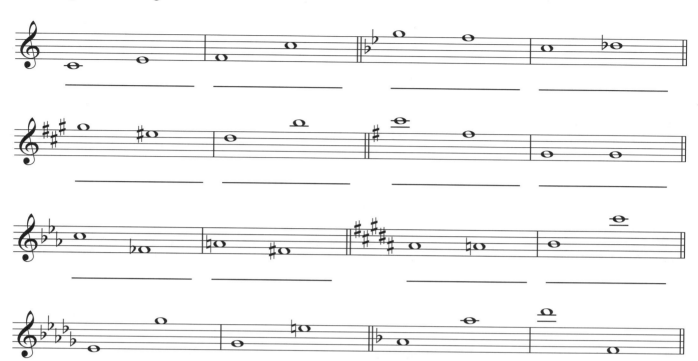

2. Provide the following intervals above the given pitch.

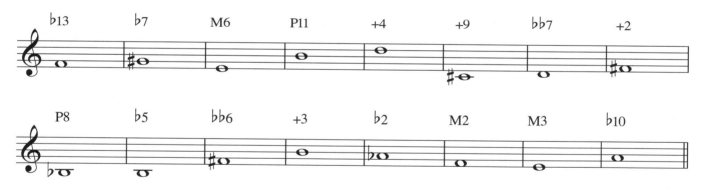

3. Write the following intervals (from any pitch).

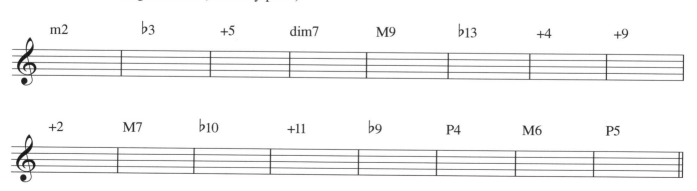

4. Write the following intervals above the given note.

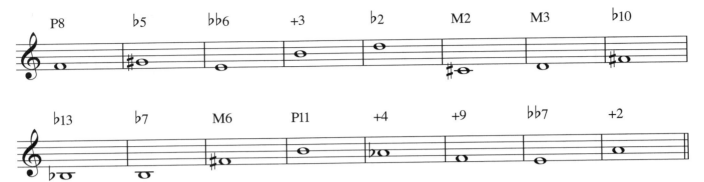

5. Identify each interval as either consonant or dissonant by writing "con" or "diss" below.

JAZZ HARMONY BASICS

Two or more notes played simultaneously form a chord. Chords are traditionally constructed by stacking 3rds on top of each other. This method of building chords is called tertian harmony. The note at the bottom of the stack of 3rds is called the root of the chord. The next note, a 3rd higher, is called the 3rd, and the next higher, a 5th above the root, is called the 5th, and so on. A complete list of chords would include 7th, 9th, 11th, and 13th chords. They are so named because of the interval between the root and the highest note in the stack of 3rds.

Triads

As the name implies, a triad consists of three notes, or two superimposed 3rds:

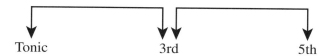

The triad type depends on the quality of the 3rds that are included in the chord. The most convenient way to build or analyze triads is to start with a major triad, by taking the 1st, 3rd, and 5th notes of the major scale. The other forms can be seen as alterations of the major triad, as shown below.

Here are triads built from the root C, and their commonly-used names.
Major Triad (1–3–5): C, CM, Cmaj

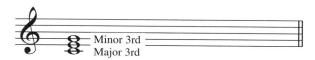

Minor Triad (1–♭3–5): C-, Cm, Cmin

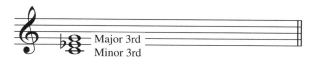

Augmented Triad (1–3–♯5): C+, Caug

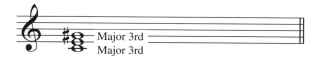

Diminished Triad (1–♭3–♭5): C°, Cdim

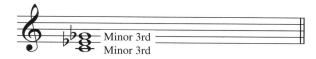

In the **suspended** triad, the 4th replaces the 3rd. Despite the implications of the word "suspension" (and the rules of consonance and dissonance), the 4th does not need to resolve to the 3rd (although it may). In jazz, unlike classical music, the suspended triad (usually called a "**sus chord**") is a fixed and stable harmonic structure unto itself.

Suspended Triad (1–4–5): C4, Csus or Csus4

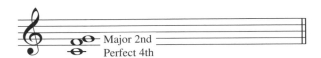

In order to hear the sonority of each triad quality, play the root in the bass with your left hand and the triad with your right hand. The resultant sound is stronger and easier to recognize when the root is reinforced in this way.

All the previous triads are said to be in **root position**: the root of the chord lies at the bottom of the triad.

Triad Inversion

Inverting a triad rearranges the notes so that the 3rd or the 5th is placed at the bottom of the triad structure. The lowest note is called the **bass**, which is not to be confused with the root. The bass is the lowest note in any chord inversion. The root is the note on which the chord is built and cannot change.

Play the triad qualities discussed so far in all twelve keys, in all possible inversions. Include them in your practice routine until you can play them without using the book or writing them down. Wind players should practice triad **arpeggios** (chords played one note at a time) in all keys and inversions.

7th Chords

7th chords provide the building blocks of jazz harmony. Unlike classical music, which relies upon the triad as the fundamental structure, jazz uses triads infrequently. Instead, most jazz styles employ 7th chords as the basic harmonic unit. A 7th chord is built by stacking three 3rds on top of one another so that the total distance from the root to the uppermost note forms the interval of a 7th. There are seven commonly-used types of 7th chords. While the content of these chords is specific and unchanging, the symbols used to designate these chords can vary substantially, as can be seen below.

- The Major 7th Chord, written: M7, maj7, or Δ
- The Minor/Major 7th Chord, written: -M7, -maj7, m(maj7), mM7, or -Δ
- The Minor 7th Chord, written: -7, min7, or m7
- The Half-Diminished 7th or m7♭5 Chord, written: m7♭5, min7(♭5), m7(♭5), or ø
- The Diminished 7th Chord, written: °7 or dim7
- The Dominant 7th Chord, written: 7
- The Suspended Dominant 7th Chord, written: 7sus or 7sus4

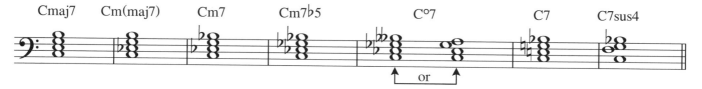

Here are the correct intervallic spellings of these chords with examples built on C.

TYPE OF CHORD	EXAMPLE	FORMULA
Major 7th	C–E–G–B	1–3–5–7
Minor 7th	C–E♭–G–B♭	1–♭3–5–♭7
Half-Diminished 7th	C–E♭–G♭–B♭	1–♭3–♭5–♭7
Diminished 7th	C–E♭–G♭–B♭♭(A)	1–♭3–♭5–♭♭7
7th or Dominant	C–E–G–B♭	1–3–5–♭7
Major/Minor 7th	C–E♭–G–B	1–♭3–5–7
Suspended Dominant	C–F–G–B♭	1–4–5–♭7

As with triads, 7th chords should be practiced in all keys, in all inversions, without reading them. Wind (and indeed all) players should practice them as arpeggiated lines in all keys and inversions.

Chord Extensions

A chord is generally extended by adding notes that increase its richness and dissonance without altering its function. These notes are called **extensions**, **tensions**, or **upper structures**; the results are called **extended chords**, and in some cases **polychords** or **polytonal/polymodal chords**.

Extensions beyond the 7th follow the same pattern of construction as 7th chords with a general rule being that if a chord tone of the triad is altered (raised or lowered), the quality is also altered, while alteration of extensions does not change the quality of the chord. Here are some examples of 7th chords with natural and altered extensions.

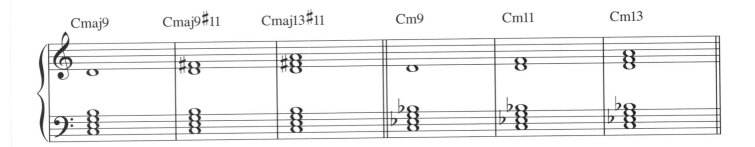

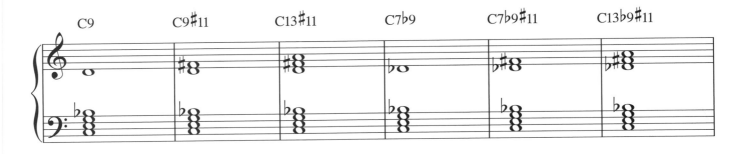

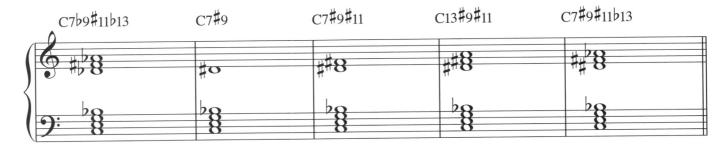

Not all possible extensions and alterations are used in jazz harmony. The ones that work with a specific chord type are said to be "available." The ear is one's best guide. The following suggestions for available extensions are intended to apply to **bebop** or **"straight-ahead"** (as opposed to **free**, **avant garde**, or **modern**) jazz harmony, and are sanctioned by more than fifty years of nearly total consensus among jazz musicians.

Major triad:
- add 6th and 9th,
- add M7 and 13,
- add ♯11 to either of the above for extra dissonance.

Minor 7th (functioning as ii):
(See Chapter 3 for more on chord function.)
- add 9,
- add 11 and/or 13 above the 9th for extra dissonance.

Minor triad (functioning as i):
- add 6 and 9,
- add M7,
- add 9 and/or 13 above for extra dissonance.

7sus4:
- add 9 and/or 13.

Dominant 7th (functioning as V7):
- add 9 and possibly 13,
- add ♭9 and possibly ♭13,
- add ♯11 to either of the above for extra dissonance. In short, V7 can take all extensions except 11 and M7.

Diminished 7th:
- may add the note a whole step above any chord tone.
- diminished chord extensions do not usually receive numbers.

Half-Diminished 7th:
- add M9,
- add 11,
- add M13 for extra dissonance.

There are many common chord types. Keep in mind that a little dissonance can go a long way, and that diminished 7th or m7♭5 chords may be dissonant enough in context without extensions.

Upper Structures

In common practice, upper structures are triads played in the right hand that have a different root from the left-hand chord. The upper structure is usually a major or a minor triad. The result is an extended chord that can be specifically referred to as a **polychord**. Upper structures are very common over dominant 7th chords, but can also occur over other chord qualities.

G13♭9

The top three notes of the upper structure, B–E–G♯, form an E major triad, whereas G♯ is really the ♭9 and E is the 13th of the G7 chord. The individual notes retain their harmonic function within G7 and are heard as a unit. The resulting sound is really in two keys at once: E and G major, thus making a **polytonality**.

To build an upper structure, play the 1, 3, and ♭7 (the 5th is usually avoided) with the left hand, and form any triad with the right hand, observing what note is played on the top of the chord or in the melody. Guitarists will likely play only the root and ♭7 as the lower part of the polychord, to free up fingers to play the upper structure.

Triads that contain the P4 (P11) or M7 in relation to the left-hand chord (the only two extensions not allowed on a dominant chord) should be avoided. The 3rd should not be placed in the left hand if it occurs in the right hand. (Occasionally, the 3rd will not appear at all.) Here are some examples on G7.

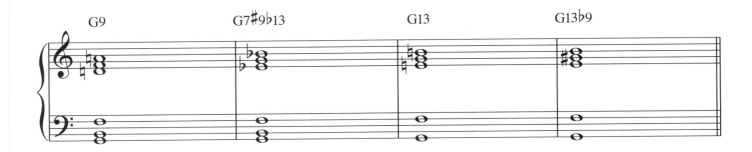

Because of the large number of extensions available on a dominant chord, it is possible to build nearly the entire chromatic scale by ascending through upper structures on the same chord.

In practice, jazz pianists and arrangers prefer simplifying upper-structure notation so as to make the chords easy to read and play. Accordingly, another way to notate the preceding examples is to indicate a left-hand chord under a right-hand triad and place a horizontal line in between:

The following upper structures are the most common examples used in jazz **comping** (accompaniment) and arranging. They should be practiced in all twelve keys.

Chords functioning as iim7 or iim7♭5:

Chords functioning as V7 (the G7 chord is played by the left hand, while the right hand plays possible triads):

Chords functioning as Imaj7:

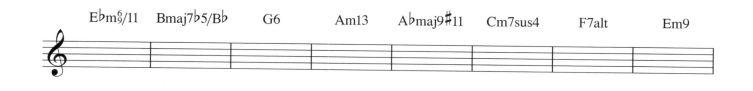

Ebm⁶/11 Bmaj7b5/Bb G6 Am13 Abmaj9#11 Cm7sus4 F7alt Em9

B°7 Bm7b5 Dm6 F+7 G9#11 F#m(maj7) Bmaj13 F°7

3. Write the tritone interval(s) found in each of the following chords.

C#7 Em⁶ F9#11 Bbmaj7b5 Ebm7b5 D13 Ab7 F#m⁶

C#°7 Eb9#5 Gm11b5 B7b9#11 Fmaj13 Abm9b5 C7sus4b9 G7alt

4. Write the 3rd and the 7th of the following chords. (Dominant 11th or sus4 chords have a P4th instead of a 3rd.)

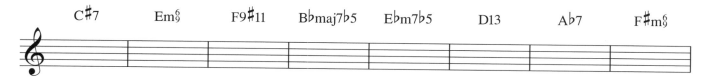

Am7 D7 Emaj7 Bbm7b5 G°7 F#m11 Abmaj9 G13b9

Eb7#9 E°7 D7alt Dbmaj13 Fm7 Bbm(maj7) Gb7 Db11

Am(maj7b5) G9sus4 Em7b5 Am9 D°7 E7b5#9 F#°7 Eb7sus4

5. Identify each chord and specify whether it is best understood as an upper structure (US), hybrid (Hyb), or slash chord (Sl). Some structures are subject to multiple interpretations.

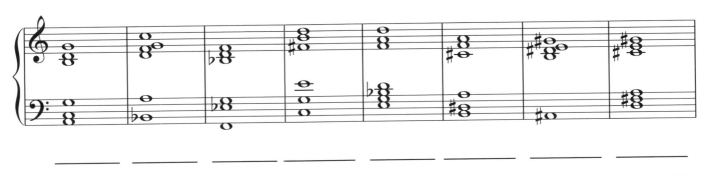

6. Identify each chord. All chords are in root position. If it contains wrong notes or inappropriate upper structures, place an "x" beneath the chord.

SCALES AND MODES

A **scale** is a stepwise arrangement of notes/pitches contained within an octave. Major and minor scales contain seven notes or **scale degrees**. A scale degree is designated by an arabic numeral indicating the position of the note within the scale.

Major Scale

In addition to recalling that there are half steps (h) between scale degrees 3–4 and 7–8, with whole steps (W) between all other pairs of notes, notice that a major scale contains a certain amount of symmetry in that it contains two identical four-note units (called **tetrachords**), separated by a whole step. Each tetrachord consists of two whole steps and a half step.

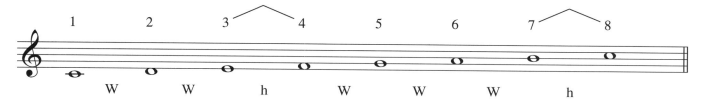

Minor Scales

There are three forms of minor scales: **natural**, **harmonic**, and **melodic**. Each starts with the same minor tetrachord (1–2–♭3–4), with variations on degrees 6 and 7 in the upper tetrachord.

Natural Minor
A natural minor scale is a scale that contains half steps between scale degrees 2–3 and 5–6.

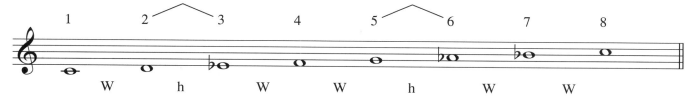

Think of the natural minor scale as the notes of a major scale starting on its 6th degree. Accordingly, the C minor scale shown above is an E♭ major scale starting on C.

Harmonic Minor
A harmonic minor scale is a form of a minor scale with half steps between 2–3, 5–6, and 7–8. The characteristic sound of this scale results from the unexpected interval between scale degrees 6–7, a whole step plus a half step (or augmented 2nd).

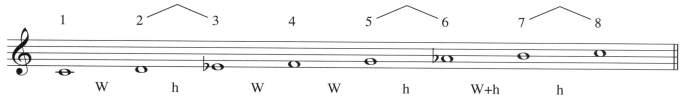

The harmonic minor scale can be thought of as a natural minor scale with a raised 7th scale degree. The 7th scale degree is typically raised in minor keys in order to provide a **leading tone** that will make the V–i chord move (also called a **cadence**) sound conclusive. The name "harmonic minor" derives from the fact that the 7th scale degree has been altered to fit the harmonic requirements of the V–i cadence.

Melodic Minor Scale

This type of minor scale is called "melodic" because is it easier to sing than harmonic minor; there is no ♯2 interval between the 6th and 7th degrees. A classical melodic minor scale has two forms: ascending and descending. The ascending form is a natural minor scale with the 6th and 7th scale degrees raised, with half steps between 2–3 and 7–8. Compare it with the major scale; the only difference is the minor 3rd. The classical descending form is simply the natural minor scale. In jazz practice, the 6th and 7th are typically raised in both the ascending and descending versions of the scale. This is sometimes referred to as the "**jazz minor**" or "real" melodic minor, and is a vital scale to learn for use in jazz improvisation. This form appears below.

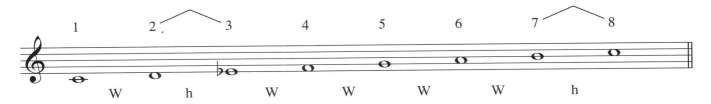

Scale Relationships

Major and minor scales may be **relative** or **parallel**. Relative major and minor scales share the same key signature but start on different notes (i.e., C major and A minor.) Parallel major and minor scales have the same starting note but different key signatures (i.e., C major and C minor).

Major and Minor Scale Diatonic Harmony

A **tonal center** consists of a scale (a **parent scale**) and a series of **diatonic** (scale-based) 7th chords created by **harmonizing** the parent scale: building chords on each step, by stacking 3rds of only scale notes.

Roman numerals are used for describing chord progressions and understanding chord functions independently of specific keys. This system designates how each chord belongs to a key. Generally, minor chord functions (minor, diminished and half-diminished chords) are indicated by lowercase Roman numerals, whereas major and dominant chord functions are indicated by uppercase Roman numerals. Added markings indicate modification of the chord from its original form. The diatonic 7th chords of the major scale are shown below.

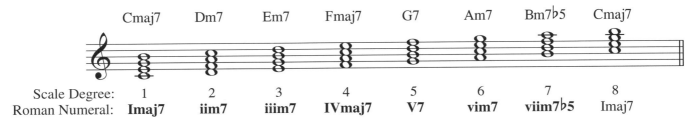

Major Scale Modes

As with chords, a scale may be inverted by keeping the same range of notes but placing a different starting pitch at the bottom; the resulting inversion is known as a **mode**.

The concept of modes is crucial to jazz improvisation. A mode contains the same seven notes of the parent scale, but adopts a different tonal center around which all the other notes revolve. The notes are equivalent to a major scale; only the starting note has changed. Modal melodies and chord progressions will emphasize this note as the tonal center. A melody based on a mode may be written with the same key signature as the parent scale, or as a major or minor key center with accidentals inserted to produce the notes of the mode.

The following table, adapted from John Mehegan, shows each mode in the key of C as a displaced scale from root to root.

CHORD	DISPLACEMENT (KEY OF C)	MODE'S NAME	QUALITY
I	C–C	Ionian	Major
ii	D–D	Dorian	Minor
iii	E–E	Phrygian	Minor
IV	F–F	Lydian	Major
V	G–G	Mixolydian	Dominant
vi	A–A	Aeolian	Minor
vii	B–B	Locrian	Minor (♭5)

The following illustration outlines the modes discussed above.

1st mode
C Ionian (**C** major)

2nd mode
D Dorian

3rd mode
E Phrygian

4th mode
F Lydian

5th mode
G Mixolydian

6th mode
A Aeolian (Natural Minor)

7th mode
B Locrian

Modal Characteristics and Colors

Each mode has one characteristic scale step that distinguishes it from either the natural minor (Aeolian mode) or major (Ionian mode) scale. The following table shows each mode's structure in comparison to the parallel major scale and its characteristic scale step, as well as its tonal and modal tones, where applicable.

MODE	STRUCTURE	CHARACTERISTIC TONE	TONAL TONE	MODAL TONE
Ionian	1, 2, 3, 4, 5, 6, 7	reference	1, 4 & 5	2, 3, 6 & 7
Dorian	1, 2, ♭3, 4, 5, 6, ♭7	6	1, 4 & 5	2, 3, 6 & 7
Phrygian	1, ♭2, ♭3, 4, 5, ♭6, ♭7	♭2	1, 4 & 5	2, 3, 6 & 7
Lydian	1, 2, 3, ♯4, 5, 6, 7	♯4	–	–
Mixolydian	1, 2, 3, 4, 5, 6, ♭7	♭7	1, 4 & 5	2, 3, 6 & 7
Aeolian	1, 2, ♭3, 4, 5, ♭6, ♭7	reference (♭6)	1, 4 & 5	2, 3, 6 & 7
Locrian	1, ♭2, ♭3, 4, ♭5, ♭6, ♭7	♭5	–	–

Notice that there are five tonal modes; all contain the same 1st, 4th, and 5th degrees. These notes are constants. Because all five modes are related through these primary tones, a jazz improviser may easily select the proper mode by changing the other, variable, notes.

Sometimes, the degree of dissonance desired will dictate mode choice. In order of decreasing tension, the modes may effectively be arranged as follows.

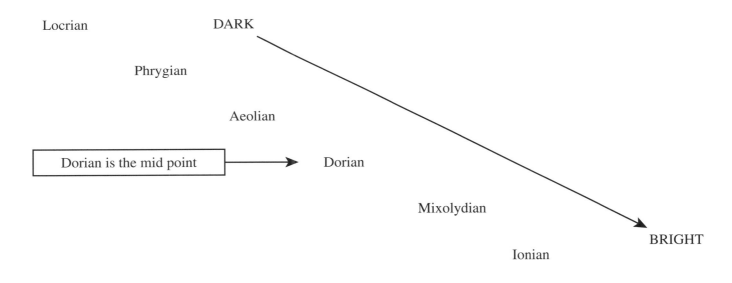

Melodic Minor Scale Modes

The various scales that result from the modes of the melodic minor scale are of fundamental importance in jazz improvisation. The seven modes that derive from the C melodic minor scale are shown below with their respective formulae.

MODE	1–2	2–3	3–4	4–5	5–6	6–7	7–8
Melodic Minor	W	h	W	W	W	W	h
Dorian ♭2	h	W	W	W	W	h	W
Lydian Augmented	W	W	W	W	h	W	h
Lydian Dominant	W	W	W	h	W	h	W
Mixolydian ♭13	W	W	h	W	h	W	W
Locrian ♮2	W	h	W	h	W	W	W
Altered	h	W	h	W	W	W	W

The applications of these modes will be discussed in detail in the context of the appropriate harmonic situations as we encounter them in later chapters.

Minor Scale Diatonic Harmony

Minor tonalities are somewhat more complex than major tonalities. A minor tonality may draw from four parent scales as a source of melodies and harmonies, while the major scale (Ionian) just uses one parent scale. In minor, the four parent scales are natural minor (Aeolian, also known as "pure" minor), Dorian, harmonic minor, and melodic minor. Dorian and melodic minor are the most frequent choices for static minor chords, with natural and harmonic minor often being employed over minor-key chord progressions.

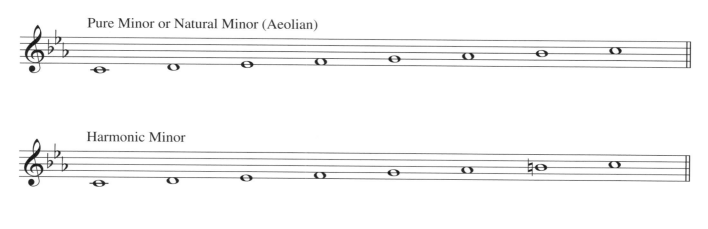

Each of these three parent scales generates its own family of diatonic chords.

Pure Minor or Natural Minor (Aeolian) Harmony

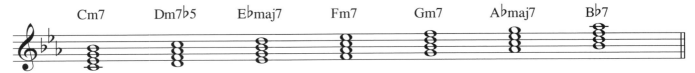

Harmonic Minor Harmony

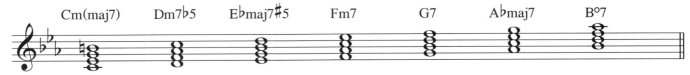

Melodic Minor Harmony

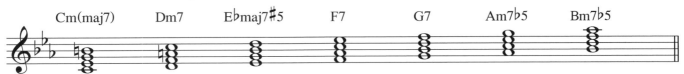

Diatonic Harmony of Modes of Harmonic Minor Scale

1. C Harmonic Minor

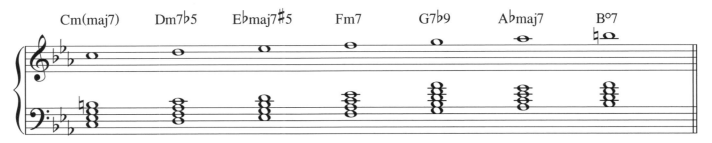

2. D Locrian (♯6)

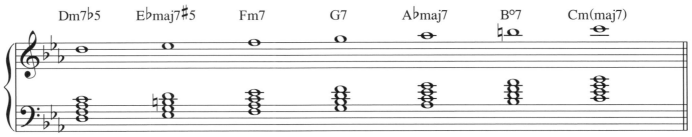

3. E♭ Ionian (♯5)

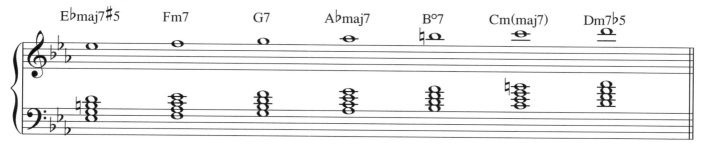

4. F Dorian (♯4)

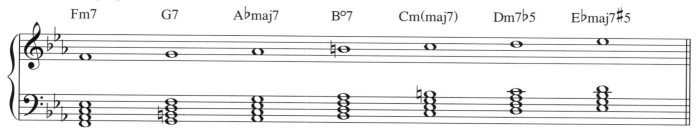

5. G Mixolydian (♭9, ♭13)

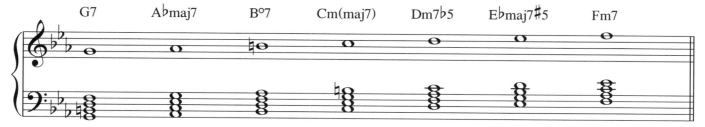

6. A♭ Lydian (♯2)

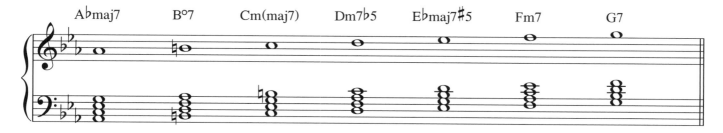

7. B Diminished (♯6, without 8)

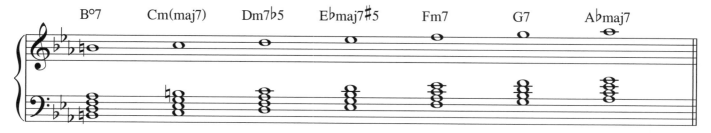

The eight-note diminished scale will be discussed later in this chapter.

Diatonic Harmony of Modes of Melodic Minor Scale

1. C Melodic Minor

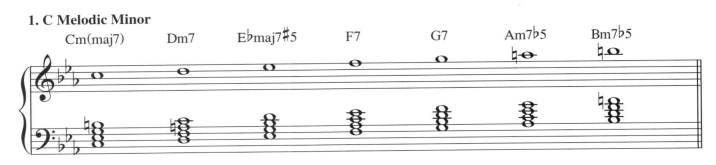

2. D Dorian (♭2)

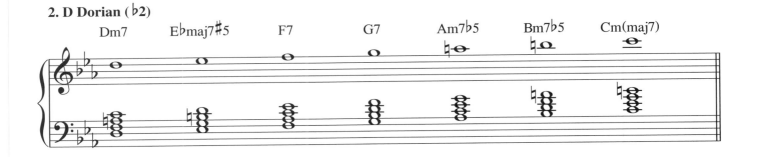

3. E♭ Augmented Lydian

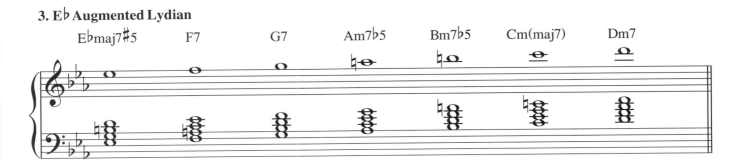

4. F Lydian (♭7)*

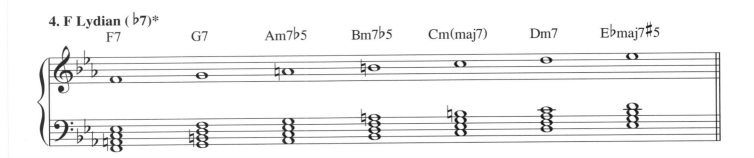

5. G Mixolydian (♭13)

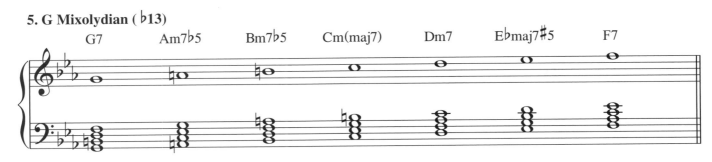

6. A Locrian (♯2)

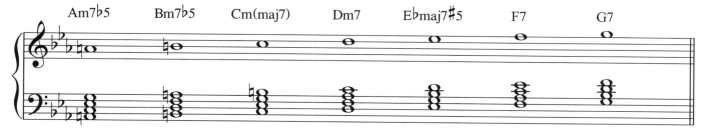

7. B Altered (B7alt)**

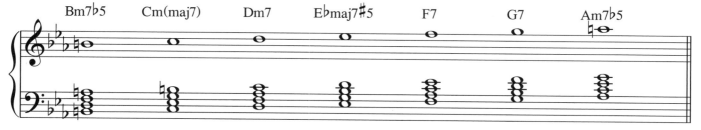

*Lydian (♭7) = Mixolydian (♯11)

**Altered = Super-Locrian (see page 32: The Altered Scale)

Pentatonic Scales

Pentatonic scales consist of five notes (from the Greek, *penta*, five). Notice that no half steps occur in any of these scales. Pentatonic scales are used in folk music throughout the world. They have also appeared in Western classical music, particularly in the works of Debussy and Ravel. Although any scale consisting of five notes may theoretically be called "pentatonic," the most common forms are the following.

Major Pentatonic Scale

In C, the major pentatonic scale is spelled: C–D–E–G–A (1–2–3–5–6). On a keyboard, the black keys form a pentatonic scale from G♭ to G♭.

Minor Pentatonic Scale

From C, this is: C–E♭–F–G–B♭ (1–♭3–4–5–♭7). On a keyboard, this corresponds to a black-key scale from E♭ to E♭.

Blues Scales

The **minor blues scale** (or simply the "**blues scale**") is similar to the minor pentatonic scale, with the addition of a ♯4. From the root of the relative major, it may also be viewed as a major pentatonic scale, with a raised 2nd (♯2) added, resulting in the **major blues scale**. The added notes are called **blue notes**, which are used for tension when improvising. The minor blues scale fits well with 7, m7 and—possibly—m7♭5 chords, whereas the major blues scale fits with maj7 chords.

C Minor Blues

E♭ Major Blues

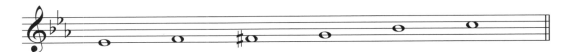

Bebop Scales

There are two types of bebop scales, the **major bebop** scale and the **bebop dominant** scale. The major bebop scale is identical to the major scale with the addition of a ♯5 or ♭6. C major bebop is spelled C–D–E–F–G–G♯(added note)–A–B–C. This scale may be used over a Cmaj7 or a C⁶ chord.

C Major Bebop

The bebop dominant scale is identical to a Mixolydian mode with the addition of a major 7th. For example, the G bebop dominant is spelled G–A–B–C–D–E–F–F♯(added note)–G–B. This scale is effective over G7, Dm7, and also Bm7♭5 chords.

G Bebop Dominant

These two scales, major bebop and bebop dominant, most often appear in descending form, which places essential tones on downbeats with the added notes on offbeats. (More examples will be discussed later.)

Symmetrical Scales

Diminished

Diminished scales are comprised entirely of alternating whole steps and half steps. As a result of this symmetrical formation, there are only two possible diminished scale modes. One begins with a whole step, and the other with a half step.

The diminished scale beginning with a whole step is called **diminished whole-half** (or simply "diminished"). It will be useful in improvisation to remember that this scale consists of two minor tetrachords (1–2–♭3–4) spaced a tritone apart. The diminished whole-half scale is used directly over a diminished chord. For instance, play C diminished whole-half over C°7.

C Diminished Whole-Half

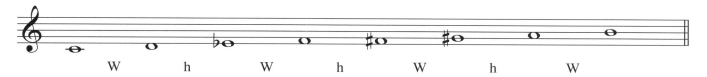

The diminished scale beginning with a half step (called **diminished half-whole** or **dominant diminished**) may be used over a dominant chord, for instance C7♭9 or C13♭9.

C Diminished Half-Whole

Because the two modes are constructed with the same intervals, just starting on different notes, you can see that C diminished whole-half is equivalent to B diminished half-whole.

The symmetrical nature of the diminished scale means that any of its notes may be considered as a root, always resulting in the same pattern of intervals between the notes, and always yielding one of the two diminished modes. Because its interval pattern repeats every three half steps, we can say there are really only three diminished scales: C, D♭, and D. A diminished scale starting on any other note is equal to one of these three.

- C diminished whole-half is equivalent to diminished whole-half scales starting on E♭, G♭, and A, and is also equivalent to half-whole scales starting on B, D, F, and A♭.

- D♭ diminished whole-half is equal to E, G, and B♭ diminished whole-half, and to E♭, G♭, A, and C diminished half-whole.

- D diminished whole-half is equal to F, A♭ and B diminished whole-half and to E, G, B♭, and D♭ diminished half-whole scales.

Knowledge of these equivalencies will ease the task of improvising over diminished chords and dominant chords.

Whole Tone

The whole-tone scale has six notes separated from one another by whole steps. Because the structure is symmetrical, there are only two whole-tone scales.

- C Whole-Tone Scale: C–D–E–F#–G#–A#
- D♭ Whole-Tone Scale: D♭–E♭–F–G–A–B

Because the scale is entirely symmetrical, all notes represent possible roots. The whole-tone scale is closely associated with French Impressionism, and many examples can be found in the works of Claude Debussy.

C Whole Tone

D♭ Whole Tone

Generally, whole tone scales are used in jazz in a similar manner to dominant diminished scales, i.e. as substitute scales for use over dominant chords, particularly when moving up a 4th.

The Altered Scale

The seventh mode of the melodic minor scale is called the **altered scale** because it contains several altered tones: ♭9, #9, #11, and ♭13. It is actually a major scale with the root raised a half step, thus: 1 ♭2 ♭3 ♭4 (= M3) ♭5 (= #4) ♭6 ♭7. In C melodic minor, we saw that the chord built on the 7th degree (B) is a half-diminished chord. It might also be considered an altered dominant 7th chord, depending upon which note is considered the 3rd of the chord: D (♭3) or E♭ (M3 or ♭4). In other words, if D is considered the 3rd, the resultant chord is Bm7♭5; if E♭ (= D#) is considered the 3rd, the resultant chord is B7♭5 (often written as B7alt).

B Altered Scale with Bm7♭5 Chord

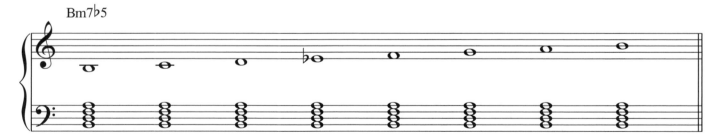

B Altered Scale with B7alt Chord (preferred in jazz practice)

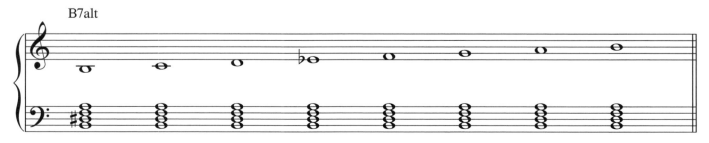

Altered Dominant Chords

In general, "altered" could mean any change to a basic chord type, and any chord that has a note that is altered from its normal position could be called an altered chord. In common jazz practice, however, the term "altered" or "alt" refers only to dominant chords and specifically means "derived from the altered scale." This scale is also known as the Super-Locrian scale, the diminished whole-tone scale, and (rarely) the Pomeroy scale. The most fundamental way to view it is as the **7th mode** of melodic minor. That is, the B altered scale equals C melodic minor starting on B.

An "altered dominant 7th" can only designate a dominant chord whose 5th and 9th have been raised or lowered by a half step, resulting in any combination of ♭9 or ♯9 with ♭5/♯11 or ♭5/♭13. Thus, when the term "alt" is used, i.e. B7alt, it generally implies a combination of *both* an altered 5th and an altered 9th.

Below is a B7alt chord that includes all the altered notes: 1, ♯11, ♭7, ♭9, 3, ♭13, 1, ♯9.

This chord shows all the possibilities for an altered dominant chord and thus has a few more notes than are normally used. If just one (but at least one) 5th and one 9th are included, there are four possible combinations for which the chord suffix "alt" would be appropriate. They're listed here with some enharmonic spellings.

- ♭5, ♭9 = ♭9, ♯11
- ♭5, ♯9 = ♯9, ♯11
- ♯5, ♭9 = ♭9, ♭13
- ♯5, ♯9 = ♯9, ♭13

Dominant chords with ♭9, ♯9 and ♯5/♭13 are derived from the altered scale, while dominant chords with combinations of a ♭9 or ♯9 with P5 or ♭5/♯11, and/or M13 come from the diminished half-whole scale. Since not all the notes are always present, part of the decision about when to use the altered scale versus dominant diminished is based on context: the chords that precede and follow the actual dominant chord. This will be discussed in Chapter 4 when we cover ii–V–I progressions. The significant observation at this point is that there is no natural 9th or natural 5th/13th in the altered chord or scale, which accounts for the unique sound of altered chords.

In short, a 7alt chord would describe any one of the following chords: 7♯5♯9, 7♯5♭9, 7♭5♭9, 7♭5♯9. Any of these chords may be played when the 7alt symbol is encountered, though it's important to be aware of the melodic note. (See Chapters 6 and 8 on jazz piano voicings and voice leading, chord substitution, and tritone substitution for specific voicings.)

Other Scales

Here are some exotic scales that may be used in jazz improvisation.

Aeolian: C–D–E♭–F–G–A♭–B♭–C
Algerian: C–D–E♭–F#–G–A♭–B–C–D–E♭–F
Arabian: C–D–E–F–G♭–A♭–B♭–C
Balinese: C–D♭–E♭–G–A♭–C
Byzantine: C–D♭–E–F–G–A♭–B–C
Chinese: F–G–A–C–D–F or C–E–F#–G–B–C
Double Harmonic: C–D♭–E–F–G–A♭–B–C
Egyptian: C–D–F–G–B♭–C
Enigmatic: C–D♭–E–F#–G#–A#–B–C
Ethiopian: G–A–B♭–C–D–E♭–F–G (B and E may be naturals. F may be F#)
Hawaiian: C–D–E♭–F–G–A–B–C
Hindu: C–D–E–F–G–A♭–B♭–C
Hirajoshi: A–B–C–E–F–A
Hungarian Gypsy: C–D–E♭–F#–G–A♭–B♭–C
Hungarian Major: C–D#–E–F#–G–A–B♭–C
Hungarian Minor: C–D–E♭–F#–G–A♭–B–C
In Sen: C–D♭–F–G–B♭–C
Iwato: B–C–E–F–A–B
Japanese: C–D♭–F–G–A♭–C
Javanese: C–D♭–E♭–F–G–A–B♭–C
Jewish: E–F–G#–A–B–C–D–E
Kumoi: C–D–E♭–G–A–C
Leading Whole Tone: C–D–E–F#–G#–A#–B–C
Locrian Major: C–D–E–F–G♭–A♭–B♭–C
Lydian Minor: C–D–E–F#–G–A♭–B♭–C
Mohammedan: C–D–E♭–F–G–A♭–B–C (= harmonic minor)
Mongolian: C–D–E–G–A–C
Neapolitan Major: C–D♭–E♭–F–G–A–B–C
Neapolitan Minor: C D♭–E♭–F–G–A♭–B–C
Oriental: C–D♭–E–F–G♭–A–B♭–C
Overtone: C–D–E–F#–G–A–B♭–C (Lydian ♭7 = G melodic minor)
Pelog: C–D♭–E♭–G–B♭–C
Persian: C–D♭–E–F–G♭–A♭–B–C
Phrygian Major: C–D♭–E–F–G–A♭–B♭–C (= F harmonic minor)
Spanish: C–D♭–E–F–G–A♭–B♭–C (= F harmonic minor)
Spanish 8 Tones: C–D♭–E♭–E–F–G–A♭–B♭–C

Chapter 3 Exercises

1. Write the following major scales. Write the name below.

2. Write the following scales.

D Harmonic Minor   E♭ Major   B Dorian

F# Locrian   D Major Blues   A♭ Lydian

F Melodic Minor   C# Whole-Tone   C Altered

B♭ Major Pentatonic   D♭ Natural Minor   G Lydian (♭7)

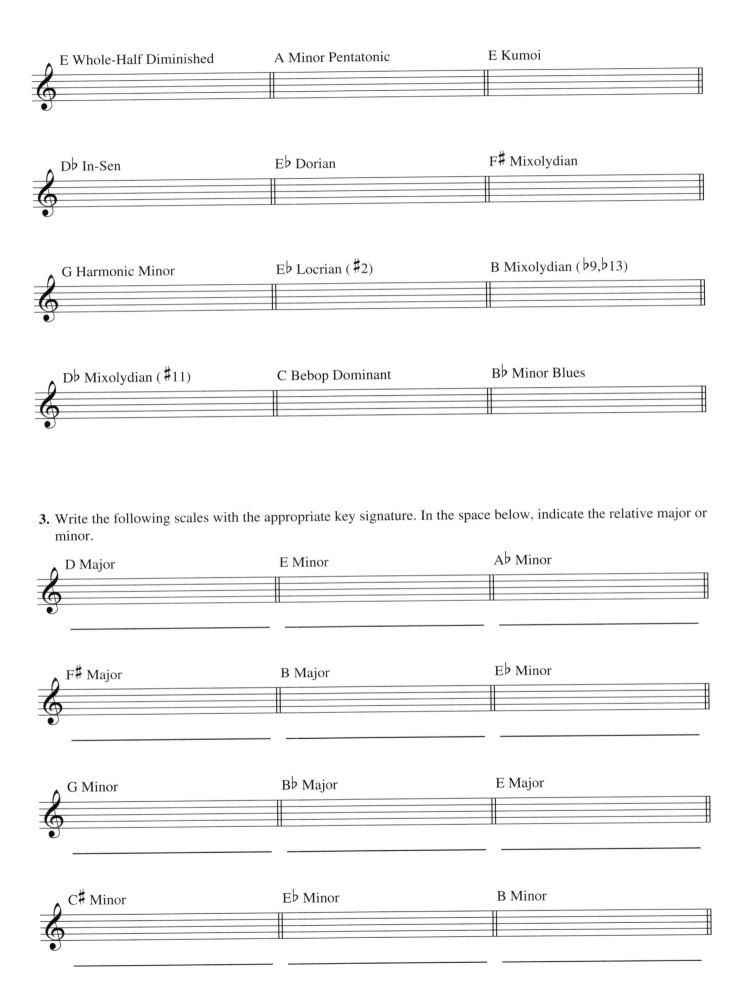

E Whole-Half Diminished   A Minor Pentatonic   E Kumoi

Db In-Sen   Eb Dorian   F# Mixolydian

G Harmonic Minor   Eb Locrian (#2)   B Mixolydian (b9, b13)

Db Mixolydian (#11)   C Bebop Dominant   Bb Minor Blues

3. Write the following scales with the appropriate key signature. In the space below, indicate the relative major or minor.

D Major   E Minor   Ab Minor

F# Major   B Major   Eb Minor

G Minor   Bb Major   E Major

C# Minor   Eb Minor   B Minor

4. Add flats or sharps to form the correct scale.

F Phrygian   F♯ Mixolydian

E Harmonic Minor   A Lydian

F Locrian   E Dorian

B Melodic Minor   E♭Major

G♯ Harmonic Minor   B Lydian

5. Write an appropriate scale for the following chords. Give the correct name.

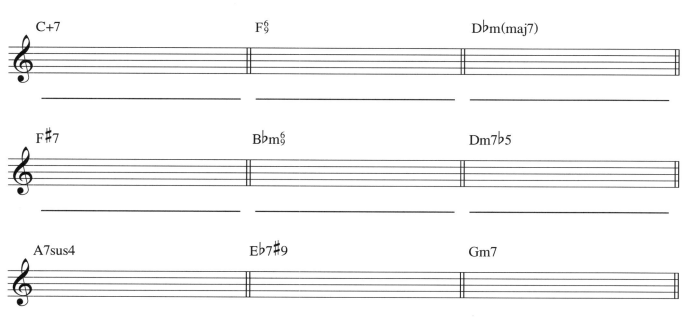

C+7   F$^6_9$ D♭m(maj7)

F♯7   B♭m$^6_9$ Dm7♭5

A7sus4   E♭7♯9   Gm7

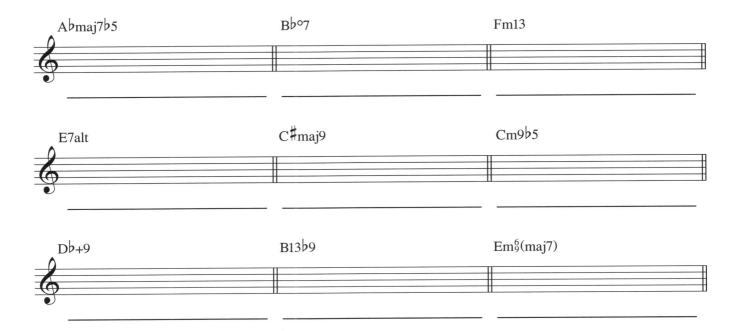

Abmaj7b5   Bb°7   Fm13

E7alt   C#maj9   Cm9b5

Db+9   B13b9   Em⁶/₉(maj7)

6. On a separate sheet of staff paper, write the modes of the following major scales and identify the characteristic tones (CT) as well as the tonal and modal tones (TT)/(MT).

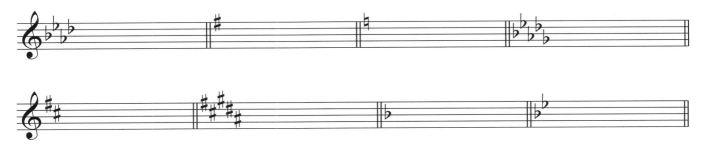

7. Harmonize the scales and provide Roman numeral analyses for exercises 1, 2, and 3.

8. What are the functions of each of these chords in the following given scales?

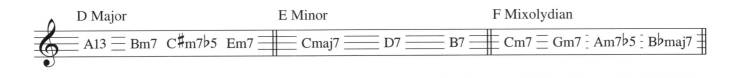

A Minor   C Lydian   Ab Major
Bm7b5 — Dm7 — E7b9   F#m7b5 — Gmaj7 — Bm7   Bbm7 — Eb7 — Ab⁶/₉

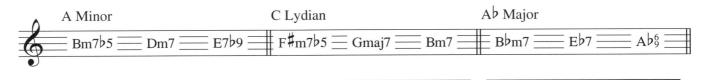

D Major   E Minor   F Mixolydian
A13 — Bm7 C#m7b5 Em7   Cmaj7 — D7 — B7   Cm7 — Gm7 : Am7b5 : Bbmaj7

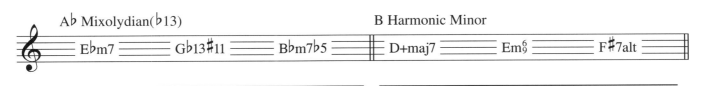

Ab Mixolydian(b13)   B Harmonic Minor
Ebm7 — Gb13#11 — Bbm7b5   D+maj7 — Em⁶/₉ — F#7alt

9. Identify the key in which the following chords will have the function indicated.

Bm7 is vim7 in the key of:

A♭m7 is iiim7 in the key of:

G♯m7♭5 is iim7♭5 in the key of:

A♭maj7 is ♭VImaj7 in the key of:

Dm7♭5 is iim7♭5 in the key of:

D♭maj7 is ♭IIImaj7 in the key of:

A♭m7 is vim7 in the key of:

F♯maj7 is IVmaj7 in the key of:

D♭7maj7 is IVmaj7 in the key of:

Cm7 is vim7 in the key of:

10. Notate the following.

The two maj7 chords in Cm.

The three m7 chords in A♭.

The two maj7 chords in G♯m.

The three m7 chords in B.

The two maj7 chords in D♭.

The three m7 chords in F♯.

The two maj7 chords in E.

The three m7 chords in D.

The two maj7 chords in Em.

The three m7 chords in F.

The two maj7 chords in C♯m.

The three m7 chords in E♭.

The two maj7 chords in C♯.

The three m7 chords in C♭.

The two maj7 chords in A♭.

The two maj7 chords in Bm.

The three m7 chords in A.

The two maj7 chords in G♭.

The three m7 chords in B♭.

The two maj7 chords in F♯m.

The two maj7 chords in A♭m.

The three m7 chords in D♭.

11. Write the following scales, with their modes on another sheet of staff paper.

F Melodic Minor   B Melodic Minor   G Harmonic Minor   D Harmonic Minor

A♭ Melodic Minor   E♭ Melodic Minor   D♭ Harmonic Minor   A Melodic Minor

12. Write the chord-scale relationship (in other words, harmonize the scale with 7th chords) for these scales and modes. Show harmonic functions.

G Ionian (Major)   F♯ Phrygian

F Lydian   G Melodic Minor

F Aeolian (Minor)   B Dorian

G Mixolydian (♭9,♭13)   B Locrian

13. Write the major pentatonic and minor pentatonic scales in all twelve keys.

14. Write the bebop dominant and bebop major scales in all twelve keys.

15. Write the Kumoi and the In Sen scales in all twelve keys.

THE II–V–I CADENCE

Chord Families

The seven diatonic chords in major keys are divided into three families in terms of their harmonic function, based on shared notes that produce the same emotional effects.

- Tonic: I, iii, vi
- Subdominant: ii, IV
- Dominant: V, vii

In minor keys, the VI chord is usually considered a member of the subdominant family.

- Tonic: i, III
- Subdominant: ii, iv, VI
- Dominant: v (or V), VII

Depending on the context of a progression, the VI chord in major or minor has the possibility of being perceived as either a tonic or subdominant, because it shares two notes with either family. For instance, when following V7, vim7 tends to sound like a chord of the tonic family. In the reverse order (e.g. vim7–V7–Imaj7), vim7 feels more like a subdominant chord.

Movement between the three families of chords is the basis for traditional Western music. Typically a harmonic sequence will start in a place of stability (the tonic), move to a place that is definitely away from it (one of the subdominant chords), then to a place of tension (a dominant), before finally providing the emotional release, or **resolution**, of returning to the tonic chord.

C–F–G–C
I–IV–V–I

Cadences

From the Latin *cadere*, to fall, a **cadence** is the movement of chords from one family (or **function**) to another. Cadences establish key centers, and their placement determines song structure, delineating ends and beginnings of song sections.

The **authentic cadence** is the movement from dominant to tonic (V–I), considered the strongest and most important chord movement in Western harmony. The **plagal** cadence (IV–I) is also very powerful. A **deceptive** cadence occurs when a V chord resolves to a chord other than the tonic, for instance V–vi.

The ii–V–I
The ii–V–I cadence has a certain level of sophistication, in that it starts on a subdominant instead of the tonic, making the key less immediately clear. The root motion is still upward by perfect 4th or downward by perfect 5th, the strongest possible in both jazz and classical music. The ii–V–I provides the cornerstone of jazz harmony. In addition, the **voice leading** (melodic lines formed by the harmony notes as the chords change, also discussed in Chapter 6) suggested by the ii–V–I cadence furnishes highly recognizable contours.

It is essential that jazz musicians be able to spot ii–V–I cadences instantly, as they are ubiquitous in jazz harmony and central to the process of improvising over changes. Familiarity with this very common chord progression will allow one to look at a set of chord changes and perceive the overall tonal structure. This will give a better idea of how the tune is put together, and how groups of chords relate to one another, instead of simply looking at and trying to remember a series of individual chords. In addition to providing the basic units of tonal organization in jazz music, ii–V–I's (and ii–V's) help us discern (and memorize) the "big picture."

The ii–V–I in C Major

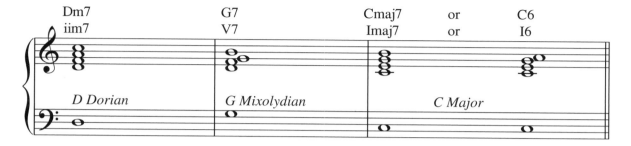

The 3rds and the 7ths of the chords are called **guide tones**. Their tendency to resolve from a point of tension to a point of rest or resolution is characteristic of jazz cadential harmony. The voice leading that results from guide tone resolution produces smooth inner lines: F to E and C to B. It is suggested that the above progression be practiced with only the 3rds and the 7ths in the right hand, resulting in a what is sometimes called a **shell voicing**. The root is already in the bass, and the 5th can be freely omitted when it is not a determinant of the quality of the chord like the 3rd or 7th.

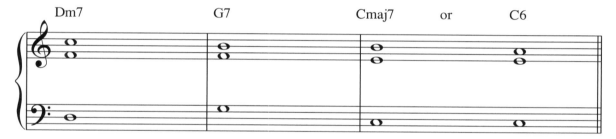

Generally, the 3rd and the 7th should be emphasized when moving from one chord to another. Conversely, the 4th should be avoided on I and V chords, and the 6th should not be emphasized on the ii chord. To do so would prematurely anticipate the arrival of these notes and dissipate the effectiveness of the progression.

Generally, a ii–V–I cadence will span either two or four measures:

| Dm7 G7 | Cmaj7 |
or
| Dm7 | G7 | Cmaj7 | |

The ii–V–i cadence in a minor key is used in much the same way as it is in a major key. It establishes the key center in similar fashion.

The ii–V–i in C Minor

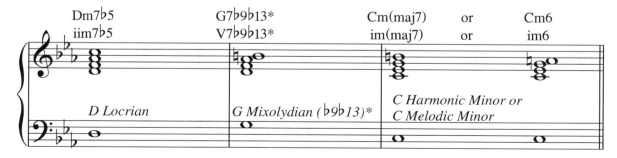

*G7♭9♭13 also refers to G7alt

The Circle of Fifths

Continued motion up a 4th or down a 5th, as in a ii–V–I, results in a **circle of 5ths** (or **circle of 4ths**) since the root will eventually come full circle and return to the starting pitch. The term **cycle of 5ths** (or **4ths**) is used interchangeably with "circle" to describe the same phenomenon.

The circle of 5ths or circle of 4ths is a graphic way to visualize all possible keys in either major or minor. It is a useful way to understand chord motion, particularly cadences, and also provides an organized manner in which to practice musical skills in all keys. Although the circle generally shows increasing sharps in a clockwise direction, normal harmonic progressions will follow a counter-clockwise motion. Thus, repeatedly descending by a fifth or ascending by a fourth, one arrives back at the starting point, having covered all the tones in the chromatic scale. The sequence C–G–D–A–E–B–F♯/G♭–D♭–A♭–E♭–B♭–F–C should be learned thoroughly in both directions for ready reference.

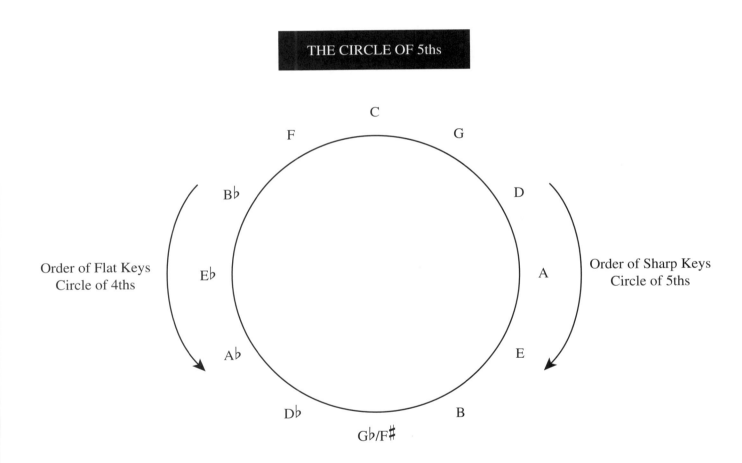

Standard Major and Minor ii–V–I Examples and Key Relationship

AUTUMN LEAVES

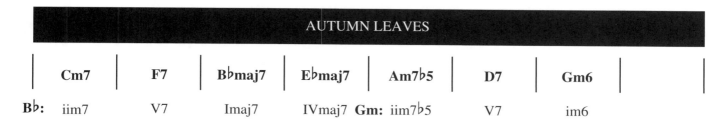

| | Cm7 | F7 | B♭maj7 | E♭maj7 | Am7♭5 | D7 | Gm6 | |

B♭: iim7   V7   Imaj7   IVmaj7   **Gm:** iim7♭5   V7   im6

BLACK ORPHEUS

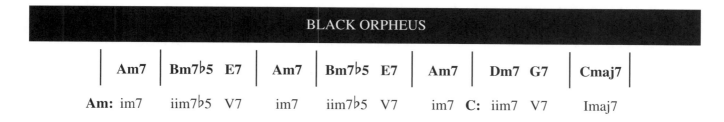

| | Am7 | Bm7♭5 | E7 | Am7 | Bm7♭5 | E7 | Am7 | Dm7 | G7 | Cmaj7 |

Am: im7   iim7♭5   V7   im7   iim7♭5   V7   im7   **C:** iim7   V7   Imaj7

THERE WILL NEVER BE ANOTHER YOU

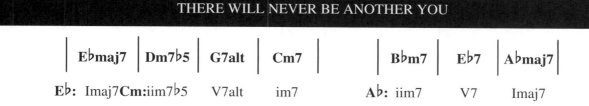

| | E♭maj7 | Dm7♭5 | G7alt | Cm7 | | B♭m7 | E♭7 | A♭maj7 |

E♭: Imaj7 **Cm:** iim7♭5   V7alt   im7   **A♭:** iim7   V7   Imaj7

THE SHADOW OF YOUR SMILE

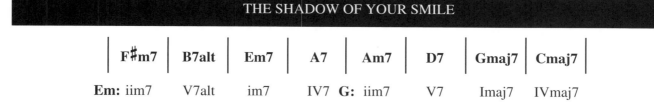

| | F♯m7 | B7alt | Em7 | A7 | Am7 | D7 | Gmaj7 | Cmaj7 |

Em: iim7   V7alt   im7   IV7   **G:** iim7   V7   Imaj7   IVmaj7

JOY SPRING

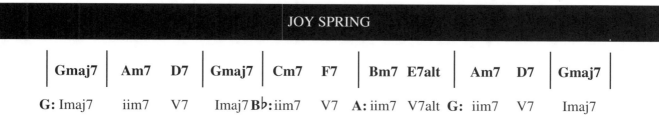

| | Gmaj7 | Am7 | D7 | Gmaj7 | Cm7 | F7 | Bm7 | E7alt | Am7 | D7 | Gmaj7 |

G: Imaj7   iim7   V7   Imaj7 **B♭:** iim7   V7   **A:** iim7   V7alt   **G:** iim7   V7   Imaj7

CONFIRMATION

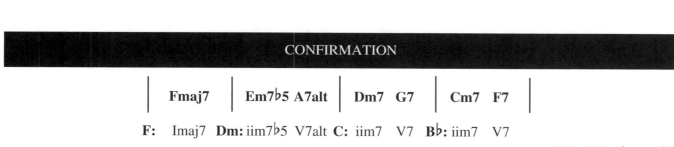

| | Fmaj7 | Em7♭5 | A7alt | Dm7 | G7 | Cm7 | F7 | |

F: Imaj7   **Dm:** iim7♭5   V7alt   **C:** iim7   V7   **B♭:** iim7   V7

Incomplete ii–V–I's

Sometimes the ii–V–I cadence works as an incomplete or unresolved ii–V which is repeated several times. This kind of sequence is closely associated with Brazilian and Afro-Cuban music styles, often played as an ostinato* (for example, a piano montuno, or repeated pattern). The **harmonic rhythm** may vary, as is shown in the following patterns.

| Dm7 G7 | Dm7 G7 |...etc.
or
| Dm7 | G7 | Dm7 | G7 |...etc.

ii–V Chains

ii–V sequences (or ii–V–I sequences) need not remain in the same key. Through a process called **chaining**, sequences may progress by either upward or downward root motion, creating a series of quick **modulations** (key changes, also discussed in Chapter 7) in parallel motion. The ii–V's are said to be **chained** and will either ascend or descend through keys that are separated by an equal distance. Here are some typical modulations used when chaining ii–V's.

- Up by M2 or Down by M2
- Up by m2 (chromatically up) or Down by m2 (chromatically down)
- Up by M3rd or Down by M3rd
- Up by m3rd or Down by m3rd

ORIGINAL SEQUENCE	ROOT MOTION	UP	DOWN
Dm7 G7	M2nd	1. Em7 A7	2. Cm7 F7
	m2nd	3. E♭m7 A♭7	4. D♭m7 G♭7
	M3rd	5. F♯m7 B7	6. B♭m7 E♭7
	m3rd	7. Fm7 B♭7	8. Bm7 E7

When the pattern is a series of ii–V's, the first V7 does not resolve to the chord that follows it, which is really the relative ii of the next dominant chord. The result is a deceptive cadence, since the V7 does not resolve to the chord a P5 or half step down as expected.

Notice the distance by which the key changes in the following examples of ii–V chains.

1. SATIN DOLL

| Dm7 G7 | Dm7 G7 | Em7 A7 | Em7 A7 |

2. AUTUMN LEAVES (last four bars)

| Gm7 C7 | Fm7 B♭7 | E♭maj7 | Am7♭5 D7 |

*An **ostinato** is a musical idea that is repeated persistently in a tune. It lends harmonic continuity and provides an established modality.

3. MILESTONES (last 2 bars of B-section)

| B♭m7   E♭7 | Bm7   E7 |

4. HALF NELSON (bars 7–8)

| Bm7   E7 | B♭m7   E♭7 | A♭maj7 |

5. GIANT STEPS (bars 8–13)

| Fm7   B♭7 | E♭maj7 | Am7   D7 | Gmaj7 | C♯m7   F♯7 | Bmaj7 |

6. HAVE YOU MET MISS JONES? (bars 17–21)

| B♭maj7 | A♭m7   D♭7 | G♭maj7 | Em7   A7 | Dmaj7 |

7. IN WALKED BUD (bars 17–24)

| Fm7   B♭7 | Fm7   B♭7 | A♭m7   D♭7 | A♭m7   D♭7 |

8. TAKE FIVE (bars 23–24)

| A♭m7   D♭7 | Fm7   B♭7 |

The same effect can be created by a series of non-functioning dominant chords only. Contiguous V's or ii–V's without resolution give a sense of anticipation or expectation to a chord progression. They are often used to delay the final resolution, thus strengthening the feeling of closure when the tonic is finally reached.

Major and Minor ii–V–I's in All Keys

The following table shows all major and minor ii–V–I cadences in every key. They should be practiced on the keyboard with both hands, without reference to music or to the chart. Once this is mastered, they should be played at random in various major and minor keys.

KEY	MAJOR			MINOR		
	ii	V	I	ii	V	i
C	Dm7	G7	Cmaj7	Dm7♭5	G7alt	Cm7
D♭	E♭m7	A♭7	D♭maj7	E♭m7♭5	A♭7alt	D♭m7
D	Em7	A7	Dmaj7	Em7♭5	A7alt	Dm7
E♭	Fm7	B♭7	E♭maj7	Fm7♭5	B♭7alt	E♭m7
E	F♯m7	B7	Emaj7	F♯m7♭5	B7alt	Em7
F	Gm7	C7	Fmaj7	Gm7♭5	C7alt	Fm7
G♭	A♭m7	D♭7	G♭maj7	A♭m7♭5	D♭7alt	G♭m7
G	Am7	D7	Gmaj7	Am7♭5	D7alt	Gm7
A♭	B♭m7	E♭7	A♭maj7	B♭m7♭5	E♭7alt	A♭m7
A	Bm7	E7	Amaj7	Bm7♭5	E7alt	Am7
B♭	Cm7	F7	B♭maj7	Cm7♭5	F7alt	B♭m7
B	C♯m7	F♯7	Bmaj7	C♯m7♭5	F♯7alt	Bm7

Turnarounds

A **turnaround** is a set of chords that occurs at the end of a section. In its simplest form, it contains four 7th chords: I–VI–ii–V. (This also known as the "I Got Rhythm" progression, or just "rhythm changes.") These chords work together to return back to the first bar, leading to the first chord of the section. A turnaround provides harmonic momentum from the end of one chorus to the beginning of the next. Here are two basic turnarounds in C major.

| Cmaj7 Am7 | Dm7 G7 |

or

| Em7 Am7 | Dm7 G7 |

In common jazz practice Am7 is usually replaced with A7alt.

| Cmaj7 A7alt | Dm7 G7 |

or

| Em7 A7alt | Dm7 G7 |

The Em7 may be also played as Em7♭5.

| Em7♭5 A7alt | Dm7 G7 |

Here are the basic turnarounds in C minor:

| Cm7 Am7♭5 | Dm7♭5 G7alt |

or

| Cm6 Am7♭5 | Dm7♭5 G7alt |

Below is a basic 12-bar blues followed by a 12-bar blues with a turnaround inserted in measures 11 and 12. The turnaround creates tension and prepares for a strong resolution back to the first measure.

Blues in C

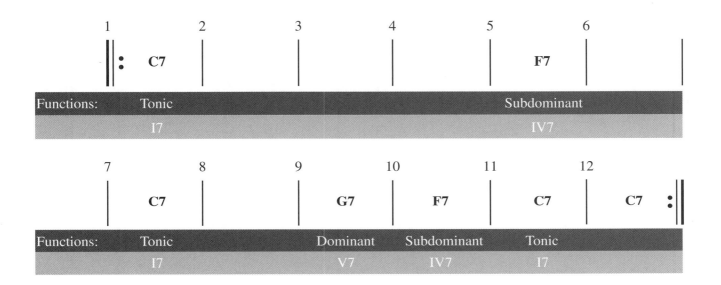

Blues in C

(with a Turnaround)

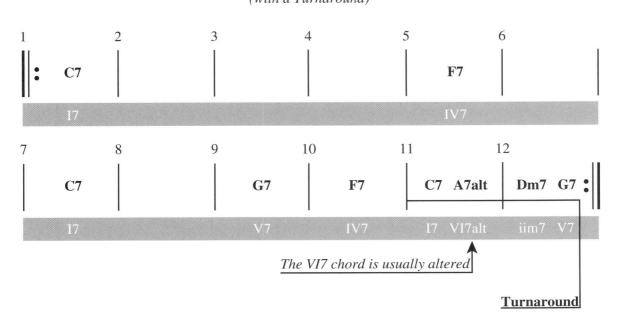

The ii–V–I Cadence and the Circle of Fifths in Classical Music

Diatonic progressions through the cycle of 5ths are found throughout the classical literature. The ii–V–I cadence in particular appears frequently in music of the baroque and romantic eras. Here are some examples that use both the cycle of 5ths and the ii–V–I cadence.

Chopin, *Etude 1, Op. 10*

meas. 37–44

meas. 67–69

Bach, *Prelude in C Major*

meas. 1–4

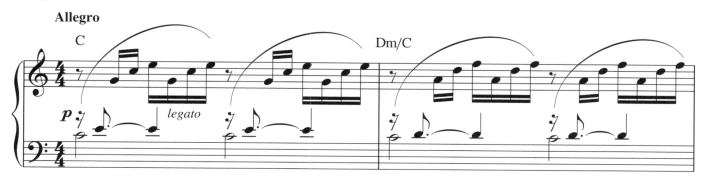

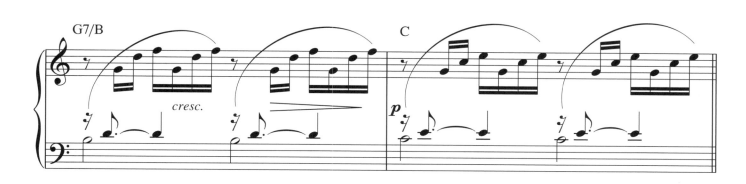

meas. 17–20

Chapter 4 Exercises

1. Write major and minor ii–V–I cadences in the following keys.

Example

2. Complete the following ii–V–I cadences.

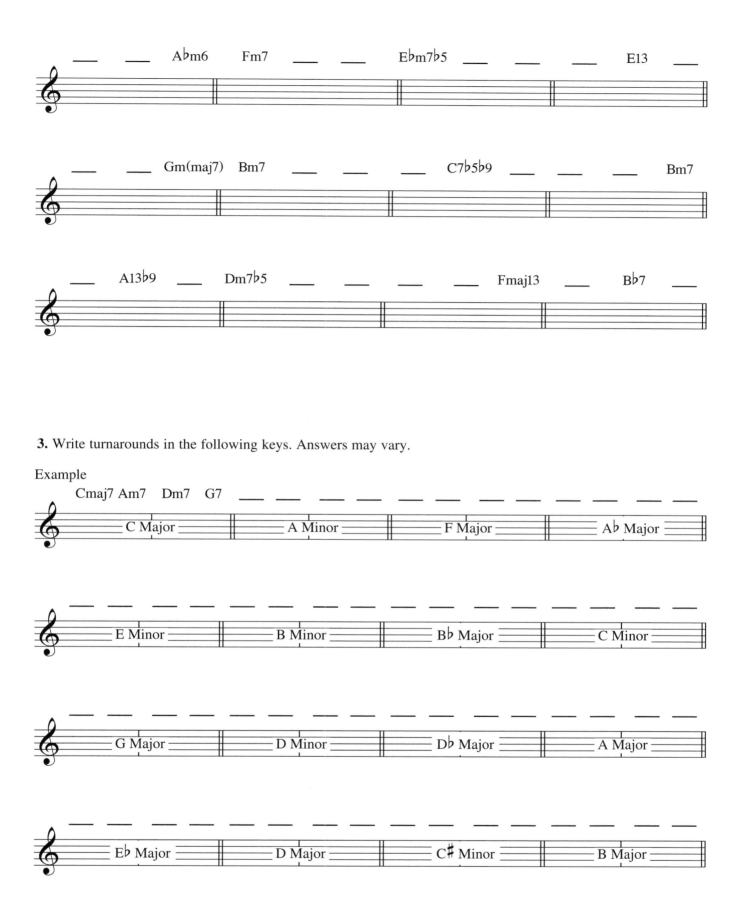

3. Write turnarounds in the following keys. Answers may vary.

Example

4. Create ii–V chains moving upward by a M3rd, then downward by a M3rd from the original.

Example

Am7 D7 C♯m7 F♯7 Fm7 B♭7 Fm7 B♭7

Dm7 G7 ___ ___ ___ ___ Bm7 E7

B♭m7 E♭7 ___ ___ ___ ___ Gm7 C7

A♭m7 D♭7 ___ ___ ___ ___ F♯m7 B7

5. Create ii–V chains moving upward by a M2nd, then downward by a M2nd from the original.

Example

Am7 D7 Bm7 E7 Gm7 C7 Fm7 B♭7

Dm7 G7 ___ ___ ___ ___ Cm7 F7

B♭m7 E♭7 ___ ___ ___ ___ Gm7 C7

A♭m7 D♭7 ___ ___ ___ ___ F♯m7 B7

6. Create ii–V chains moving up and down chromatically.

Example

Am7 D7 B♭m7 E♭7 A♭m7 D♭7   Fm7 B♭7 __ __ __ __

Dm7 G7 __ __ __ __ Em7 A7 __ __ __ __

B♭m7 E♭7 __ __ __ __ Gm7 C7 __ __ __ __

A♭m7 D♭7 __ __ __ __ F♯m7 B7 __ __ __ __

CHAPTER 5:

HARMONIC ANALYSIS

Harmonic analysis helps us to understand a musical work's harmonic and melodic structure. A working knowledge of the harmonic principles that govern chord motion is of great value in creating chord progressions that sound smooth and logical. This not only facilitates the process of composition, but also assists in reharmonizing existing melodies in order to create fresh or more colorful sounds. **Reharmonization**, also known as **chord substitution**, is extremely common in jazz as a way of personalizing an existing chord progression.

Analytical Markings

Besides using Roman numerals to indicate how chords function in key centers, some other conventions are helpful in harmonic analysis.

Draw an arrow if any dominant 7th chord (including altered dominant chords) goes down by perfect 5th to any kind of chord. The arrow indicates a **functioning dominant chord**: one that moves to its expected resolution (down by a 5th). Those that do not are called **non-functioning** dominants and receive no arrow.

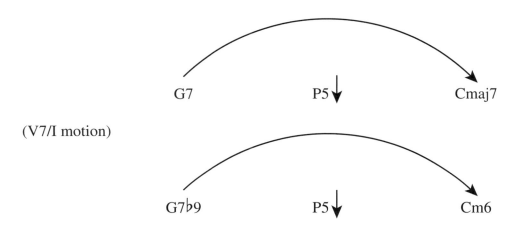

(V7/I motion)

Draw a dotted arrow if any dominant 7th (including altered dominants) goes down by a minor 2nd to any kind of chord.

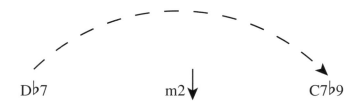

Draw a bracket beneath if any m7 or m7♭5 chord goes up by perfect 4th to any dominant 7th (including altered dominant chords).

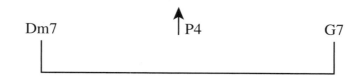

(ii–V7 motion)

Complete II–V–I

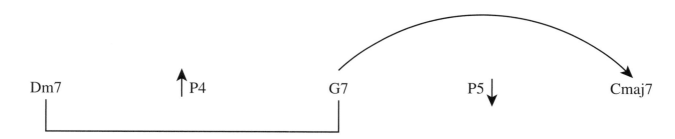

Complete II–V–i

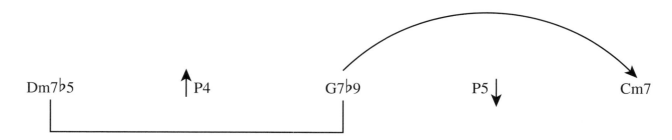

Structural Divisions

Standard jazz tunes generally incorporate an easily recognizable formal design. Typically, an overall thirty-two-bar structure is subdivided into four eight-bar sections. These sections are somewhat independent of one another and usually either parallel or contrast strongly with other sections. This design affects melody as well as chord changes. Common structural schemes include **AABA** and **ABAC**, where each letter represents an eight-bar section. The structural divisions between sections are significant points of demarcation and strongly influence the way harmonic motion is perceived, as can be seen below.

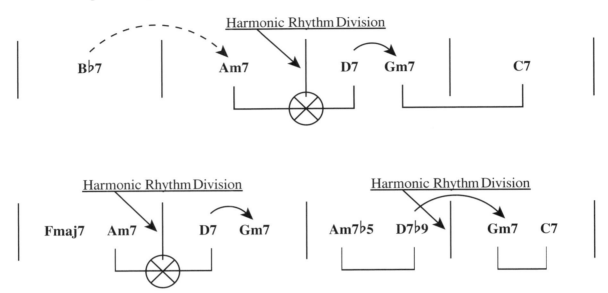

Dominant functions are not affected when they cross a structural division. Resolution by descending 5th still occurs. However, structural divisions disrupt ii–V7 motion. As shown in the above examples, if the ii–V7 motion occurs across a structural division, it is no longer perceived as ii–V7 motion. Thus, in both examples, Am7 will sound like an extension of Fmaj7 because it serves as a diatonic chord with tonic function. Therefore, it should not be analyzed with a bracket, which we have crossed out in the diagram.

Generally, to qualify as a ii–V7 progression, the minor 7th chord needs to occur on the strong beat or measure of the prevailing harmonic motion. For example, when chords occur one to a measure, ii chords would most likely fall on the odd-numbered measures with the V7s on even numbers. If the harmonic motion is defined by the half note, ii chords usually fall on the first half of the measure. Minor 7th chords occurring on the second half of the measure are probably not part of ii–V7 progressions.

Secondary Dominants

Secondary dominant chords are dominant chords that, when functioning, resolve to a diatonic chord other than the tonic. The dominant chord that does resolve to the tonic—V7—may be thought of as the primary dominant chord. A given key contains only one primary dominant chord—the chord built on the 5th scale degree, which contains only diatonic notes.

Dominant chords that are built on other scale degrees contain one or more nondiatonic chord tones:

- the raised 3rd required to change a minor 7th chord (ii, iii, or vi) to a dominant chord,
- the flatted 7th required to change a major 7th chord (I or IV) to a dominant chord, or
- the raised 3rd and 5th required to change the m7♭5 chord (vii) to a dominant chord.

Secondary dominants generally resolve to the diatonic chord a perfect 5th below. For instance, an A7 chord that occurs in the key of C tends to resolve to Dm7, the ii chord. Although it is possible to analyze the A7 as VI7, showing that the chord quality differs from vi7, the chord's function is better understood by labelling it **V7/ii** ("five of two").

Diatonic Chords in C Major

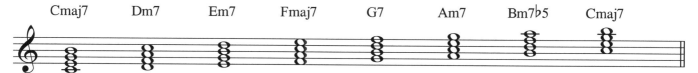

Motion of Secondary Dominants in C Major

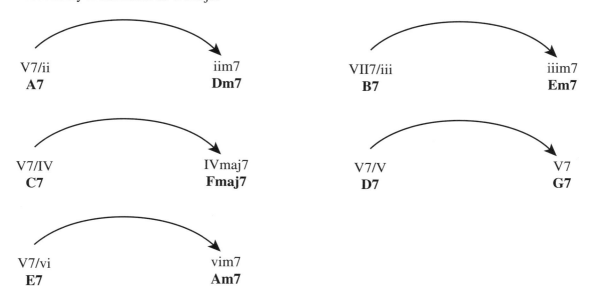

Any of these extra dominant chords creates the momentary feeling that the diatonic chord towards which it resolves is the tonic chord in a new key. This chord is said to be **tonicized**. The tonicization effect is temporary: in most cases the overall key does not change. One diatonic chord, viimi7♭5, cannot function as a tonic even temporarily, so its secondary dominant ("V7/vii") is not used in major keys.

The term "secondary dominant" still applies even in cases where the dominant chord is **non-functioning** (it does not resolve to its expected target). For instance, in the key of C, A7 is still called V7/ii even if it is not followed by Dm7 but by another chord in the key.

Finally, not every dominant chord that can occur in a given key other than V is necessarily a secondary dominant. For example, IV7 (F7) in the key of C is not a secondary dominant chord, because its resolution by a descending 5th would lead to ♭VII (B♭maj7), which is not a diatonic chord in C major. There are other possible analyses for IV7 that we'll see in Chapters 7 and 8.

Secondary dominants can also occur in minor keys. As we saw in Chapter 3, the 7th degree of the minor scale is usually raised when building the chord on step V in minor harmony, resulting in a dominant chord on this degree for a stronger resolution to I. This, the V chord, is considered the dominant chord in the minor key, although another chord of dominant quality occurs diatonically on step VII.

Diatonic Chords in A Minor (with V7 replacing vm7)

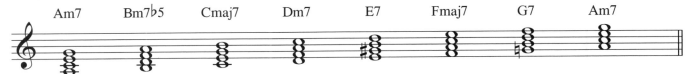

Motion of Secondary Dominants in A Minor

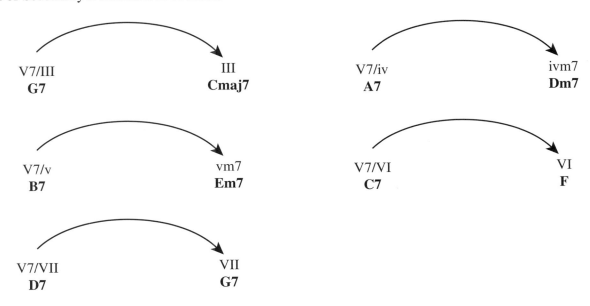

| V7/III | III | V7/iv | ivm7 |
| G7 | Cmaj7 | A7 | Dm7 |

| V7/v | vm7 | V7/VI | VI |
| B7 | Em7 | C7 | F |

| V7/VII | VII |
| D7 | G7 |

Again, V7/ii is not used in the minor mode, since ii is a m7♭5 chord, which cannot be tonicized.

Diminished Chords Functioning as Dominants

Diminished 7th chords, as we learned in Chapter 3, may function as rootless 7♭9 chords. The diminished 7th chord occurs naturally on the seventh step of harmonic minor tonality, with the label vii°7. The same label is used when diminished chords function as secondary dominants.

An important difference in the analysis of a diminished 7th chord is that in order to be considered a functioning secondary dominant, it must be followed by one of its intended targets: a diatonic chord a half step above any of its tones. (Remember that any tone in a dim7 chord may be thought of as its root—see page 104.)

Motion of Diminished Chords with Secondary Dominant Function in C Major

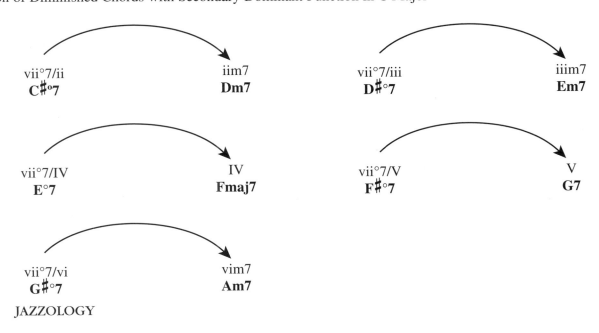

| vii°7/ii | iim7 | vii°7/iii | iiim7 |
| C#°7 | Dm7 | D#°7 | Em7 |

| vii°7/IV | IV | vii°7/V | V |
| E°7 | Fmaj7 | F#°7 | G7 |

| vii°7/vi | vim7 |
| G#°7 | Am7 |

Motion of Diminished Chords with Secondary Dominant Function in A minor

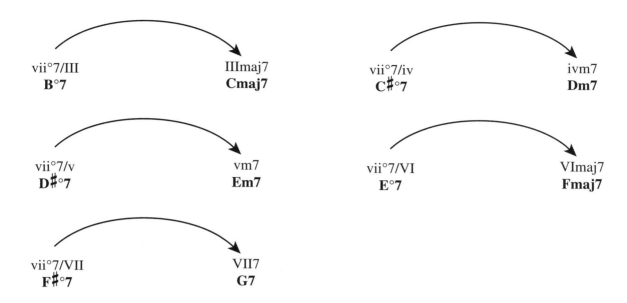

Backcycling Dominants

These are two or more dominant chords that follow the circle of 5ths until they reach the **target chord**—usually I. The final point of resolution of this series of secondary dominants may be delayed for quite some time. The example below shows a typical "rhythm changes" bridge in B♭. The target chord after this section is B♭maj7, which is Imaj7 in the key of B♭.

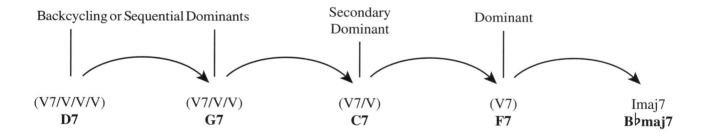

Roman numeral analysis does not work well for these cycles of dominant seventh chords, and is usually reserved for diatonic and secondary dominant chords. If used for backcycling dominants, functions should be enclosed in parentheses. Backcycling dominants are sometimes called **sequential dominants** or **extended dominant** chords, though this last term is potentially confusing and should be avoided, as it is already used to mean chords with added tension notes.

Related ii's

Any dominant chord may be preceded by its related minor 7th chord (iim7), which is found a perfect 4th below. Roman numeral analysis is not necessary, but brackets are needed to show that the pair belongs together. The example below is an arrangement where related iim7 chords are applied.

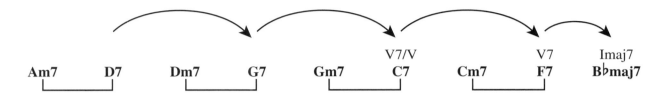

This kind of reharmonization was common during the bebop era.

Contiguous Dominants

Contiguous dominants consist of a series of non-functional dominant chords or ii–V's. They generally occur in one of the following patterns: ascending by half step, whole step, minor 3rd, or major 3rd; or, descending by minor 3rd or major 3rd. When the pattern is a series of ii–V's, the first V7 does not resolve to the chord that follows it, which is really the relative ii of the next dominant chord. The result is a deceptive cadence, since the V7 does not resolve to the chord a perfect 5th or half step down as expected. Contiguous dominants actually outline a series of brief modulations. Suggesting or implying a new key without actually moving to and establishing the new key is called **tonicization**.

The technique actually dates back to the Romantic period and was common with Schumann, Chopin, and Brahms. In many works of this period, modulations tended to become more frequent and shorter, resulting in passages where the music had little chance to settle or come to rest in the new key. Of course, the best way to imply a new key without going there is to use the key's dominant chord, or, better, a dominant preceded by a subdominant chord. To add structure and logic to such passages, composers would frequently move through suggested keys in a predictable way, such as moving through the scale degrees or moving by a fixed interval.

The procedure has become much more codified in jazz theory, generally manifesting itself in a series of V's or ii–V's that move through keys at a fixed interval. Because contiguous dominants lack immediate resolution, they instil a sense of anticipation or expectation to a chord progression. They are often used to delay the final resolution, thus strengthening the feeling of closure when the tonic is finally reached. Examples of contiguous dominants are shown on the next page.

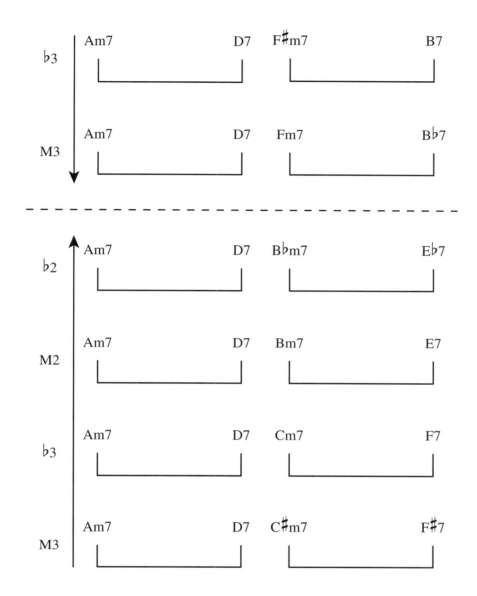

Chapter 5 Exercises

1. a. Show major and relative minor II–V–I cadences using the following key signatures and analyze using brackets and arrows.
   b. List all possible secondary dominants in these keys on another sheet.
   c. Identify the harmonic function of each secondary dominant.

Example

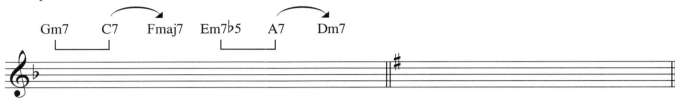

2. a. Complete the following and fill in the blanks.
   b. What kind of dominant chords are these?
   c. Find all possible secondary dominants in these keys.

Example

3. Complete the following chord progressions and add harmonic analyses.

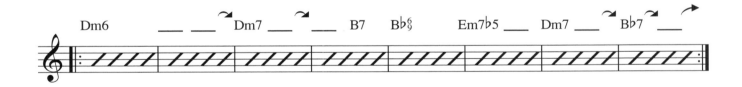

4. Identify the key in which the following chords will have the function indicated. Use enharmonic equivalents where convenient.

G7 is V7/V in the key of:
D♭7 is V7/IV in the key of:
F♯7 is V7/ii in the key of:
E7 is V7/IV in the key of:
B°7 is vii°7/V in the key of:
C♯7 is V7/V in the key of:
B♭7 is V7/vi in the key of:
D♯°7 is vii°7/iii in the key of:
F♯°7 is vii°7/iii in the key of:
E♭7 is V7/V in the key of:
D7 is V7/vi in the key of:

5. Analyze the following progressions indicating chord function, considering harmonic structure.

a. || Dm7 G7 | Dm7 G7 | Em7 A7 | Em7 A7 |

    | Dm7 G7 | A♭m7 D♭7 | C | Em7 |

    | A7 | | Dm | ||

b. || C | Am7 | D7 | |

    | Dm7 | G7 | C   Am7 | D7 G7 ||

c. || A♭ | Fm7 | B♭7 E♭7 | B♭7 E♭7 ||

d. || G♯m7 C♯7 | F♯m7 B7 | Em7 A7 | Dm7 G7 ||

e. || B7 | Em7 A7 | Dm7 G7 | C ||

f. || B7 | Em7 | A7   D7 | G7   C ||

g. || B7   Em7 | A7 | Am7 D7 | Dm7 G7 ||

h. || B7 | Em7 | A7 | Dm7 G7 ||

i. || B7 | | Em7 | A7 ||

j. || C   C7 | F | Fm7 B♭7 | A7 ||

k. || C   C7 | F   Fm7 | B♭7 | A7 ||

6. Locate the following tunes in a reliable source. Study, analyze, and play them. It is recommended that they be learned thoroughly and ultimately memorized.

- "Blue Bossa"
- "Autumn Leaves"
- "Tune Up"
- "Confirmation"
- "Caravan"
- "Giant Steps"
- "Body and Soul"
- "Manha do Carnaval"
- "Countdown"

- "All the Things You Are"
- "Blues for Alice"
- "I Got Rhythm"
- "Nardis"
- "Bluesette"
- "Waltz for Debby"
- "Joy Spring"
- "Song for My Father"

II–V–I PIANO VOICINGS AND VOICE LEADING

The **voicing** of a chord is the exact vertical arrangement of its tones. The term is commonly used by pianists and guitarists to indicate how chord tones are distributed when comping for improvisers. Keyboard voicings may be played by either one or both hands.

Why study voicings? In jazz practice, a large repertoire of voicings is necessary; comping instruments (such as piano, guitar, vibes, or organ) rarely play chords in ascending order (1–3–5–7–9, etc). This is for various reasons:

- Using only root position chords will result in excessive parallel 5ths, which can sound like a monotonous drone. Simply put, a relentless string of root-position chords tends to sound boring. The result will be perceived as unrefined and decidedly "uncool."

- Successive root-position chords force the hands to move too much, because the roots of chords often move by 5ths rather than linearly.

- Using only root position chords results in poor voice leading. Inner voices do not resolve in a smooth and logical fashion. (Voice leading will be discussed later in this chapter.)

As a basic example of chord voicing, a major seventh chord will often be played as 1–7–3–5, where the 3rd and 5th are raised an octave from their original positions. This is just one of a vast number of possibilities for voicing this chord.

Jazz piano voicings are divided into two basic types, **rooted voicings** and **rootless voicings**.

Rooted Voicings

Sometimes called "Bud Powell voicings," these left-hand piano voicings place the root deep in the bass and provide a solid harmonic foundation, obviating the need for a bass player. You may play rooted voicings as: 1–3–5–7, 1–3–7 (known as a shell voicing), or just 1–7 (or even 1–3), depending upon the chord's quality. Here are Cmaj7 rooted voicings.

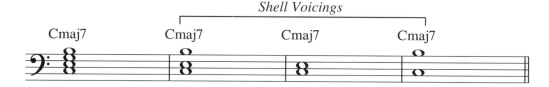

Rootless Voicings

As the name implies, rootless voicings have the root omitted. They are the preferred voicing technique when jamming or comping with a rhythm section, and most often used when a bassist is present. They work equally well with non-tonal/modal music.

> The 5th is often omitted. If included, it will generally be on top of the voicing.

Rootless and especially left-hand piano voicings are commonly employed as three- or four-note voicings.

Three-Note Voicings

Chords can be voiced with three notes as follows.

Major ii–V–I cadence

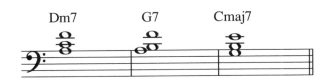

Minor ii–V–i cadence

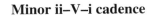

Four-Note One-Hand Voicings

Four-note voicings are the most common left-hand piano chord voicings because of their richness. They are also known as "Bill Evans" voicings. They may be classified into two categories: **type A** and **type B**. Both are four-note close voicings and each is the inversion of the other. They were made popular by Bill Evans and Wynton Kelly, and can be used as building blocks for many other voicings. The following configurations must be learned thoroughly.

Type A: 3–5–7–9
Type B: 7–9–3–5

Major Rootless Voicings

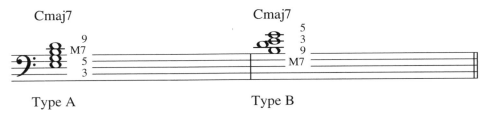

Other Common Rootless Voicings for Major Chords

Type A: 3–5–6–9 or 3–6–7–9
Type B: 6–9–3–5

Minor Rootless Voicings

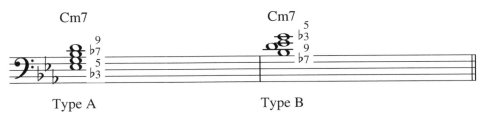

Other Common Rootless Voicings for Minor Chords

Type A: ♭3–5–6–9

Type B: 6–9–♭3–5

Dominant Rootless Voicings

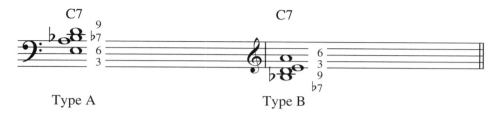

> The 5th is often replaced by the 6th (13th) in order to provide a typical jazz color. Of course, three-note voicings such as 3–7–9 or 7–3–13 will not include the 5th.

Altered Dominant Rootless Voicings

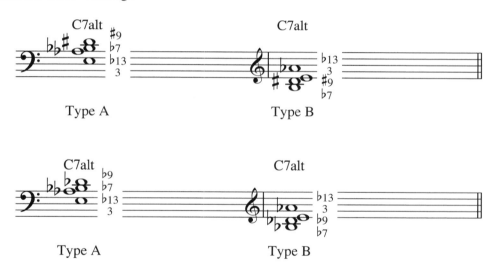

The altered dominant is most often encountered in the minor ii–V–i cadence.

Dm7♭5	G7alt	Cm7 or Cm6
iim7♭5	V7alt	im7 or im6

It is especially prominent as a secondary dominant in the major ii–V–I cadence.

Cmaj7 A7alt	Dm7 G7
Imaj7 VI7alt	iim7 V7

Half-diminished (m7♭5) voicings are less often extended than the other types, and the root is more often included.

Half-Diminished Voicings

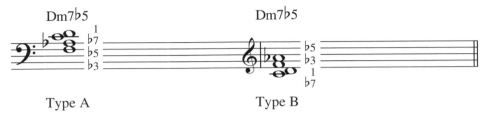

Other Common Voicings for Half-Diminished Chords

Type A: ♭3–♭5–♭7–9
or
Type A: ♭3–♭5–♭7–♭9

Type B: ♭7–9–♭3–♭5
or
Type B: ♭7–♭9–♭3–♭5

Voice Leading and the ii–V–I Cadence

Voice leading refers to the creation of smooth motion between inner voices by maintaining adjacent tones when moving from one chord to another. In other words, each inner voice is connected to the next through common tones or stepwise movement. Voice leading allows us to hear the chord resolutions we expect, but with very little movement between adjacent chord tones. With good voice leading, harmony notes form lines that progress smoothly and strengthen the harmonic continuity.

The following examples will help you to visualize and memorize voice-leading rules by using just guide tones around the circle of fifths. You may play either 3–7 or (inverted) 7–3. Pay particular attention to how the guide tones switch when moving from one chord to another around the circle.

Dominant Chords around the Circle

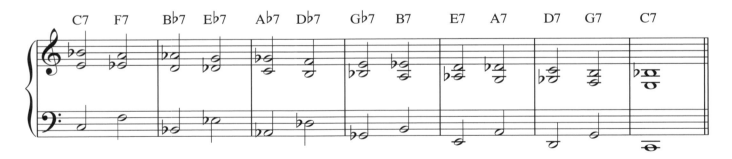

Major Chords around the Circle

Minor Chords around the Circle

One-Hand Voicings

In jazz practice, extra tension notes are often added in the ii–V–I cadence.

Major Key Extended ii–V–I Voicings

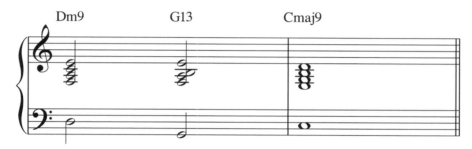

is preferable to

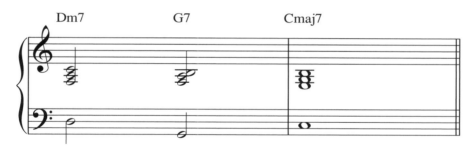

Notice how type A follows type B and how type B follows type A in the following examples.

One-Hand Voicings

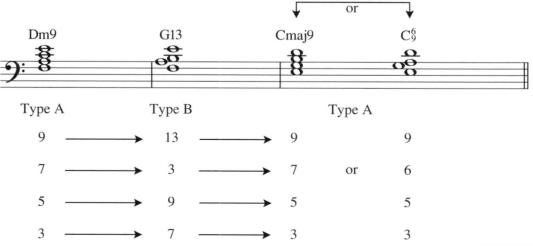

Type A		Type B			Type A		
9	→	13	→	9			9
7	→	3	→	7	or		6
5	→	9	→	5			5
3	→	7	→	3			3

Inverted One-Hand Voicings

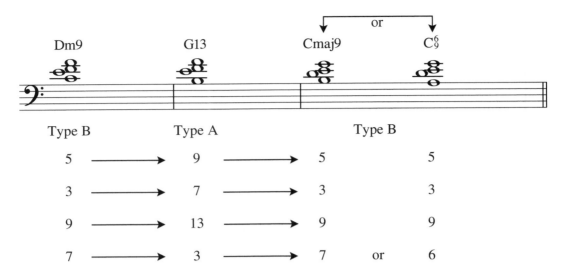

Type B	Type A	Type B	
5 ⟶	9 ⟶	5	5
3 ⟶	7 ⟶	3	3
9 ⟶	13 ⟶	9	9
7 ⟶	3 ⟶	7 or	6

We may summarize the voice-leading rules as follows. (Arrows represent inner-voice exchange.)

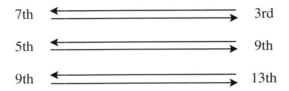

7th ⟷ 3rd

5th ⟷ 9th

9th ⟷ 13th

G13♭9 may be substituted for G13. This produces a more poignant effect. (The dominant diminished scale may be used over the G13♭9 chord.)

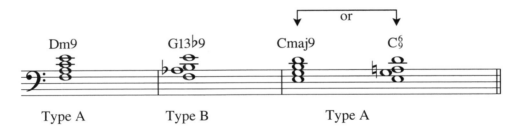

Type A Type B Type A

Inversion

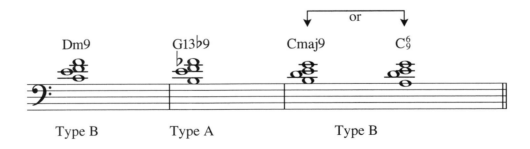

Type B Type A Type B

Other Inversion

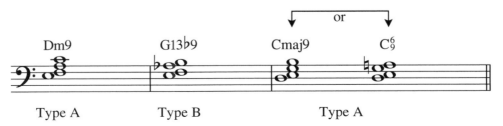

Type A Type B Type A

Minor Key Extended ii–V–i Voicings

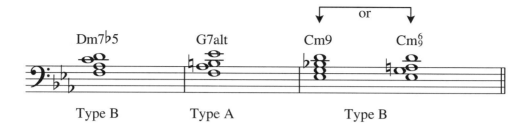

Inversion

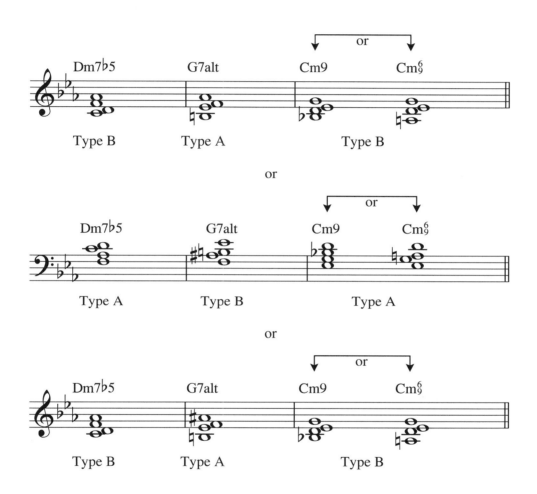

or

Other Inversion

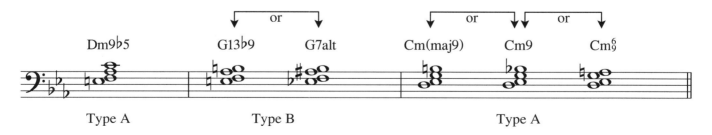

Alternative Voicings for Minor Keys

You can alternate between the ♭3rd and the 4th when voicing the ii in a minor ii–V–i cadence. This is very effective for iim7♭5. Following are six options for voicing a half-diminished chord.

Instead of:

you may play:

♭3–♭5–♭7–1

4–♭5–♭7–1 or 4–♭5–♭7–9/♭9

♭5–♭7–1–♭3

♭5–♭7–1–4 or ♭5–♭7–9/♭9–4

1–♭3–♭5–♭7

1–4–♭5–♭7 or 9–4–♭5–♭7

On iv of a minor key, a m7♭5 chord may be substituted for the diatonic min7 chord. The ♭5 of the substitute chord is equivalent to the M7 of the overall key, implying harmonic minor. A m7♭5 chord may be also be inserted on VI in a minor key, implying the Dorian mode.

On ♭VI, ♭VII and ♭III of a minor key, you might play a maj7♯5 chord or a maj7♭5 chord instead of the diatonic maj7 chord.

Points to Remember:
- Type A voicings have a more open sound for major and minor chords.

- Type B voicings have a more open sound for dominant chords.

- Some dominant voicings are duplicates of other voicings. In the following examples, illustrated in the key of F major, the voicing of a dominant chord will be the same as:

1) an altered dominant having a root a tritone away. Both type A and type B voicings for C13 are also voicings for an altered dominant chord a tritone away (F♯7alt).
2) a m7♭5 chord a M3rd above. Both type A and type B voicings for C13 are also voicings for Em11♭5.
3) a **suspended-phrygian** chord a m3rd below. Both type A and type B voicings for C13 are also voicings for A7sus4♭9.
4) a minor chord a 4th below. Both type A and type B voicings for C13 are voicings for Gm⁶.

Notice that these voicings belong to G melodic minor.

Left-Hand Voicing Rules
- If the root movement is linear—by M2nd or by m2nd—keep the same voicing.

- If the root movement is by 4th or 5th, the voicing should be switched from type A to type B or vice versa.

- If the root movement is by M3rd or by m3rd, the voicing is either retained or switched, at the player's discretion.

Comping Ranges for Rootless Voicings

A too-dark or "muddy" sound results if a voicing is played too low; a thin or "tinny" sound results if a voicing is played too high. Generally, good voicing practice dictates that the lowest note (the bass) should be one octave below middle C and the highest note one octave above.

Keep the left pinky (lowest note) no lower than D♭ below middle C. In particular, do not place the 3rd or 7th of the chord below the D♭ below middle C in the left hand (this applies to left-hand and open forms). Type A voicings are suited to this situation.

Keep the left thumb (highest note) no higher than B above middle C. Do not place the 3rd or 7th of the chord too high. This can result in a thin sound and will restrict the soloing range. Thus, there is a one-and-one-half octave range in which to play rootless voicings. Below this, the voicings may sound muddy, and above, tinny.

Left-Handed Rootless Voicing – Preferred Range

The comping range for the right hand can be just about anywhere, but you have to gauge the appropriateness by good taste. In general, voicings should probably be played with the lowest note within an octave of either side of middle C on the piano. In other words, the range of chord voicings should fall between the C below middle C and the C on the second ledger line above the treble clef. There are exceptions, however, so let the ear be the final judge. (See Chapter 9 for rhythmic patterns to be used when comping with the left hand, right hand, and both hands.)

Rootless Voicings for the Blues

An interesting model that reflects root movement by 4th or 5th is the 12-bar blues progression. The following illustration shows rootless voicings in a standard blues in F. The chord qualities throughout are dominant chords. Key centers are F, B♭ and C. Chord functions are I7, IV7, and V7.

Blues in F
Starting with Type A Voicing

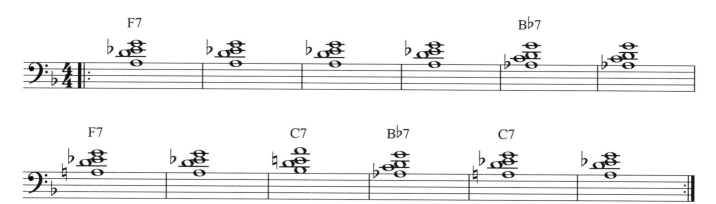

Blues in F
Starting with Type B Voicing

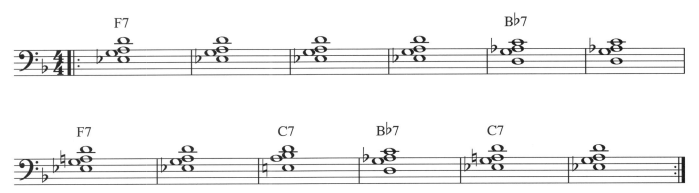

Now look at the following examples where the basic blues progression is embellished with ii–V's in measures 4 and 9, a diminished passing chord in measure 6, and a turnaround starting in measure 11, creating a standard **jazz-blues** progression. Notice how voicings flow from one to another, illustrating how proper voice leading works. These are excellent rootless voicings for playing 12-bar blues. Transpose the model into all twelve keys and play.

Blues in F
Voiced Starting with Type A

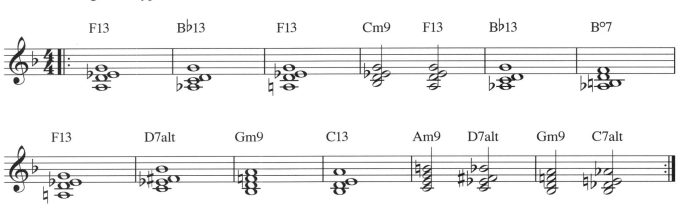

Blues in F
Voiced Starting with Type B

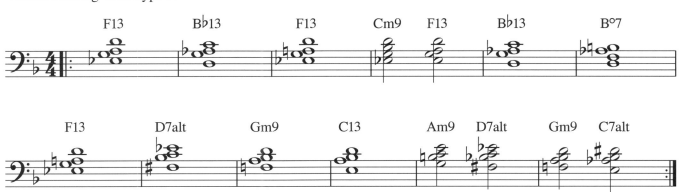

Two-Hand Voicings

Four-Note Voicings

Two-hand voicings create a full sound of unduplicated notes by increasing spacing or by dropping one or more notes from close voicing to a position one octave below. The most common technique is called **drop 2**. The second voice from the top is repositioned an octave below.

Type 1

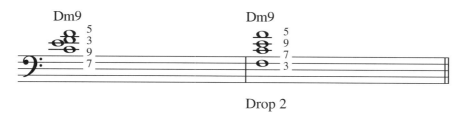

Drop 2

Type 2

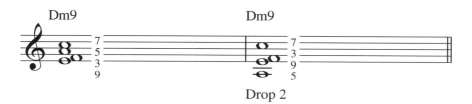

Drop 2

Type 3

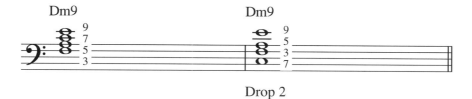

Drop 2

Type 4

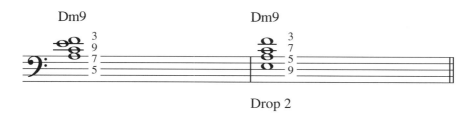

Drop 2

Major ii–V–I with Two-Hand Drop-2 Voicings

Type 1

Type 2

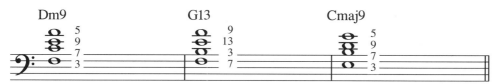

Type 3

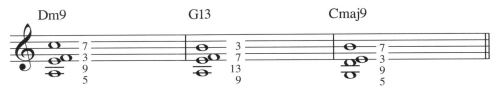

Type 4

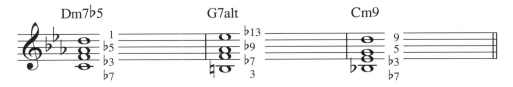

Minor ii–V–i with Two-Hand Drop-2 Voicings

Type 1

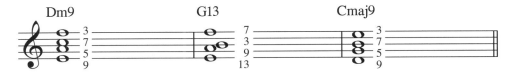

Type 2

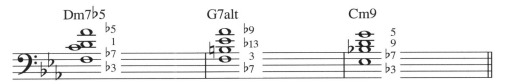

Type 3

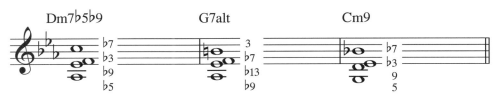

Type 4

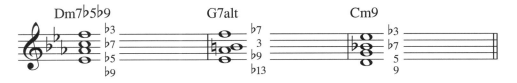

Characteristics and Range

Drop-2 voicings sound both full and transparent, especially in the midrange, which extends from about the F one octave plus a 5th below middle C to the G one octave plus a 5th above middle C. Chords that have F as the lowest note include Fmaj7, F7, Fm7, A♭6, F6 (Dm7) and Fm6 (Dm7♭5). Chords with G as the highest note include: G6 (Em7), E♭7, E°7, and Em7♭5 (Gm6). The following example shows one possible chord at each end of the range.

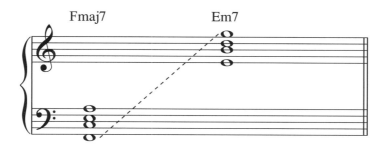

Drop-2 as well as **drop 2–4** voicings are used when accompanying a soloist or a singer, as well as when soloing, because their open structure produces a rich sound. Here are examples of major and minor ii–V–I progressions with drop 2–4 voicings, where the second and fourth notes from the top are dropped by an octave.

Type 1

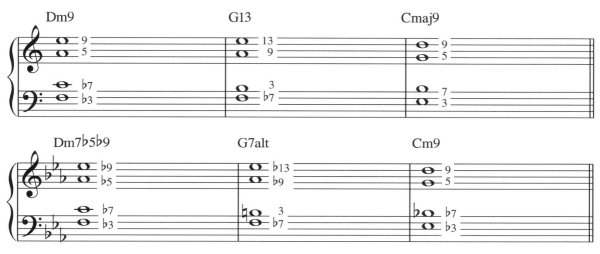

Type 2

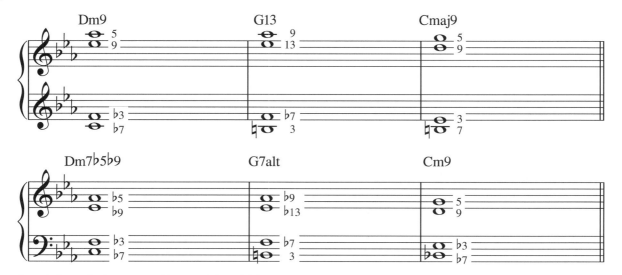

Drop 3 and **drop 2–3** are usually considered big-band arranging techniques, but may also be used when comping.

Modal Voicings

Modal voicings were made popular by McCoy Tyner, a jazz pianist who used modal harmony or **quartal harmony** extensively in his comping, as well as in his compositions. Pianist Joanne Brackeen displays a similar style. Both players incorporate a great deal of quartal harmony in their voicings, resulting in a preponderance of 4ths. This creates a distinctly modal sound. The use of modal harmonies is yet another arranging technique, found in modal tunes such as "So What," "Moaning," "Milestones," "Impressions," "Maiden Voyage," "Footprints," "My Favorite Things," "Blue in Green," and "Little Sunflower," to name a few. All of these tunes are characterized by the inclusion of 4ths in the structure of the chords. Modal tunes are also characterized by static, non-functional harmony.

Quartal Voicings

Also called **fourth voicings**, these voicings are built by stacking perfect 4ths or augmented 4ths based on the different degrees of the key center, played over the same root. They make most sense in modal music, as they can establish a tonal center without reference to function. Stacked 4ths result in open chords that are less dense than harmonic structures built on 3rds.

Modal voicings may be left-hand voicings or two-hand voicings. They are most often employed in the Dorian mode, with minor chords, or with suspended chords. One way to reinforce a particular chord or scale is to slide voicings up or down in parallel motion while intervallic relationships between notes remain constant relative to the melodic line. This creates a sense of motion between comping and voicings while the harmony remains static. Known variously as **planing**, **side-stepping**, or **parallelism**, this technique can be applied to either chromatic or diatonic motion.

Here is an example of chromatic planing in a salsa break.

Quartal voicings such as the following are quite effective, especially when supporting a pentatonic melodic line.

* Key signature denotes C Dorian.

Below is a descending line harmonized with quartals in convincing modal fashion.

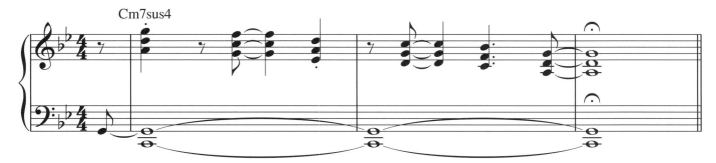

"So What" Voicings

This type of voicing, m7sus4, consists of a series of three P4ths with a 3rd on top. These chords are often played as an alternative to quartal voicings. An authentic example occurs in "So What" by Miles Davis.

"So What" voicings may use both diatonic and chromatic planing.

The following example might provide an effective eight-bar introduction to Mal Waldron's "Soul Eyes."

Tonal Quartal Voicings for ii–V–I Cadences

Most often, quartal voicings derive from pentatonic scales. (Any pentatonic scale can be arranged in a series of fourths.) Of the many quartal voicings available on a given chord, some will sound acceptable while others should be avoided because they conflict with the harmony or the melody. Incomplete quartal voicings may occur as long as the basic chord sound is clearly implied. When playing quartal voicings, avoid tones that are only used in modal contexts and would not likely occur in a tonal framework. For example, ♭9th intervals are generally avoided in tonal quartal voicings, since they have no clear tonal implications.

Left-hand quartal voicings are often 3-note voicings consisting of either perfect or augmented 4ths.

Tonal Quartal Voicings for the ii–V–I Cadence

Imaj7: 2–5–1, 3–6–9, 6–9–5, 7–3–6, or ♯4–7–3 (rare)

iim7: 1–4–♭7, 2–5–1, ♭3–6–9 (effective in modal contexts but avoided in tonal contexts because of its ambiguity), 4–♭7–♭3, 5–1–4, or 6–9–5

V7: ♭7–3–6

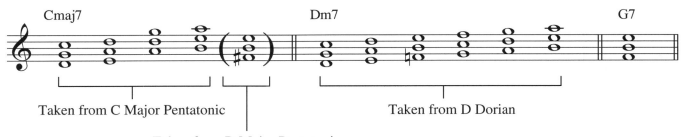

Taken from C Major Pentatonic   Taken from D Dorian

Taken from D Major Pentatonic

Here is an example of left-hand quartal voicings in a major ii–V–I.

Minor Key Quartal Voicings

im⁶/₉ or m7: ♭3–6–9, ♭7–♭3–6 (rare and avoided), 4–♭7–♭3

iim7♭5: 1–♭5–♭7, ♭5–1–4, ♭7–♭3–♭13 (rare), or ♭3–♭13–♭9 (rare)

V7alt: ♭7–3–♭13 or 3–♭7–♯9

Here is an example of left-hand quartal voicings in a minor ii–V–i.

Two-Hand Quartal Voicings

A common approach to two-hand quartal voicings consists of playing guide tones or 3-note rootless voicings with the left hand while the right hand stacks 4ths. Sometimes when both hands are connected, the left hand may stack 4ths too, especially when voicing Imaj7, im⁶/₉, or im7, and V7. The use of both hands in quartal voicings is encountered in the modal comping of McCoy Tyner, Bill Evans, and Randy Weston.

Right-Hand Quartal Voicings in Major Keys

Imaj7: 2–5–1, 3–6–9, 6–9–5, 7–3–6, or #4–7–3

iim7: 1–4–♭7, 2–5–1, 4–♭7–♭3, 5–1–4, or 6–9–5

V7: 13–9–5, 9–5–1, or 5–13–9 (same quartals as for iim7)

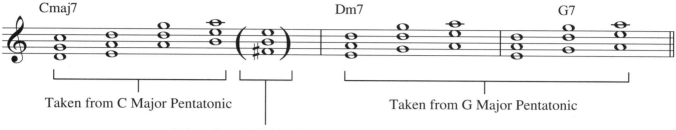

Taken from C Major Pentatonic

Taken from D Major Pentatonic

Taken from G Major Pentatonic

These are examples of two-hand quartal voicings over major ii–V–I cadences.

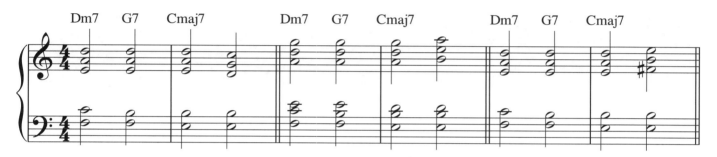

Right-Hand Quartal Voicings in Minor Keys

im⁶/₉ or m7: 2–5–1, 5–1–4, or 6–9–5

iim7♭5: 1–4–♭7, 4–1–♭3, or ♭7–♭3–♭13

V7alt: ♭7–3–♭13, #9–♭13–♭9, or ♭13–♭9–#11

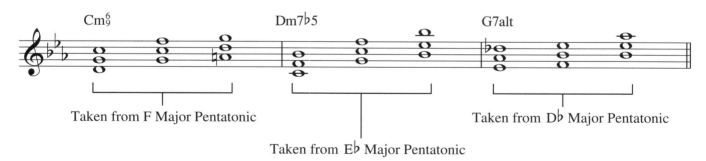

Taken from F Major Pentatonic

Taken from E♭ Major Pentatonic

Taken from D♭ Major Pentatonic

Here is an example of two-hand quartal voicings over a minor ii–V–i cadence.

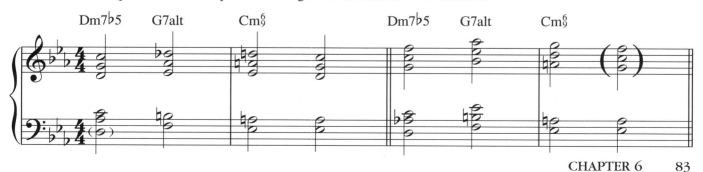

Some other permutations could be:

When playing 3-note type B voicings over an altered dominant, make sure to include the ♭9 in the left hand (3–♭7–♭9) and never (3–♭7–9). Over Imaj7 the left hand may alternate between the 5th and the 6th: 7–3–5 or 7–3–6.

The following chart shows some effective voicings that have been used by many jazz pianists. They are useful in all two-handed comping situations. They may be enlarged into five- or six-note voicings.

CHORD QUALITY	LEFT HAND	RIGHT HAND
Maj7	3–6, 7–3–6	9–5–7, ♯11–7–3
Maj7	3–5–7	9–3–1, 9–13–9
Maj7	3–6, 3–6–9	9–5–7, 9–♯11–7, 6–9–5, 7–3–6
m7	♭3–5–♭7, ♭7–♭3–5	9–5–1, 5–1–11, 6–9–5
m7	♭3–6, ♭3–6–9	9–5–1, 6–9–5
m7	♭3–♭7–9	5–1–11, 5–9–11
m7	1–4–♭7	♭3–5, ♭3–5–9, ♭3–6–9
m7♭5	1–♭5–♭7, ♭5–1–11	♭3–♭13–♭9, 11–♭7–♭3, ♭7–♭3–♭13
m7♭5	1–♭5–♭7, ♭5–1–11	9–11–♭13
m7♭5	1–4–♭5–♭7	9–11, ♭3–♭13, ♭13–♭9–♭5
7	♭7–3–13	9–5–1, 9–5–9, 9–13–9
7	3–♭7	9–5–1, 3–13–9, 13–9–5
7	3–♭7–9	3–5–1, 3–13–1
7	♭7–3–13, ♭7–3–♭13	♭9–3–13, ♭9–♯11–♭7, ♯9–♭13–13
7	1–♭7	3–13–1, 3–13–9

cont. ⟶

CHORD QUALITY	LEFT HAND	RIGHT HAND
7♯11	1–♭7, 1–3–♭7, 3–♭7–9	9–♯11–13, ♯11–13–9
7sus4	1–♭7	9–11–13, 11–13–9, 13–9–11
7sus4	1–4–♭7	9–5–1, 5–1–4, 13–9–5, 4–13–9
7alt	1–♭7	3–♭13–1, 3–♭13–♭9, 3–♭13–♯9
7alt	♭7–3–♭13	♭9–♯11–♭7 or ♯9–♭13–1
7alt	♭7–3–♭13	♯9–♭13–♭9, ♭13–♭9–♯11
7♯9	3–♭7–♭9, 3–♭7–♯9	5–♭7–♯9, ♭7–♯9–5
7alt	3–♭7–♭9, 3–♭7–♯9	♯5–♭7–♯9, ♯11–♭7–♯9, ♭7–♯9–♯11
7alt	3–♭7–♭9, 3–♭7–♯9	♭7–♯9–♭13, ♭13–♭9–♯11

Cluster Voicings

In classical music this concept is referred to as **secundal harmony**. **Clusters**, also called **tone clusters**, consist of collections of pitches that are closely arranged by stacking major or minor 2nds instead of 3rds or larger intervals. Any vertical aggregation of notes containing more than two adjacent tones can be called a cluster. Clusters provide maximum density and can represent either dissonances or more tonal consonances, providing a tight and compact arrangement of the notes. (In jazz these notes will almost always be members of a particular scale, chord, or mode. In classical music they need not be.) Clusters usually sound best when played at soft to medium volume. Bill Evans and Thelonious Monk were pioneers in using clusters as chord voicings.

Clusters are not normally used in ii–V–I cadences and are not conventional piano voicings. Nevertheless, they can be very effective in some contexts and can spice up some melodic lines. By inverting the notes in a cluster (or by dispersing them into different octaves), the voicing can be opened up to create some interesting results (such as quartal harmonies), but at the expense of losing the characteristic tight sonority of the cluster.

Some ii–V–I cadences in C major with cluster voicings are shown below.

There are endless permutations. The best approach is to pack the chord tones plus optional tones as closely as possible and experiment at the piano to find smooth resolutions. Dissonances neither have nor require rules, except: 1) never have a m2 on the top of the voicing—this makes a poor cluster sound; 2) low range limits should not go below E♭ below middle C for a M2nd cluster (E♭–F) and E for a m2nd cluster (E–F).

Below are examples studied previously in this book that include clusters. Notice the cluster voicings played over G13, G13♭9 and over C⁶₉.

Clusters in Major ii–V–I

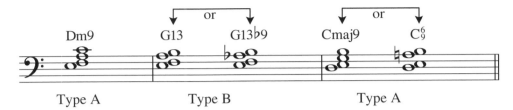

Type A   Type B   Type A

Clusters sound particularly effective in minor contexts, especially over iim7♭5.

Clusters in Minor ii–V–i

Other common cluster voicings occur in the Phrygian mode. Below is an E Phrygian or Esus4♭9 voicing, and an inversion of an E7sus4 chord.

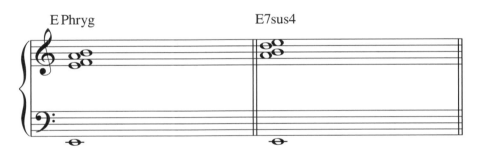

Observe that the cluster voicing played over iim7♭5 in the previous minor ii–V–i cadence (4–♭5–♭7–1) is the same cluster voicing for an E Phrygian, which played from the root becomes 1–♭2–4–5. This may imply the sound of an E Phrygian mode. Thus the voicing is called "E Phryg," often written as Esus4♭9. It also implies a cluster voicing for the following chords: G13, Dm⁶₉, Fmaj7♭5, and D♭7alt.

The suspended cluster voicing structure for E7sus4 (4–5–♭7–1) may imply other sonorities, such as the following chords: D⁶₉ or Dm⁶₉, Fmaj7(♭5, 6), G(add⁶₉), Asus4(add9), Bm7sus4, D♭7alt.

Fragment Voicings
Also known as **partial voicings**, these incomplete constructions consist of just three notes, including a half step (or less often, a whole step) on the bottom. Because of their weak and ambiguous sound, they work especially well over 3/4 meter tunes, which lack the strong metrical pulse of 2 and 4 associated with common time. Fragment voicings derive from early twentieth-century French composers, especially Eric Satie, Claude Debussy, Maurice Ravel, and Gabriel Fauré. In essence, the harmony is suggested rather than defined. This is accomplished by omitting some chord tones to achieve a desired musical effect. This concept has influenced many jazz pianists, including Bill Evans, Keith Jarrett, Chick Corea, Thelonious Monk, Clare Fischer, and Herbie Hancock. The technique derives from the playing style of the great jazz pianist and innovator Bill Evans, whose original harmonic approach (dominated by rootless and cluster voicings) had an important impact on the playing of modern jazz pianists. Examples of fragment voicings can be heard on many of his recordings.

The following are typical fragment voicings.

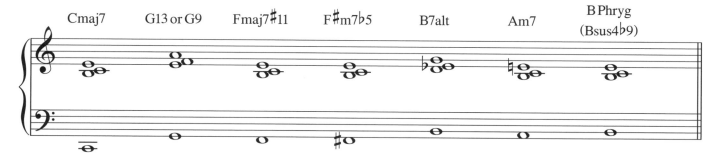

Notice how several chords share the same simple voicing. Consequently, a limited number of voicings can have many applications. Here is an excerpt from an original composition.

In Three Days

© 1998 Nor Eddine Bahha

Another example of these 3-note voicings may be found in Stuart Isacoff's tune, "Justice."

Fragment Chord Summary

CHORD QUALITY	FRAGMENT VOICING CHOICES
M7	M7–1–3 or 2–3–5 or ♯4–5–M7
m7	♭7–1–♭3 or 2–♭3–5
m7♭5	4–♭5–♭7
°7	9–♭3–♭5 or 4–♭5–13
7	♭7–1–3 or 13–♭7–9 or 13–♭7–♭9
7sus4	4–5–♭7
7sus4♭9	1–♭2–4
7alt	♭7–1–3 or ♯9–3–♭13
m⁶⁄₉; ⁶⁄₉	5–6–9

You may notice that Bill Evans type B voicings combine portions of two three-note groupings, including two fragments in one voicing.

Chapter 6 Exercises

1. Voice the following chords using 3rd and 7th guide tones with 3-note voicings, 4-note voicings, drop 2, and drop 2–4. For the purposes of these exercises suggested range limits may be exceeded.

Example

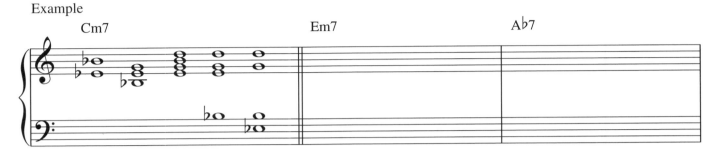

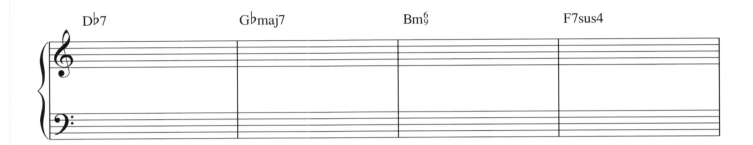

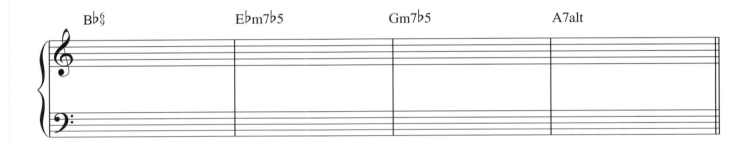

2. Voice the following three turnarounds with 3rd and 7th guide tones, then again on separate staff paper with 3-note voicings, 4-note voicings, drop 2, and drop 2–4. Use both inversions, types A and B.

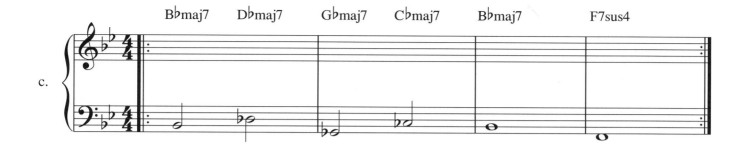

3. Select several jazz tunes of your choice and apply some of the voicings discussed in this chapter. See the voicing examples in the appendix for more options.

MODULATIONS AND MODAL INTERCHANGE

Modulations are changes of key. They may be as subtle as the brief suggestion of a new tonal center, or as significant as the permanent establishment of a new key. Modulations occur frequently in most jazz standards and can be as short as one measure or less.

To be considered a true modulation, the new key has to be verified by a cadence, typically involving V–I chord motion. Sometimes chords other than the tonic (I) chord are briefly emphasized in a chord progression, without the existence of a confirming cadence. This is referred to as tonicization, implying that a new tonic has been suggested without a true modulation to that key. Any ii–V creates an instance of tonicization, as shown in the following example, which tonicizes the key of A.

V–I Tonicization

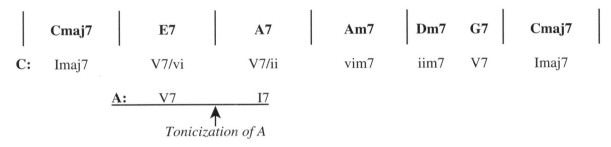

ii–V Tonicizations

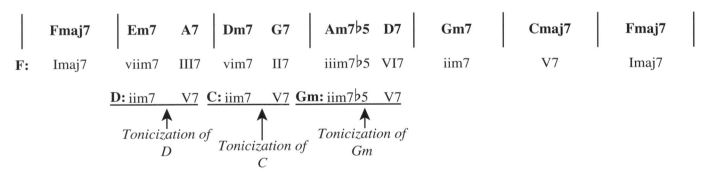

If another key becomes firmly established and actually replaces the original key by means of a confirming cadence, a true modulation has occurred. The following shows a modulation from C to A.

Cmaj7	C7	Fmaj7	E7	Amaj7	Bm7	E7	Amaj7
C: Imaj7	V7/IV	IVmaj7	A: V7	Imaj7	iim7	V7	Imaj7

Types of Modulations

Modulations occur in many ways, but most may be categorized into one of these four types.
- Direct
- Prepared
- Pivot Chord
- Transitional

In **direct** (also called **unprepared** or **abrupt**) **modulation**, the key changes from chord to chord without preparation, giving the impression that the music is suddenly in a new key.

Major Key to Major Key Direct Modulation

Minor Key to Minor Key Direct Modulation

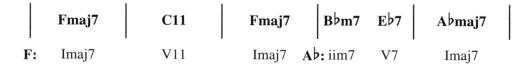

The modulation may also occur after the V7.
Major Key to Major Key

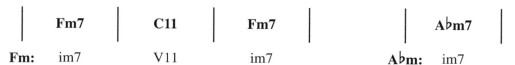

Minor Key to Minor Key

A good example of direct modulation is found in John Coltrane's "Giant Steps," which will be discussed in greater detail later.

In **prepared modulation**, a V7, a ii–V, or a vii°7 sets up the arrival of the new key.

Major Key to Major Key Prepared Modulation Using ii–V

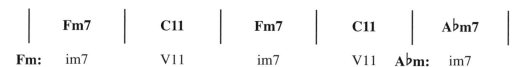

Minor Key to Minor Key Prepared Modulation Using ii–V

Each tone of a diminished 7th chord may resolve to the chord one half step above. However, the symmetrical structure of a diminished chord results in four enharmonic equivalents for any given chord: i°7 = ♭iii°7 = #iv°7 = vi°7 (i.e. F°7 = A♭°7 = B°7 = D°7). This results in four possible key-area resolutions: ♭II, III, V, ♭VII (G♭, A, C, and E♭, or G♭m, Am, Cm, and E♭m).

Prepared Modulations Using the °7 Chord

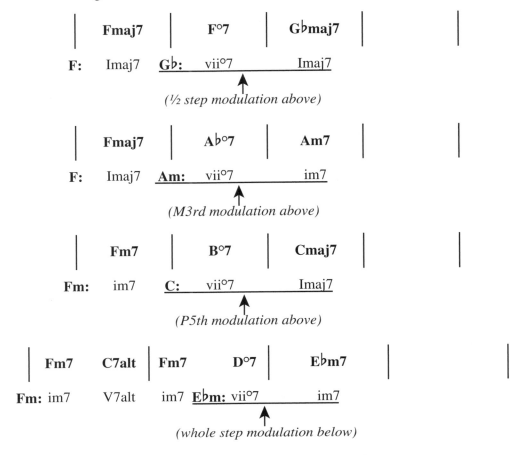

In **pivot chord modulation** a common chord that is diatonic to both the old and new keys serves as a link or "pivot" between the two adjacent tonal areas. It is not necessary to change the key signature when a piece modulates, although this can happen sometimes to facilitate easier reading of a melody.

In the progression below, the entire Cm7–F7 unit has a dual function, acting as vim7–II7 in E♭, and acting as iim7–V7 in B♭.

	Fm7	B♭7	E♭maj7	A♭maj7	Cm7	F7	B♭maj7	
E♭:	iim7	V7	Imaj7	IVmaj7	vim7	II7		
					B♭: iim7	V7	Imaj7	

Similarly, in the following example, the Am7–D7 is functioning both as iiim7–VI7 in F and iim7–V7 in G.

	Gm7	C7	Fmaj7	B♭maj7	Am7	D7	Gmaj7	
F:	iim7	V7	Imaj7	IVmaj7	iiim7	VI7		
					G: iim7	V7	Imaj7	

Pivot chord modulation works the same way in minor keys.

	Ebm6		Fm7b5	Bb7	Ebm	Ebm/Db	Cm7b5	F7		Bbm7	
Ebm:	im6		iim7b5	V7	im	(im)	vim7b5	II7		vm7	
			Bbm:	ivm	(ivm)		iim7b5	V7		im7	

Some modulations employ only the V7 instead of the entire ii–V7 cadence between keys.

	Dm7	G7		Cmaj		B7		Em7	
C:	iim7	V7		Imaj7		V7/iii		iiim7	
		Em:		bVImaj7		V7		im7	

The Cmaj7 chord is diatonic to both C major and E minor. The progression begins with ii–V–I in C major, but then the Cmaj7 becomes the bVImaj7 in E minor, resulting in a bVImaj7–V7–im7 progression in E minor.

A **transitional modulation** occurs when, following a cycle of chromatic ii–V's or sequential dominants (or sequential dominant substitutes), the music winds up in a different key from where it started. A series of progressive sequences, maintaining fixed horizontal relationships between chords, arrives at a destination different from the starting point.

	Fm7	Bb7		Ebmaj7		Em7	A7		Ebm7	Ab7		Dm7	G7		Cmaj7	
Eb:	iim7	V7		Imaj7	D:	iim7	V7	Db:	iim7	V7	C:	iim7	V7		Imaj7	

The changes go chromatically through three key areas, each suggested by a ii–V pair. The tonicized areas are D major, descending by half step to Db major, then down another half step to the final destination in C major. An example of transitional modulation is found in Coltrane's "Moment's Notice."

	Em7	A7		Fm7	Bb7		Ebmaj7		Abm7	Db7		Dm7	G7		Ebm7	Ab7		Dbmaj7	
D:	iim7	V7	Eb:	iim7	V7		IM7	Gb:	iim7	V7	C:	iim7	V7	Db:	iim7	V7		Imaj7	

The first eight measures of "Along Came Betty" provide another example of transitional modulation. (It also contains a tritone substitute, which we'll cover in Chapter 8.)

	Bbm7		Bm7		Bbm7		Bm7	E7		Amaj7		Ab7		Gmaj7		F#7	
Ab:	iim7	A:	iim7	Ab:	iim7	A:	iim7	V7		Imaj7	G:	SV7/I		Imaj7	F:	SV7/I	

Most tunes do not contain actual modulations. They may appear to change key, but it's usually best to analyze in the original key. A good example is "Just Friends," in G major.

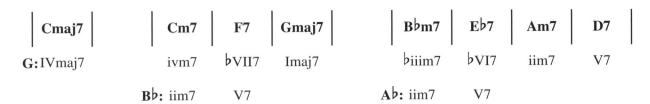

	Cmaj7			Cm7	F7	Gmaj7		Bbm7	Eb7	Am7	D7	
G: IVmaj7				ivm7	bVII7	Imaj7		biiim7	bVI7	iim7	V7	
			Bb: iim7	V7				**Ab:** iim7	V7			

The chord functions begin with IVmaj7, then ivm7 (it's possible to remain on the same chord quality, IVmaj7), moving to its related V7, producing bVII7 from the perspective of the original key. This is called the **back-door cadence** (bVII7–Imaj7) leading to G major: ivm7–bVII–Imaj7 or IVmaj7–bVII7–Imaj7, and analyzed as a sub-dominant cadence. In other words, the tonic chord is preceded, not by the V7 a 5th higher, but by a 7th chord (bVII7) a whole step lower. Some examples of this sequence are found in Miles Davis's "Half Nelson," Charlie Parker's "Yardbird Suite," Tadd Dameron's "Lady Bird," and Errol Garner's "Misty."

Other types of modulation are **parallel V–I** and **ii–V chains** modulation, as mentioned in Chapter 4. Any consecutive set of several parallel V–I's or parallel ii–V's creates "modulation" to many foreign keys, even though the I chord may be heard only briefly or not at all.

"Giant Steps"
V–I Chains Modulation

	Bmaj7	D7	Gmaj7	Bb7	Ebmaj7		Am7	D7	
	B: Imaj7	**G:** V7	Imaj7	**Eb:** V7	Imaj7		**G:** iim7	V7	

"Bluesette"
ii–V Chains Modulation

	Bbmaj7			Am7b5		D7		Gm7		C7		Fm7		Bb7	
Bb: Imaj7			**Gm:** iim7b5			V7	**F:**	iim7		V7	**Eb:**	iim7		V7	

Modal Interchange

Modal interchange (sometimes referred to as **borrowed harmonies**, **mode mixture**, or just **mixture**) is the use of a chord from a **parallel** (having the same root) mode or scale. Chords are "borrowed" from the parallel key and directly inserted into the original key, replacing expected functions. Chords that occur naturally in the natural or harmonic minor scale are commonly used in the parallel major. Borrowed chords have "altered" tones that do not belong to the original key signature, but that occur naturally in the parallel mode. By borrowing chords from parallel minor, the major scale expands its resources by adding the three variant notes of the natural minor scale (b3, b6, and b7). Arrangers and composers use modal interchange in order to create, to add, and to emphasize new colors in a composition, as well as to simplify modulations to certain foreign keys (specifically, to those keys that are closely related to the parallel minor or major of the key in which the piece or section started).

Chords that include ♭6—vii°7, iim7♭5, ivm, and vim6—are very commonly borrowed in major key progressions.
| Dm7 B°7 | Cmaj7 |

| Dm7♭5 G7♭9 | Cmaj7 | ("Night and Day")

| Dm7 Fm | Cmaj7 |

| Dm7 Fm6 | Cmaj7 |

| Dm7 Fm/G | Cmaj7 |

| Dm7 Fm6/G | Cmaj7 |

Chords that contain ♭3 are also commonly borrowed: im7, ♭VImaj7, and ♭IIImaj7.
| Cmaj7 Cm7 | Cmaj7 |

| Cmaj7 A♭maj7 | Cmaj7 |

| Cmaj7 E♭maj7 | Cmaj7 |

A half-diminished 7th chord can function as iim7♭5 in a major key.
| Cmaj7 | Dm7♭5/C | Cmaj7 |

A very common borrowing situation (classically—though not exactly accurately—termed the **Phrygian cadence**) occurs when a major or dominant V chord is approached via ivm6 in first inversion.
| Cmaj7 | Fm6/A♭ G7 | Cmaj7 |
      or
| Cmaj7 | Fm⁶/A♭ G7 | Cmaj7 |

Common Chord Borrowing Examples
These examples illustrate how common major-key cadences may be creatively modified with modal interchange.

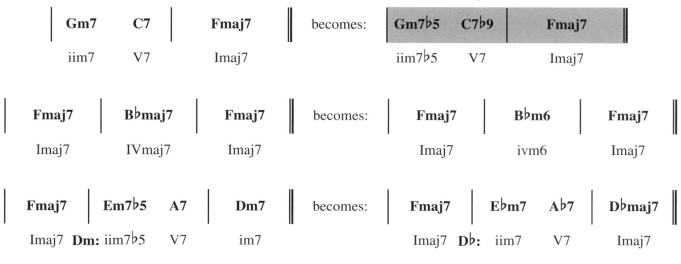

Beyond these relatively commonplace examples lie virtually endless possible parallel mode functions. Here is a chart of those available to major keys.

Major	Imaj7	iim7	iiim7	IVmaj7	V7	vim7	viim7♭5
Harmonic Minor	im(maj7)	iim7♭5	♭IIImaj7(♯5)	ivm7	V7♭9	♭VImaj7	vii°7
Melodic Minor	im(maj7)	iim7	♭IIImaj7(♯5)	IV7(♯11)	V9	vim7♭5	viim7♭5
Natural Minor	im7	iim7♭5	♭IIImaj7	ivm7	vm7	♭VImaj7	♭VII7
Dorian	im7	iim7	♭IIImaj7	IV7	vm7	vim7♭5	♭VIImaj7
Phrygian	im7	♭IImaj7	♭III7	ivm7	vm7♭5	♭VImaj7	♭viim7
Lydian	Imaj7	II7	iiim7	♯ivm7♭5	Vmaj7	vim7	viim7
Mixolydian	I7	iim7	iiim7♭5	IVmaj7	vm7	vim7	VIImaj7
Locrian	im7♭5	♭IImaj7	♭iiim7	ivm7	♭Vmaj7	♭VI7	♭viim7
Scale Degree	I	II	III	IV	V	VI	VII

Modal Interchange in Minor Keys

Chords may also be borrowed from the parallel major when in a minor key, though this is less common than the opposite situation. The most commonly borrowed chord in minor keys is I or Imaj7, called the **Picardy 3rd**. (This chord often occurs in the final cadence of a song.)

Picardy 3rd

$\frac{3}{4}$ Cm7	E♭maj7	A♭maj7	Dm7♭5 G7alt	Cmaj7 ‖

Cm: im7   ♭IIImaj7   ♭VImaj7   iim7♭5 V7 **C:** Imaj7

Other diatonic functions can be borrowed from major to minor as well. Here the diationic iim7 chord is borrowed from E major.

ìThe Shadow of Yo ur Smile"

F♯m7 B7	Em7	

E: iim7   V7   im7

Chapter 7 Exercises

1. Identify tonicization and modulation in the following.

   a. | Cmaj7 | Am7 | C7 | Fmaj7 | Em7 A7 | Dm7 G7 | A♭maj7 | ||

   b. | Dmaj7 | Em7 | F♯m7 | Gm7 C7 | F♯m7♭5 B7 | Em7 E♭7 | A♭m7 | A7 ||

   c. | E♭maj7 | C♯m7 F♯7 | Bmaj7 | B♭7sus4 | Am7 | B♭7sus4 | A7sus4 | D7sus4 | Gmaj7 ||

   d. | Cmaj7 | E7 | C7 | Fmaj7 | A♭7 | D♭maj7 | C7alt | Fm7 | Dm7♭5 D♭7 | Cmaj7 ||

2. Provide four examples of direct modulation.

3. Provide four examples of prepared modulation.

4. Provide four examples of pivot chord modulation.

5. Provide four examples of transitional modulation.

6. Look for tunes that use direct, prepared, pivot chord, and transitional modulation. Extract the examples and provide harmonic analyses.

7. Name the parallel major and minor keys that contain the respective chord functions shown below. Assume enharmonic equivalents when necessary.

Example

	Cm7		**Emaj7**				
A♭:	iiim7	**A♭m:**	♭VImaj7				

C♯m7	Fmaj7			D♯m7	Gm7
Cmaj7	G♯m7			Cmaj7	E♭maj7
D♭maj7	Cm7			Cm7	Bm7
Gmaj7	B♭maj7			Em7	A♭maj7
Fm7	G♭m7			B♭m7	Bm7
Bmaj7	Dmaj7			B♭m7	Dmaj7
Am7	B♭m7			Dm7	G♭maj7
E♭maj7	G♭maj7			G♯m7	Cmaj7
F♯m7	Gm7			C♯m7	Dm7
A♭maj7	Bmaj7			Cm7	C♯m7

D♭maj7	Emaj7
Amaj7	F#maj7
Amaj7	Cmaj7
Amaj7	Fm7
Gm7	Bmaj7
Dmaj7	Cmaj7
Dmaj7	Emaj7

8. Find five tunes in any style that use modal interchange and extract the examples. Provide harmonic analysis for each.

CHAPTER

REHARMONIZATION

Chord substitution is a procedure for increasing the harmonic interest of a tune. While the word "substitution" implies a one-for-one exchange of chords, this is not always the case. Since chord substitution may result in a totally new harmonic rhythm, with either more or fewer chords than the original, some theorists feel that **reharmonization** is a better description of the process. In any case, nearly all jazz standards incorporate substitute chords. Some affect the underlying harmonic structure very little, and may be utilized by the soloist without the support of the rhythm section. Others result in a more significant restructuring of the harmonic progression of the tune and require the support of the rhythm section.

Following are some basic but effective chord substitutions that are commonly used by most jazz composers, accompanists and arrangers.

Diatonic Substitution in Tonal Contexts

iiim7 and vim7 may freely substitute for Imaj7; these three functions may interchange because they all act as tonic chords, which define the key area. Moving between tonic chords adds color and variety without a real change in harmonic function.

Cmaj7	**Cmaj7**	becomes:	**Cmaj7**	**Am7**	or	**Cmaj7**	**Em7**
Imaj7	Imaj7		Imaj7	vim7		Imaj7	iiim7

Similarly, iim7 may substitute for IVmaj7. Both iim7 and IVmaj7 contain the stable tonic of the key along with the unstable 4th, functioning as subdominant chords, and may be interchanged.

Fmaj7	**G7**	**Cmaj7**	becomes:	**Dm7**	**G7**	**Cmaj7**
IVmaj7	V7	Imaj7		iim7	V7	Imaj7

Finally, V7 and viim7♭5 contain both the unstable 4th degree and the major 7th (or **leading tone**). These two notes are a tritone apart, causing these chords to be highly unstable. Accordingly, they function as the dominant chords of the key, and may be substituted for one another.

Dm7	**G7**	**Cmaj7**	becomes:	**Dm7**	**Bm7♭5**	**Cmaj7**
iim7	V7	Imaj7		iim7	viim7♭5	Imaj7

Diatonic substitution follows similar practice in minor keys, with chords in the same families substituting for each other.

Substitutions in Modal Contexts

In functional harmony, chords are categorized according to their tendency to resolve in certain ways. This is primarily based upon the presence or absence of specific notes that signal voice-leading expectations within the overall key. Thus Cmaj7 and Am7 are substitutes for one another in the key of C major, despite their different qualities and associated chord scales.

Modal jazz relies upon a completely different method of organizing harmony. Modal chord "progressions" are chosen for their individual colors or sounds, not for their tendency to move to other chords within the overall key. Thus a "diatonic" substitution for a specific chord in modal jazz is not chosen based upon any tendency to resolve in any specific way. Instead, modal substitutions must produce the same sound as the original. This is generally achieved by choosing a chord that utilizes the same scale.

For example, if a tune or section of a tune is based on F Lydian and the chord is Bm7♭5, a possible substitution would be Cmaj7. This is not because ♯ivm7♭5 stands in for Vmaj7 in any functional sense in a Lydian context, but simply because they share the same **chord scale**. Other possibilities would be Dm7, Em7, Fmaj7, G7, and Am7. In short, any chord built on a note in the mode, and containing only the notes of that mode, is a possible substitution.

A serious consideration when using substitute chords in modal harmony is to avoid chords that will suggest functional harmony and destroy the modal quality. For example, if a modal area were in the key of B Locrian, the substitution of Cmaj7 for Bm7♭5 would almost certainly vitiate any sense of modality, effectively forcing the key into C major.

Tritone Substitution

Also referred to as **flat five substitution** (abbreviated ♭**5 sub**), this device is used extensively in reharmonization. In it, a dominant chord is replaced or followed with another one whose root is a tritone away. The tritone sub is one of the basic cadences of jazz, both as a two-chord structure, and as a variation of the ii–V–I cadence, which then becomes ii–♭II–I. The interchange is possible because V7 and ♭II7 share the same tritone: the 3rd of one is the ♭7th of the other. (These notes are also the unstable 7th and 4th degrees of the parent key.)

The ♭5 sub for G7—V in the key of C—is D♭7. Either chord resolves easily to Cmaj7.

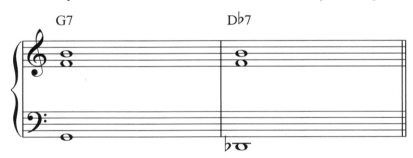

The tritone substitute chord is often preceded by its relative iim7, which here is a minor 7th chord built on the ♭6th degree of the key.

Dm7	G7	Cmaj7	becomes:	Dm7	G7	A♭m7	D♭7	Cmaj7
iim7	V7	Imaj7		iim7	V7	♭vim7	♭II7	Imaj7

A better analytical symbol for ♭II7 is **SubV7/I** (or just **SV7/I** for short), indicating that the V of I is the chord being replaced.

Dm7	G7	A♭m7	D♭7	Cmaj7
iim7	V7	♭vim7	**SV7/I**	Imaj7

"SV7/ " may also be followed by any diatonic chord name for which secondary dominants are used, giving us symbols such as SV7/ii, SV7/iii, SV7/IV, etc., indicating tritone subs for all the secondary dominant functions. In C major, SV7/ii is the tritone sub for V7/ii (A7), which is E♭7. SV7/iii is the tritone sub for V7/iii (B7), which is F7, and so on for SubV7/IV, /V, and /vi.

SV7/I resolves chromatically by half step, making a very strong motion to the tonic chord. When diatonic substitutes stand in for either the ii7 or the Imaj7, the result is descending motion by major 3rd.

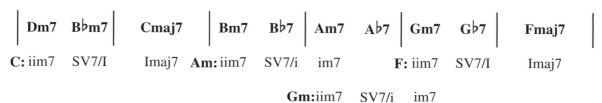

| Dm7 | B♭m7 | Am7 | or | Fmaj7 | D♭7 | Cmaj7 | or | Fmaj7 | D♭7 | Am7 |
| iim7 | SV7/I | vim7 | | IVmaj7 | SV7/I | Imaj7 | | IVmaj7 | SV7/I | vim7 |

A common use of tritone substitution is demonstrated by the following chord progression, which employs a chromatically descending bass line.

| Dm7 | B♭m7 | Cmaj7 | Bm7 | B♭7 | Am7 | A♭7 | Gm7 | G♭7 | Fmaj7 |
| C: iim7 | SV7/I | Imaj7 | Am: iim7 | SV7/i | im7 | | F: iim7 | SV7/I | Imaj7 |

Gm: iim7   SV7/i   im7

Unaltered SubV7 chords (or those with ♭5/♯11 as their only alteration) always take the **Lydian ♭7** scale, the fourth mode of the melodic minor scale. This scale is also known as **Lydian Dominant**, and occasionally as **Mixolydian ♯11**. Lydian ♭7 is enharmonic to the altered scale of the V7 a tritone away. In other words, the same notes are played over G7alt or D♭7 when resolving to C.

A♭ Melodic Minor, Modes 7 and 4

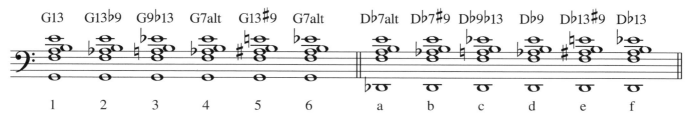

G Altered Scale   D♭ Lydian ♭7 Scale

Any voicing that works over V7 will also work over its SubV7. Each chord voicing on the left (1–6) in the following diagram may interchange with the corresponding one on the right (a–f), in alternation or as a substitute.

Because the notes are the same in the respective G7 and D♭7 chords in the diagram, a scale that fits the extensions or alterations of one chord will also fit those in the other.

- Over G13 or D♭7alt, you can play G Lydian ♭7, which equals D♭ altered (or D melodic minor). The 13th of G (E) is the ♯9 of D♭.

- Over G13♭9 or D♭7♯9, play the A♭ diminished scale, producing dominant diminished over both chords.

- Over G9♭13 or D♭9♭13, play the whole tone scale. Both chords will receive the correct ♭5/♯11 and natural 9.

- Over G7alt or D♭9, play A♭ melodic minor to produce G altered or D♭ Lydian ♭7. Again, this also fits if a ♭5/♯11 is present on D♭9.

- Over G13♯9 or D♭13♯9, play A♭ diminished.

- Over G7♯9♭13 or D♭13, play A♭ melodic minor to produce G altered, or D♭ Lydian ♭7.

Tritone substitution also provides a method for improvising **outside** of the harmony, by outlining a melodic line that is a tritone away from the expected diatonic dominant (or vice versa).

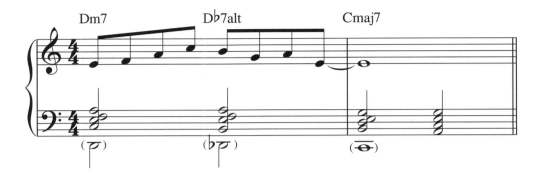

or the opposite:

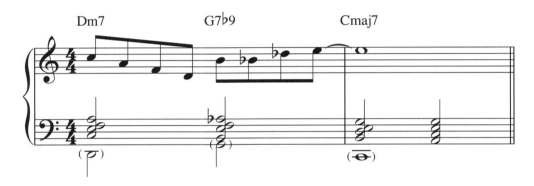

John Coltrane often substituted the ii–V a tritone away for the original ii–V cadence. For example, the progression

	Dm7 G7		Cmaj7			
	iim7 V7		Imaj7			

would become:

	A♭m7 D♭7		Cmaj7			
G♭:	iim7 V7	C:	Imaj7			

Mixture of the sub ii–V with the original often occurs, as in Duke Ellington's "Satin Doll."

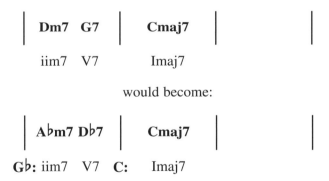

The SubV7 chord may serve as a pivot chord in a modulation to a foreign key.

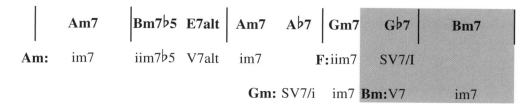

	Am7	Bm7♭5	E7alt	Am7	A♭7	Gm7	G♭7	Bm7
Am:	im7	iim7♭5	V7alt	im7		F:iim7	SV7/I	
				Gm: SV7/i	im7	Bm:V7		im7

Changing Chord Quality

A dominant 7th chord may substitute for a maj7 or a m7 chord on the same root, providing more harmonic possibilities when comping and improvising. Here is chord quality change applied to a diatonic turnaround in C major.

Minor to Dominant Chord Quality Change

	Cmaj7	Am7	Dm7	G7	becomes:	Cmaj7	A7	D7	G7
	Imaj7	vim7	iim7	V7		Imaj7	VI7	II7	V7

Taking this procedure a step further, replacing the expected VI7, II7, and V7 chords with their appropriate tritone subs results in the **Tad Dameron turnaround**.

	Cmaj7	E♭7	A♭7	D♭7
	Imaj7	SV7/ii	SV7/V	SV7/I

A common modification of this progression occurs when maj7 chords are substituted for the dominants.

	Cmaj7	E♭maj7	A♭maj7	D♭maj7
	Imaj7	♭IIImaj7	♭VImaj7	♭IImaj7

Numerous instances of chord quality substitution appear in the jazz and standard song literature. Here are some notable examples.

- "Just Friends"   first four bars
- "Sophisticated Lady"   last two bars of the bridge
- "'Round Midnight"   last two bars of the bridge
- "Wave"   between the first two A sections
- "Chega de Saudade"   the bridge, where Dm7 becomes Dmaj7

Substituting a m6 or m(maj7) Chord for a m7 Chord

This technique resembles chord quality substitution. Following a ii–V cadence to a minor 7th chord, the minor 7th may be changed to a m6 or m(maj7) in the following measure, melody permitting. The effect is to continue the harmonic rhythm, giving the impression that the chord progression changes regularly on each measure, while, in fact, only the quality has changed. The last four bars of the A section of "Autumn Leaves" furnishes an example.

	Am7♭5	D7alt	Gm(maj7)	Gm6
	iim7♭5	V7alt	im(maj7)	im6

Passing Chords

Any chord that moves between one diatonic chord and another one nearby may be loosely termed a **passing chord**. A diatonic passing chord may be inserted into a pre-existing progression that moves by a third in order to create more movement.

| Cmaj7 | Em7 | Dm7 | G7 |

A diatonic passing chord may be inserted between I and iii.

| Cmaj7 Dm7 | Em7 | Dm7 | G7 |

The easiest passing chords to recognize move chromatically, with the passing chord quality usually matching that of the chord above or below. Here is the same progression with a chromatic passing chord between iiim7 and iim7.

| Cmaj7 | Em7 E♭m7 | Dm7 | G7 |

Adding Extra Chords

Whenever Imaj7 moves to VI7, two additional chords may be inserted to strengthen the progression. Below we'll examine some possible modifications of a simple turnaround in C major.

Cmaj7 B7	B♭7 A7	Dm7	G7
Imaj7 V7/iii	SV7/vi V7/ii	iim7	V7

Replacing the III7 with its tritone sub results in smooth bass movement and parallel dominant double passing chords: two passing chords in a row—B7 and B♭7—between Cmaj7 and A7. B7 is a secondary dominant of Em.

Cmaj7 B7	B♭7 A7	Dm7	G7
Imaj7 V7/iii	SV7/vi V7/ii	iim7	V7

Notice that each chord receives the same metric placement and time duration. The turnaround to the first section of "Satin Doll" (measures 7 and 8) furnishes an example of the progression shown directly above (parallel dominant double passing chords). Another example is found in the Latin jazz standard "Aquarela di Brazil." The same turnaround may also result from a modification of the following chord progression.

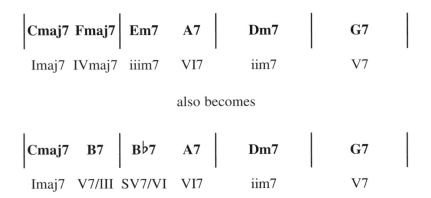

Cmaj7 Fmaj7	Em7 A7	Dm7	G7
Imaj7 IVmaj7	iiim7 VI7	iim7	V7

also becomes

Cmaj7 B7	B♭7 A7	Dm7	G7
Imaj7 V7/III	SV7/VI VI7	iim7	V7

As noted before, the qualities of the chords may be altered.

Parallel Major Double Passing Chords

| Cmaj7 Bmaj7 | B♭maj7 A7 | Dm7 | G7 |

or

Parallel Minor Double Passing Chords

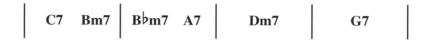

| C7   Bm7 | B♭m7 A7 | Dm7 | G7 |

Diminished Chord Functions

As noted in Chapter 5, any functioning dominant 7th chord may be replaced by its related vii°7. When resolving to their intended targets, these are technically not passing chords, as they perform the dominant function in a cadence. In practice, whenever a diminished chord is built on a non-diatonic step and also leads to a diatonic chord, it may be called a passing chord.

These are the most common places to put diminished passing chords in a major key:
- on the ♯1 or ♭2 scale degree leading to iim7,
- on the ♭3 scale degree leading to iim7 or to iiim7,
- on the ♯4 scale degree leading to V7,
- on the ♯5 scale degree leading to vim7.

All diminished chords usually sound best with the diminished whole-half scale as the source for melodic notes or extended arrangements. Diminished chords functioning as vii°7 may also take the harmonic minor scale based on the root of their target chord as an improvisational choice if that chord immediately follows and is minor. If the target chord is a major or dominant chord, the diminished scale is usually best, though any scale devised with the intent to tonicize the target chord and that includes the notes of the diminished chord may be explored.

In the following turnaround, notice the chromatic bass line between Imaj7 and iim7.

| Cmaj7 A7♭9 | Dm7   G7 | becomes: | Cmaj7 C♯°7 | Dm7   G7 |
| Imaj7 VI7♭9   iim7   V7 | | | Imaj7 vii°7/ii   iim7   V7 |

A chord may change to a diminished chord on the same root as an embellishment.

| Cmaj7 C°7 | Dm7   G7 | or: | Em7   E♭°7 | Dm7   G7 |
| Imaj7   i°7   iim7   V7 | | | iiim7   ♭iii°7   iim7   V7 |

i°7 is an embellishing chord of Imaj7. ♭iii°7 has a similar function as i°7 since both are a m3rd apart. Notice how each one moves smoothly to iim7. Refer to measures 13–15 of "Chega de Saudade" and measure 22 of "Body and Soul" for two of the many examples of embellishing diminished chords found in the literature.

Diminished Substitution

The equivalencies of the diminished scales we examined in Chapter 3 also apply to the related chords. Each of the twelve possible diminished chords and the twelve possible dominant $7\flat9$ chords are equivalent in some inversion to one of three diminished 7th chords: $C°7$, $D\flat°7$, or $D°7$.

- $C°7 = E\flat°7 = G\flat°7 = A°7 = D7\flat9 = F7\flat9 = A\flat7\flat9 = B7\flat9$

- $D\flat°7 = E°7 = G°7 = B\flat°7 = E\flat7\flat9 = F\sharp7\flat9 = A7\flat9 = C7\flat9$

- $D°7 = F°7 = A\flat°7 = B°7 = E7\flat9 = G7\flat9 = B\flat7\flat9 = C\sharp7\flat9$

Here are dominant chords obtained by the diminished substitution method.

Gm7 C7	**Fmaj7**	may become:	**Gm7 Eb7** **Fmaj7**
iim7 V7	Imaj7		iim7 bVII7 Imaj7
		or:	**Gm7 Gb7** **Fmaj7**
			iim7 SV7/I Imaj7
		or:	**Gm7 A7** **Fmaj7**
			iim7 III7 Imaj7

Any vii°7 chord may resolve to three other minor (or major) key areas other than its related one. For example $B°7$, $D°7$, $F°7$, or $A\flat°7$ may resolve to any of the following:

- Cm6 or Cmaj7

- $E\flat$m6 or $E\flat$maj7

- $F\sharp$m6 or $F\sharp$maj7

- Am6 or Amaj7

By the same token, the related $V7\flat9$ can work the same way.

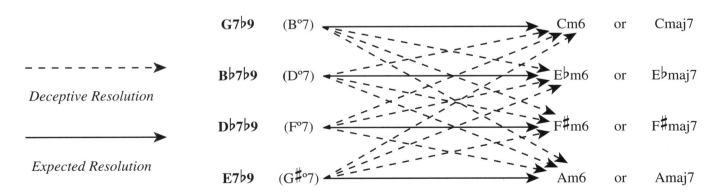

Like the $G7\flat9$ chord, $B\flat7\flat9$, $D\flat7\flat9$, and $E7\flat9$ could also resolve **deceptively** to one of the keys on the right.

We have seen that if we add the related ii to a V7, new harmonies may be created. Thus new deceptive cadences may occur as new reharmonizations for the previous diminished chords.

| Dm7♭5 G7♭9 | as reharmonization for B°7
| Fm7♭5 B♭7♭9 | as reharmonization for D°7
| A♭m7♭5 D♭7♭9 | as reharmonization for F°7
| Bm7♭5 E7♭9 | as reharmonization for G♯°7

All the above minor ii–V cadences may resolve authentically or deceptively to one of four key areas: Cm6 or Cmaj7, E♭m6 or E♭maj7, F♯m6 or F♯maj7, and Am6 or Amaj7.

V7♭9 of iim7: a Leading Chord

A straightforward example of diminished substitution, a secondary dominant chord may be inserted before iim7 in any lengthy ii–V–I cadence, thus creating a renewed tension toward iim7.

| **Dm7** | **G7** | **Cmaj7** | | becomes: | **Dm7 A7♭9** | **Dm7 G7** | **Cmaj7** | |
| iim7 | V7 | Imaj7 | | | iim7 V7♭9/ii | iim7 V7 | Imaj7 | |

This technique is mostly used when comping; it allows a new confirmation of the ii. "Body and Soul" is a very good example, as is Spencer William's "I've Found a New Baby," excerpted here.

| **Cm7 G7♭9** | **Cm7** | **C7♭9** |
| **Cm:** im7 V7♭9 | im7 | **Fm:** V7♭9 |

Side-Stepping

Also called **side-slipping**, this technique can be applied to any lengthy ii–V–I cadence. As it is most commonly used, a chromatic ii–V progression a half step above or below is inserted, which then moves back to the first key area. This effect intensifies harmonic interest and is often used on repeated ii–V's.

| **Dm7** | **G7** | **Cmaj7** | | becomes: | **E♭m7 A♭7** | **Dm7 G7** | **Cmaj7** | |
| **C:** iim7 | V7 | Imaj7 | | | **D♭:**iim7 V7 | **C:** iim7 V7 | Imaj7 | |

Side-stepping is not necessarily a chromatic phenomenon. Sometimes the ii–V–I cadence may be replaced by another ii–V that side-steps by a M3rd below or m3rd above.

Side-Stepping by Major 3rd Below: "'Round Midnight" in D Minor, Meas. 3–5

| **Dm7**   **G7** | **B♭m7** **E♭7**   **Am7** **D7** | **Gm7** |
| **C:** iim7   V7 | **A♭:** iim7   V7 **G:** iim7   V7 **Gm:** im7 |

Side-Stepping by Minor 3rd Above

| **Dm7 G7** | **Fm7 B♭7** | **Dm7 G7** | **Cmaj7** |
| **C:** iim7 V7 | **E♭:** iim7 V7 | **C:** iim7 V7 | Imaj7 |

Side-stepping is also used in modal tunes as a device for creating tension and release, through the use of dissonance. Miles Davis's "So What" provides a good model for this technique.

Added ii–V's

Any chord may be preceded by a pair of ii–V's. They may be chained together in series and may be mixed with tritone subs.

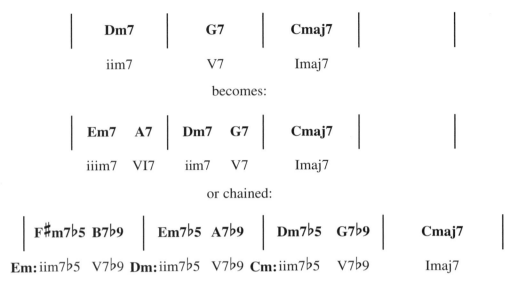

	Dm7		G7		Cmaj7			
	iim7		V7		Imaj7			

becomes:

	Em7 A7		Dm7 G7		Cmaj7			
	iiim7 VI7		iim7 V7		Imaj7			

or chained:

	F#m7b5 B7b9		Em7b5 A7b9		Dm7b5 G7b9		Cmaj7	
Em:	iim7b5 V7b9	Dm:	iim7b5 V7b9	Cm:	iim7b5 V7b9		Imaj7	

(Charlie) "Parker's Blues" contains many chained ii–V7's.

	Fmaj7		Em7 A7		Dm7 G7		Cm7 F7		Bbmaj7	
F:	Imaj7	D:	iim7 V7	C:	iim7 V7	Bb:	iim7 V7		Imaj7	

Here is the same progression with tritone subs added.

	Fmaj7		Em7 Eb7		Dm7 Db7		Cm7 B7		Bbmaj7	
F:	Imaj7	D:	iim7 SV7/I	C:	iim7 SV7/I	Bb:	iim7 SV7/I		Imaj7	

CESH

This acronym stands for **chromatic embellishment of static harmony** or **contrapuntal elaboration of static harmony**. Sometimes the technique is simply called **line cliché**. A moving chromatic line is introduced in what would normally be a static progression. Following is an example with a descending chromatic line over two measures of a static Dm7 chord.

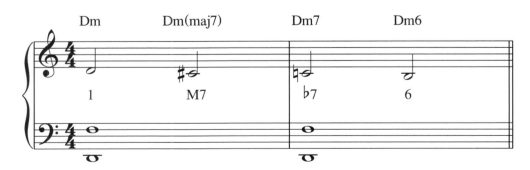

The same series of chromatically moving notes works well on a II–V sequence.

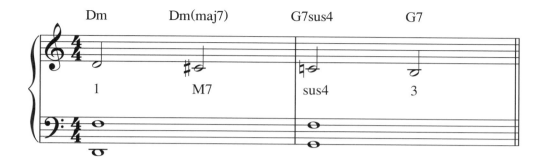

CESH may ascend as well as descend.

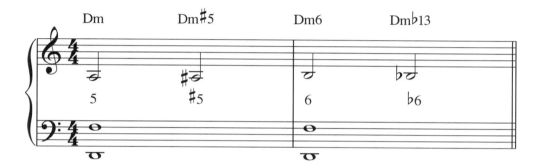

Dm♯5 or Dm♭13 are the same chord as Dm♭6 or even B♭/D. Arrangers, composers, and improvisers frequently resort to this device when a minor chord encompasses two or four bars. "'Round Midnight" is an example where this substitution occurs.

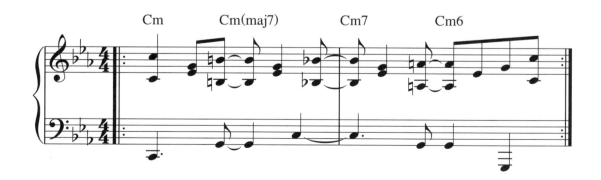

In Latin music, the chromatic descending bass line is mostly encountered as a reharmonization of a lengthy minor (or major) chord, as in the first 4 bars of the Latin standard "Besame Mucho."

Sometimes the bass remains while the chromatic descending line occurs in both the intermediate voice and the upper voice. Here is a typical Latin montuno pattern where CESH is doubled.

Or in a II–V sequence:

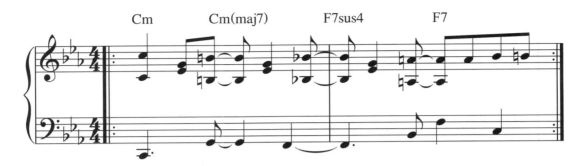

This device is often used in improvisation, especially in bebop.

"Summer of Forty-Two," "My Funny Valentine," "It Don't Mean a Thing," "In a Sentimental Mood," and "In Walked Bud" are good examples of CESH. Sometimes CESH is utilized as a 4- or 8-bar introduction to a tune.

Kosma, "Manha Do Carnival" ("Black Orpheus")

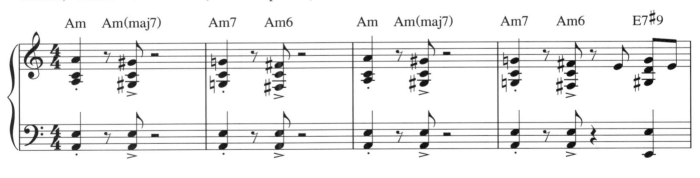

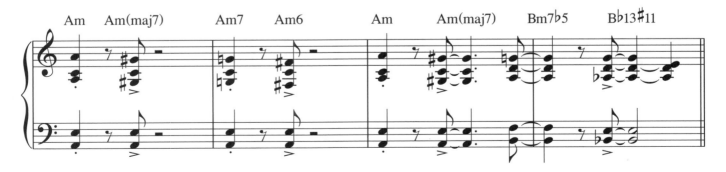

Coltrane Substitutions

These are among the most complex substitutions in jazz harmony. Variously known as **'Trane changes**, **Giant Steps** changes, or **'Trane substitutes**, this technique incorporates a process of key centers moving through a cycle of major or minor thirds. John Coltrane was the innovator of this challenging technique of harmonization, and it appears in several of his famous compositions, including "Giant Steps" and "Countdown."

An examination of the first 4 bars of Coltrane's "Countdown" in C reveals how Coltrane employed a very useful formula to replace a standard four-bar ii–V–I.

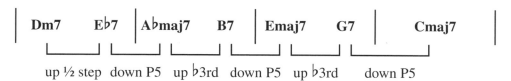

| Dm7 | Eb7 | Abmaj7 | B7 | Emaj7 | G7 | Cmaj7 | |

up ½ step   down P5   up b3rd   down P5   up b3rd   down P5

The **"Countdown" formula** may be applied whenever a ii–V–I cadence encompasses four measures. The basic idea is to modulate by major thirds or by minor thirds. While the concept is simple, the difficulty lies in applying the formula effectively to a progression. It is helpful to begin by determining the key in which the progression needs to end, then work backwards from there. By going up or down a series of thirds from that point, it is possible to determine which keys will fit the melody. Coltrane would also frequently reverse the process, altering the melody to fit the progression he had chosen.

Let's break down the process of modifying the ii–V–I to include a series of key centers modulating down by major 3rds. Begin with a simple ii–V–I cadence.

| Dm7 | G7 | Cmaj7 | |
| iim7 | V7 | Imaj7 | |

Determine the keys that lie a major 3rd away. These divide the octave from C to C into three equally sized parts.

| Cmaj7 | Abmaj7 | Emaj7 | Cmaj7 |
| C: Imaj7 | Ab: Imaj7 | E: Imaj7 | C: Imaj7 |

Each I chord is then preceded by its V.

| Cmaj7 | Eb7 | Abmaj7 | B7 | Emaj7 | G7 | Cmaj7 |
| C: Imaj7 | Eb: V7 | Imaj7 | E: V7 | Imaj7 | C: V7 | Imaj7 |

We can put the iim7 of C back at the beginning.

| Dm7 | Bbm7 Eb7 | Abmaj7 | F#m7 B7 | Emaj7 | Dm7 G7 | Cmaj7 | |
| C: iim7 | Ab: iim7 V7 | Imaj7 | E: iim7 V7 | Imaj7 | C: iim7 V7 | Imaj7 | |

Extending the idea by preceding each V with its relative ii we get:

Dm7	**B♭m7 E♭7**	**A♭maj7**	**F♯m7 B7**	**Emaj7**	**Dm7 G7**	**Cmaj7**
C: iim7	A♭: iim7 V7	Imaj7	E: iim7 V7	Imaj7	C: iim7 V7	Imaj7

It's also possible to apply tritone substitution and/or modal interchange to Coltrane changes.

| Dm7♭5 A7 | A♭maj7 F7 | Emaj7 D♭7 | Cmaj7 |

All of these techniques may be applied to minor keys as well. It takes practice to become fluent at improvising and comping over Coltrane changes, because they go by fast. There aren't many choices of good lines to go with them. "Giant Steps" and "Countdown" provide good models. Effective improvisational strategies include arpeggios, symmetric lines, pentatonic scales, and similar constructions.

A V7 May Resolve to Any Chord: More Deceptive Cadences

Through a combination of the principles discussed in this chapter, a dominant chord can move to practically any other chord. It can be fascinating to hear a V7 resolve unexpectedly in a tune, leaving the listener convinced that the progression sounds right, but lacking an immediate explanation as to why. Obviously, it is a simple task to assign Roman numerals to any progression, but that does little to explain why an unusual progression is effective and convincing. For the purpose of applying what one has learned it is far better to have an understanding of the theory that controls the motion of dominant chords. Then one is able to understand both the "how" and the "why." Many musicians learn how progressions work, but fail to reach the deeper level of understanding that comes with comprehending why chords move as they do.

"How" may be viewed as the Roman numeral formula for analyzing chord progressions. All one needs to remember is what goes where. "Why" requires an abstract understanding of the source of a given chord progression. An understanding of *why* chords move as they do will facilitate remembering *how* they move.

While differences of opinion are bound to occur, harmonic motion can only be understood by explaining that motion in clear and logical terms.

A V7 can resolve to tonic family chords (I, iii, vi in major, or i, ♭III in minor) by

- P5th down to I or i, the dominant function.
- whole step up to vim7, or possibly to VImaj7 as a back-door cadence, in which case the proper designation would be ♭VII7/I.
- half step down to I or i as SubV7/I or SubV7/i.
- m3rd down to iiim7 or maj3rd down to ♭IIImaj7.

A V7 can also move to a chord of the subdominant family (ii or IV in major, iim7♭5, iv, or ♭VI in minor) by

- P4th down to iim7 or iim7♭5.
- whole step down to IVmaj7 or ivm7.
- half step up to ♭VImaj7.

A V7 can move to any other chord in the dominant family or any of their substitutes derived by diminished substitution

- to a dominant chord up or down a minor 3rd.
- to a dominant chord up or down a tritone.
- to a min7♭5 up a major 3rd.
- to a °7 chord up a half step, up a maj 3rd, up a 5th, or up a ♭7th.

A V7 may resolve with these other possible harmonic motions:

- to a major or minor chord up a minor 3rd.
- to a major or minor chord up a major 3rd.
- to a major or minor chord up or down a tritone.
- by a whole step up to vim7.

Below are some unusual progressions involving dominant chords. It is quite simple to employ them, but why do they work? Why do they sound both convincing and deceptive?

Half Step Up, Usually to im6 or im7

It sounds unusual to hear VII7 resolve to Cm6 rather than to its usual target chord (Em7, Em6, or Emaj7). One possibility for explaining why B7 may resolve to Cm6 is to consider it a variation of a plagal (IV–I) cadence rather than an authentic (V–I) cadence.

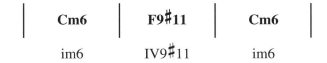

By replacing the F7 with its tritone substitute, B7, we get the following cadence, characterized by ascending half-step motion in the bass.

Up or Down a Tritone
While this is occasionally used in jazz, there is no agreement among theorists as to why it works. It simply sounds convincing, or as Debussy might say, follows the "rule of hearing." Some hear it as a "near miss" to the expected target down a 5th, while others hear it as an incomplete tritone sub, making it essentially the same chord as the original dominant 7th, except that the tendency for resolution has been lost.

Up a Minor 3rd or Major 3rd
Dominant chord resolution upwards by either minor or major 3rd is not common, but it does occur. The logic of these progressions can be understood by following the steps below.

In this example we'll analyze a dominant chord resolving up by a minor 3rd.

B♭m7 could also be B♭maj7 if there is chord quality substitution.

Consider this major ii–V–I cadence in G♭.

	Abm7	D♭7	G♭maj7	
	iim7	V7	Imaj7	

We'll insert iiim7 as a diatonic substitute for Imaj7.

	Abm7	D♭7	B♭m7	
	iim7	V7	iiim7	

Now replace the V7 with its tritone sub.

	Abm7	G7	B♭m7	
	iim7	SV7/I	iiim7	

Now we'll examine a dominant chord resolving up by a major 3rd.

	G7	Bm7	
	V7/I	VIIm7	

Bm7 could also be Bmaj7 if we have a chord quality change.

Consider a plagal cadence in B minor.

	Bm6	E7	Bm6	
	im6	IV7	im6	

We learned that the E7 chord may act as a diminished substitution for G7 and vice versa. If E7 is IV7, then G7 is ♭VI7.

	Bm6	G7	Bm6	
	im6	♭IV7	im6	

Chapter 8 Exercises

1. Each pair of chords below derives from the chord scale indicated. Show one applicable substitute chord for each chord listed. Remember that function does not apply in modal contexts.

   Fm7 and B♭7 (F Dorian)

   Gmaj7 and D7 (G Ionian)

   Am7♭5 and E♭maj7 (E♭ Lydian)

   C♯m7 and G♯m7♭5 (A Major)

   Cm7 and B♭maj7 (D Phrygian)

   Fm7♭5 and A♭m§ (A♭ Mel. Min.)

   Gmaj7 and A7 (D Major)

   Cm(maj7) and B°7 (C Harm. Min.)

   B7alt and F13(♯11) (B Altered)

   F♯m7♭5 and Cmaj7(♭5) (F♯ Locrian)

   Fm7♭5 and E♭7 (D♭ Lydian ♭7)

   Em7 and Am7 (E Minor)

   G♭maj7 and A♭7 (B♭ Minor)

   Fmaj7 and G7 (F Lydian)

2. Provide tritone substitutes for the following dominant chords.

   A♭7   D7   B7   E♭7   G7   C♯7   F7   B♭7   A7   C7   E7

3. Provide tritone substitutions for the following chord progression. Show harmonic analysis.

   | Gm7 | Am7♭5 D7alt | Gm7 C7 | Fm7 B♭7 | E♭maj7 | Em7♭5 A7alt |

   | Dm7♭5 G7alt | Cm7 G7♭9 | C7 F7 | B♭7 A7 | A♭7 D7alt | Gm(maj7) ||

4. a. Provide chord quality change substitutions for the above chord progression (exercise 3) with harmonic analysis.

   b. Compose a chord progression for F minor blues that includes these chord quality changes: major for minor, dominant for major.

   c. Analyze each new chord progression.

   d. Make new chord progressions from the above by using diatonic and tritone substitutions.

5. Apply diminished 7th chords over the progression given in exercise 3.

6. Make diminished substitutions over the progression given in exercise 3.

7. Add ii–V's to the following chord progressions and provide harmonic analyses.

a. | Gm7　　　　　 |　　　　　 |　　　　　 |　　　　　 |

　　| E♭maj7　　　 |　　　　 | Cm7　　　 |　　　 |

　　| F7　　　 | A7　　 | D7alt　　 | Gmaj7　　 ‖

b. | Fmaj7　　　　 |　　　　 |　　　　 |　　　　 |

　　| B♭maj7　　　 |　　　 | A♭maj7　　 |　　 | Fmaj7　　　 ‖

c. | Gmaj7　　　 |　 | E♭maj7　　 |　　 |

　　| Bmaj7　　　 |　 | A♭m6　　 |　　 |

　　| Fm6　　　 |　 | Dm6　　 |　　 |

　　| B♭maj7　　 |　 | Gm6　　 |　　 ‖

8. Create CESH over the above chord progressions given in exercise 7. (New chords maybe inserted freely.)

9. Provide six examples of John Coltrane substitutions: three from tunes that already incorporate the progression, and three that do not but are suitable for Coltrane changes. (Do not include Coltrane's own works.)

10. Reharmonize the diminished 7th chords you applied to the progression in exercise 5.

CHAPTER 9

JAZZ PIANO COMPING

The Rhythm Section

The standard rhythm section consists of piano, bass, and drums. There are also many rhythm sections that use guitar or vibes. Each of these instruments has a specific role to play in providing support for the soloists. Additionally, they function equally well as solo instruments themselves.

Comping

Providing accompaniment for soloists (comping) is a primary function of the rhythm section. Comping provides an improvised background involving both chordal and rhythmic components. This connection of rhythm and voicings may be referred to as **rhythmic voicings**. When comping, a musician must support, complement, and give energy to the soloist while providing rhythmic variety.

In terms of chordal textures, one should look to jazz pianists, vibraphonists, and guitarists for inspiration. The best way to learn to comp is to listen to experienced pianists and guitarists.

When comping, musicians must remember to:

- keep a steady tempo,
- listen to the rhythm section,
- maintain simplicity and clarity,
- vary the rhythmic patterns,
- change or alternate voicings,
- make use of space, balance, velocity, and sustained sonorities, and,
- utilize chord substitutions.

Although comping is improvised, certain musical elements may be planned ahead of time. For instance, in order to avoid potential harmonic conflicts, the soloist and rhythm section will sometimes discuss and agree upon certain voicings and extensions prior to the performance. Below is an example of a harmonic clash that could have been averted through prior discussion. The D natural played by the saxophone conflicts with the D♭ played by the piano.

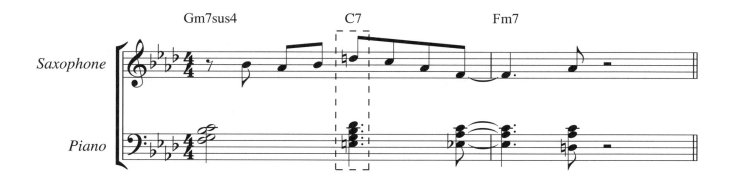

The clash is avoided in the example below by selecting a voicing more appropriate to the improvised line.

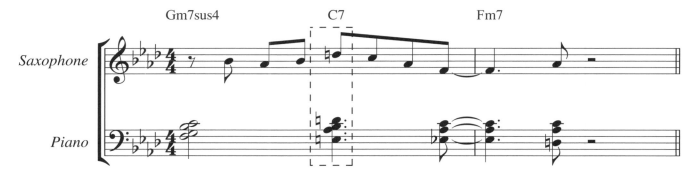

Similarly, the soloist might have chosen to play the following line, in order to match an agreed-upon ♭9 on the C7.

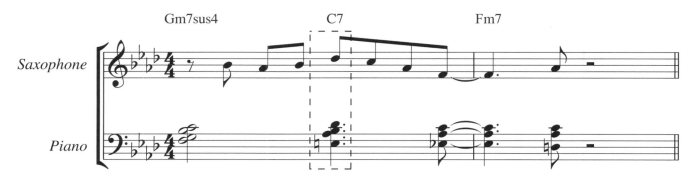

Comping is an art form as well as a cooperative effort. Musicians who comp must use their ears in order to make creative choices. However, when comping chords behind a soloist, it is also important to "stay out of the way." Initially, 9ths, 11ths, and 13ths should be avoided, until it becomes clear in which direction the soloist is going to go. For example, if the rhythm section plays a ♭9 on a dominant chord, then the soloist doesn't have the freedom to play a natural 9. It is not the place of the rhythm section to limit the soloist. Accordingly, comping should at first be restricted to the guide tones (3rds and 7ths) of the chords, until the soloist makes known his or her harmonic preferences. This may involve more than upper structures. A soloist might choose to play a ♭5th on a dominant chord, in which case the comper might choose to play it too, or to omit the 5th in his chord. In sum, expert comping requires careful and attentive listening to the soloist at all times.

Voicings: Which Notes To Avoid

MODE	CHORD FUNCTIONS	AVOID NOTE(S)
Major, Mixolydian	Imaj7, V7	P4
Dorian, Aeolian	iim7, vim7	6 (13), ♭6 (♭13)
Phrygian, Locrian	iiim7, viim7♭5	♭2 (♭9)
Lydian	IVmaj7	none
Lydian ♭7, Altered, Diminished, Half-Diminished	V7, iim7♭5	none

Comping Examples

When comping, pianists, vibraphonists, and guitarists employ a myriad of rhythms. The following examples illustrate some useful comping rhythms in both swing and Latin contexts. They should be practiced at a steady tempo and combined in various ways. Practice with a metronome is recommended. In traditional jazz swing situations (this does not apply to Latin jazz), do not repeat rhythmic patterns as you might when establishing a groove in rock, R&B, or other styles. Comping should play a supportive role, adding needed harmonic content and varied rhythmic accents in an ongoing interactive conversation, without unduly drawing attention away from the soloist.

Swing Comping Rhythms

Latin Comping Rhythms

Jazz Waltz Comping Rhythms

Tips for Improving Left-Hand Comping

1. Practice comping along to a tune using the left hand only. The *Hal Leonard Jazz Play-Along* series is highly recommended. Each volume includes CD audio with removable piano tracks so you can play along with the rhythm section.

2. Left-hand voicings must be 100% secure. Try just playing the changes to a tune you are working on a few times with a variety of left-hand voicings before you start trying to practice solos on it.

3. When comping for yourself, make it a rule that your left hand plays only when your right hand doesn't. This will help to get away from just thumping chords in on the downbeat all the time, and can also help your right-hand phrasing. Once you are confident with this, you can start to put the left hand in elsewhere.

4. Make sure that you aren't always playing the chord on the beat. Focus on anticipating the beat to give your solos a sense of forward motion. As you get better at this, start to look at other rhythmic displacements. (Bill Evans is an excellent model.)

5. Don't feel as if you need to play every chord change with your left hand. The professionals don't. Listen to a variety of styles and players and pay careful attention to what they are doing. *All the answers are in your record collection.*

6. Remember that the primary role of the left hand when soloing is to accompany and punctuate your ideas. Make sure your comping isn't encroaching on what your right hand is doing.

7. When learning how to comp, it is easy to get caught up in voicings and substitutions. The most dazzling ingenious voicings will sound simply ridiculous if not connected to the context of the music.

8. Pay attention to how the comping fits rhythmically with the rest of the musicians and with the soloist. Simplicity is often the best approach.

Lead Sheets

Jazz musicians, particularly students and young players, often use lead sheets as a source for tunes with which they are not familiar. A lead sheet typically contains melody, chord symbols, and lyrics. It is intended to represent the general framework and form of a jazz tune. This non-specific formatting provides just enough information for the musicians' personal interpretations to take precedence. In the improvisational spirit of the jazz idiom, this notational approach also lends unbiased representations of tunes that have had myriad variations performed and recorded over the last century.

Collections of jazz lead sheets, known as "fake books," typically consist of the standard jazz repertoire and are used by many musicians and professionals as efficient and useful charts for practice, rehearsal, and on-stage performance. Many fake books are in violation of copyright law, but the *Real Book (Volumes I – III)*, published by Hal Leonard, presents a giant collection of fully legal and highly accurate lead sheets for an affordable price.

Another source for information on jazz tunes is, of course, audio recordings. However, learning from recordings poses some inherent problems. It can be confusing or disorienting to hear a tune reinterpreted by various musicians with divergent styles, particularly when one is not intimately familiar with the tune. Musicians often seek to make a tune their own by finding unique harmonies and playing the melody in a personal way. Indeed, it sometimes requires a bit of research to locate the original version of the tune the way the composer conceived it. Therefore, even with ample recordings available, lead sheets are very handy, if not essential, to those who study or perform jazz.

Advanced pianists can not only "fake" by knowing the tune and listening, but can also play directly from chord symbols. The following example demonstrates how a pianist interprets and fakes the chord changes from a given lead sheet.

JAZZOLOGY

By NOR EDDINE BAHHA
with BOB RAWLINS

1. Place chords on beats 1 and 3.
2. If a melodic note is anticipated, anticipate the chord as well.
3. When the melodic line is active the accompaniment should be inactive, and vice versa.

Notice the voice-leading in the comping of the following example.

JAZZOLOGY

By NOR EDDINE BAHHA
with BOB RAWLINS

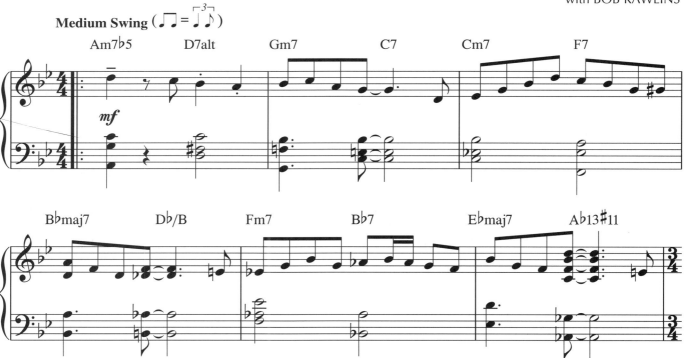

In the above example, the comping avoids interfering with the melody by playing only the necessary guide tones (3rds and 7ths). It is, however, permissible to play or double the melody in the upper voicings. The next example shows more sophisticated voicings.

JAZZOLOGY

By NOR EDDINE BAHHA
with BOB RAWLINS

In measure 1, Am7♭5 has been reharmonized as Am11, which adds color while maintaining the function. In measures 3 and 5 the harmony is outlined by the melody and the bass so there is no need to play chords. This produces the effect of hidden or linear harmony. The same process is used in the first part of measures 7 through 9.

The following example demonstrates how to comp with a bassist. Common left-hand rootless voicings are quite effective in this context.

JAZZOLOGY

By NOR EDDINE BAHHA
with BOB RAWLINS

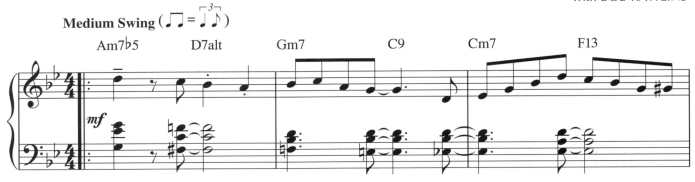

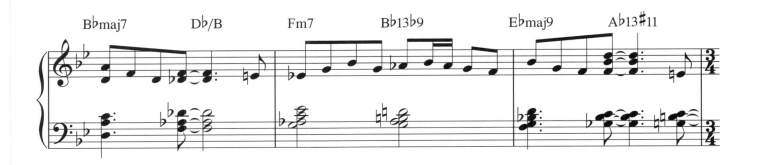

Notice how the voicings anticipate and consolidate the rhythm used within the melody.

Though these examples are enough to get you well on the way to comping appropriately, there is much more to learn when it comes to comping in various substyles of jazz. Numerous books are available dealing extensively with voicing and comping in various contexts, such as swing, rock, and Latin, offering examples that have been employed by jazz masters.

Chapter 9 Exercises

1. Play the rhythmic patterns included in this chapter in connection with the various kinds of voicings given in the appendix. Use a metronome.

2. If at all possible, practice comping with other musicians.

JAZZ TUNE FORMS

A typical performance of a jazz standard follows the scheme shown below:

1. An **introduction**,
2. The **head** or the main melody, often called the "A" section,
3. The **bridge** or "B" section, which usually provides a contrasting melody before returning to the main melody,
4. Open-ended repetition of the overall form with improvisation,
5. A conclusion or ending consisting of a final statement of the entire tune.

Tonal Tunes

12-Bar Blues Form

The blues is a 12-bar form divided into three sections, each containing four bars. The first part consists of four measures of a I7 chord. The second consists of two bars of the IV7 chord and two bars of the I7 chord. The third part consists of one bar of the V7 chord, one bar of IV7 and two bars of the I7 chord. The entire form is shown below, with the thematic formula shown above the harmonic framework.

Blues in F

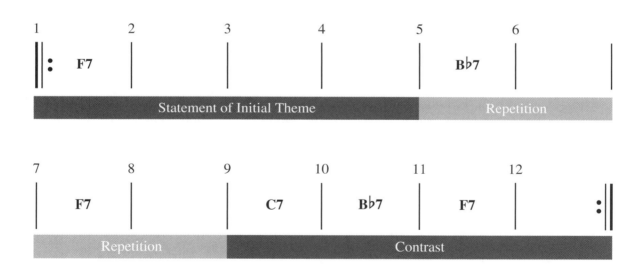

Here is a mathematical formula for remembering standard 12-bar blues form.

12-bar blues = [4 bars I7] + [2 bars IV7 + 2 bars I7] + [1 bar V7 +1 bar IV7 + 2 bars I7]

Thirty-Two-Bar AABA Form

This is the most common standard form in popular music as well as in jazz. It consists of thirty-two bars divided into four eight-measure sections:

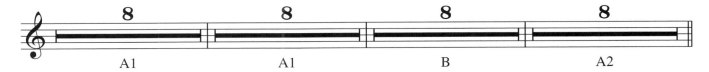

- The "A" section is played twice (A1, A1).
- The "B" section is called the **bridge**, **middle eight**, or **release**.
- Another "A" section (A2) played as a conclusion, usually with an alternative or optional ending or coda.

Following is a typical AABA song form.

A: || Cmaj7 | B♭m7 E♭7 | A♭maj7 | Dm7♭5 G7alt | Cm6 | Dm7♭5 G7alt | Cmaj7 | Cmaj7 C13♭9 ||

A: || Cmaj7 | B♭m7 E♭7 | A♭maj7 | Dm7♭5 G7alt | Cm6 | Dm7♭5 G7alt | Cmaj7 | Cmaj7 C9♯5 ||

B: || Fmaj7 | E♭m7 A♭7 | D♭maj7 | Gm7♭5 C7alt | Fm6 | Gm7♭5 C7alt | Fm6 | Dm7♭5 G7alt ||

A: || Cmaj7 | B♭m7 E♭7 | A♭maj7 | Dm7♭5 G7alt | Cm6 | Dm7♭5 G7alt | C6 | C6 ||

More examples include "Satin Doll," "Take the A Train," "Body and Soul," "'Round Midnight," "September in the Rain," "Caravan," "Nardis," "Well You Needn't," and countless others.

Rhythm Changes

The unique AABA form known as **rhythm changes** takes its name from Gershwin's "I Got Rhythm." Published in 1930, the tune quickly became a favorite among jazz musicians, ultimately inspiring a wealth of new songs based on similar harmonic sequences. In essence, the structure is characterized by a common major turnaround in the A section followed by a series of secondary dominants in the bridge. This circle of fifths starts on III of the key, working its way around to V, which prepares for the return to I. Rhythm changes in B♭ (with the most common substitutions) are shown below.

Rhythm Changes

A: || B♭maj7 G7 | Cm7 F7 | B♭maj7 G7 | Cm7 F7 | Fm7 B♭7 | E♭maj7 A♭7 | Dm7 G7 | Cm7 F7 ||

A: || B♭maj7 G7 | Cm7 F7 | B♭maj7 G7 | Cm7 F7 | Fm7 B♭7 | E♭maj7 A♭7 | Cm7 F7 | B♭maj7 ||

B: || Am7 | D7 | Dm7 | G7 | Gm7 | C7 | Cm7 | F7 ||

A: || B♭maj7 G7 | Cm7 F7 | B♭maj7 G7 | Cm7 F7 | Fm7 B♭7 | E♭maj7 A♭7 | Cm7 F7 | B♭maj7 ||

Some **contrafact** (set to the same chord changes) examples include "Oleo," "Salt Peanuts," "Anthropology," and "Cotton Tail." The importance of rhythm changes in jazz history cannot be overstated. Arguably, the form's importance as an improvisational vehicle is second only to that of the blues.

AB, AABC, ABAC, ABC, and ABCD Forms

Many other structural approaches appear in jazz and popular songs. The table below shows other common schemes and some tunes based on each form. Keep in mind that interpretations of form can vary. It is not always clear if a modified recurrence of a melody should be indicated as a repeated section or a new section with a new letter designation. (For example, "Bye Bye Blackbird" could as well be shown as AA1BA2, where A1 and A2 represent modified occurrences of the main melody.)

AB	AABC	ABAC	ABC	ABCD
Giant Steps Tune Up Blue Bossa Lady Bird	I Concentrate on You Alone Together Autumn Leaves	Four ESP Soul Eyes	Afro-Centric Mercy, Mercy, Mercy Solar Someday My Prince Will Come	Black Orpheus (or Manha do Carnival) Bye Bye Blackbird

Modal and Polytonal Tunes

Modal Tunes and Harmony

Modal jazz typically utilizes few chords (sometimes just one chord) which may be sustained for long periods of time. Chord durations of four, six, eight, or sixteen measures are common. Despite limited harmonic motion, modal jazz allows for enhanced improvisational freedom, providing opportunities for the soloist to develop and explore various tensions and dissonances. In addition to its slower **harmonic rhythm** (the speed at which the chords change), much modal jazz incorporates unexpected or sudden shifting and displacement of chords, including planing and side-stepping. Such harmonic motion is governed by color, not function, resulting in chord sequences that sometimes appear not to be related to one another. It is thus the responsibility of the improviser to emphasize common tones and reveal the logic behind chord motion in modal contexts.

Consider the following:

| Dm7sus4 Fm7sus4 | Em7sus4 E♭m7sus4 | Dm7sus4 |

In this modal sequence it would be better to emphasize the notes F or C in order to ensure smooth connections between the harmonies. In some modal tunes, a few identical chords are sequenced and sustained for long durations. Miles Davis's "So What" consists of sixteen bars of Dm7 followed by eight bars of E♭m7 and finally another eight bars of Dm7. The feeling of tension and release is controlled by the relationship between tense chords (dissonances) and weak chords (consonances). The effect is not as pronounced as in traditional harmony; listen for it as the 7sus4 chords move to the maj7 chord in the next example.

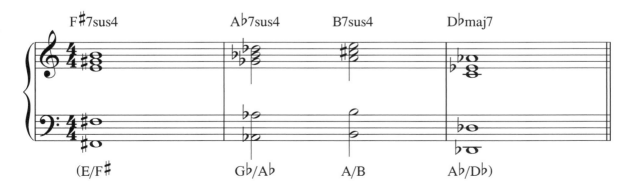

Modal harmony is often characterized by the use of chord voicings that follow the related modes. Two of the seven modes, however, are not generally used. Ionian is major, and thus does not produce the expected modal sound. Locrian contains a diminished fifth instead of a perfect fifth and therefore is not effective in establishing an extended modal area. Thus, most modal tunes employ Dorian, Phrygian, Lydian, Mixolydian, or Aeolian, although other nondiatonic scales are also possible. Examples of modal tunes include "So What," "Footprints," "Impressions," and "Maiden Voyage."

Polytonal Tunes
Polytonality refers to the procedure of using more than one key center in a composition or voicing. Functional harmony may or may not be present. Some theorists call the presence of two or more tonal centers the **multi-tonic system**. Jazz tunes that include more than one tonal center give the impression of floating through multiple keys. Examples include "Giant Steps," "Ladybird," "Have You Met Miss Jones," and Chick Corea's "Day Waves."

Chapter 10 Exercise

Select several standard tunes from a reliable source and identify each tune's form.

CHAPTER 11

OTHER ARRANGING TECHNIQUES

In recent years, contemporary music composers and arrangers have relied extensively on the following devices.

- Rooted/rootless voicings
- Modal and/or tonal quartal voicings, "So What" voicings, upper structures, polychords, hybrid chords
- Modulations
- Modal interchange
- New options in chord construction, including clusters and fragment or partial voicings
- CESH (line cliché)
- Tritone and other substitutions

It is essential for pianists and non-pianists alike to learn chord voicings on the piano or keyboard. So-called "arranger's piano" is an extremely useful tool for hearing and seeing how chords fit together and how chord-scale relationships are constructed. The examples provided in this book categorize many practical skills under the rubric of "arranging." All chord voicings discussed thus far may be scored for various combinations of instruments and ensembles.

In addition to the procedures mentioned above, we will consider other less-common arranging devices. Often taken for granted, these subtle techniques can do much to enrich and expand a musician's harmonic vocabulary.

Constant Structures

Constant structures are chord progressions that comprise three or more chords of the same quality. Pioneered by Herbie Hancock and Bill Evans, constant structures provide a cohesive combination of functional and non-functional sounds that produce the effect of a free and shifting tonal center.

$\begin{array}{c}4\\4\end{array}$ | Fmaj7 | A♭maj7 | D♭maj7 | G♭maj7 | C13sus ‖

$\begin{array}{c}3\\4\end{array}$ | Cm7 E♭m7 | A♭m7 | D♭m7 E♭m7 | Fm7 G7alt ‖

$\begin{array}{c}3\\4\end{array}$ | E♭maj7 D♭maj7 | C♭maj7 Amaj7 | A♭maj7 F♯maj7 | Fm7 B♭7 ‖

Pedal Point

Pedal point is one of the earliest devices for creating dissonance to be found in Western music. It consists of a sustained note (typically in the bass—hence the reference to the pedal notes of the organ) that is held through changing harmonies in the other parts. The pedal note need not be literally sustained; it may appear in patterned or non-patterned rhythmic configurations that can actually include rests. Nevertheless, the aural effect of a sustained pitch must be clear. A pedal point can also appear in middle or upper parts but in any case will be on the tonic or dominant pitch in the vast majority of instances. The overall effect of pedal point is to create tension and increase harmonic interest. The first four bars of "Green Dolphin Street" provide an excellent example.

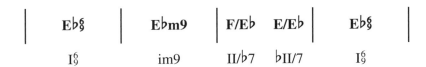

The passage below effectively lends itself to pedal-point treatment.

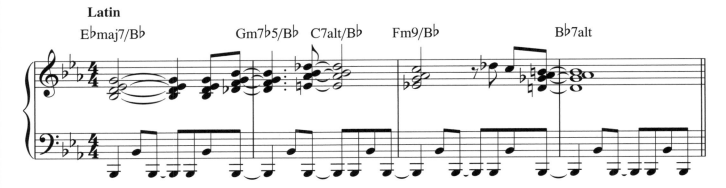

These are tunes that customarily include pedal point:
- Hanks Tresser's "A La Mode"
- Josef Zawinul's "Birdland"
- Duke Ellington's "Satin Doll" (Intro)
- Stevie Wonder's "Too High" (Intro)
- Bill Evans's "Skidoo"
- Herbie Hancock's "Dolphin Dance"
- Pat Metheny's "Lakes"
- John Coltrane's "Naima"
- Eddie Harris's "Freedom Jazz Dance"

Ostinato

An ostinato is any clearly defined melodic or rhythmic pattern that is repeated persistently. In jazz, ostinato patterns may be of various lengths and are generally found in the bass line. (Do not confuse ostinato with **vamp**, which refers to a short repeated chord progression, often serving as the introduction to a performance.) Ostinato has become a favorite technique of contemporary jazz writers. It appears frequently in modal and Latin jazz, as well as in African traditional music, such as Moroccan Gnawa music. Ostinato must be employed judiciously, as its overuse can quickly lead to monotony. Examples include "So What," "A Night in Tunisia," "Take Five," "Maiden Voyage," and "Cantaloupe Island."

A similar example occurs in the following piano arrangement of "Bania," a standard piece in the Moroccan traditional music of Gnawa. (Notice how the harmony "floats" while the left-hand bass line maintains a steady rhythmic feel.)

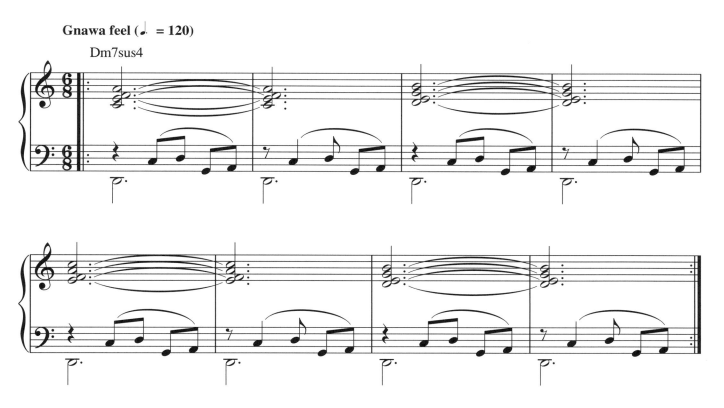

Here are two examples of ostinato found in traditional Moroccan Gnawa.

Shallaban

Bania

Pedal and ostinato are particularly suited to modal harmony, as their relentless, repetitive character help to establish and confirm the modal center.

Reharmonizing a Melody

Many of the voicings studied thus far are appropriate and effective for harmonizing or reharmonizing melodies. The discussion that follows examines specific situations involving various types of melodic motion. In order to select chords that effectively support a given melodic line, it is first necessary to analyze the type of motion involved. Melodies that are static (consisting of sustained or repeated notes) will receive different treatment from those that incorporate diatonic or chromatic motion.

Harmonizing Sustained or Repeated Melody Notes

Sustained or repeated notes strongly suggest the use of chromatic harmony, which is attained by using an ascending or descending chromatic bass line. Dominant substitutes and chromatic diminished chords with an oblique or a contrary motion may be implied.

The above example furnishes a decided improvement over the following.

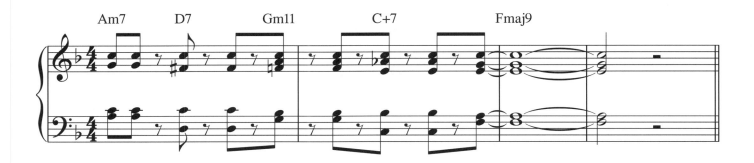

Several of Jobim's tunes exemplify this concept, including "One Note Samba," "How Insensitive," "Desafinado," and "Corcovado." However, when the notes are repeated or sustained (as in modal contexts), diatonic or chromatic planing can strengthen and consolidate the melodic line.

Another Time

Notice how harmonic activity increases when the melody is less active.

Harmonizing Chromatic or Diatonically Symmetric Melodies

One effective approach to chromatic or diatonically symmetric melodies is for all lines to move in parallel motion. In this case, the harmony should chromatically follow the melodic line. An alternative is to employ contrary harmonic motion. In this instance, sequential dominants, dominant substitutes, block chords, and constant structures may be implied. Quartal harmonies are also suitable for chromatic melodies, resulting in an open harmonic texture devoid of strong directional implications.

This technique is called **parallel reharmonization** (or **planing**): all the voices move by the same interval. Notice the constant structures that occur, providing a rich and compelling harmonic texture.

A specialized form of the constant-structure approach is known as **block-chord** style.

The following melodic line, somewhat reminiscent of Stevie Wonder, displays a descending stepwise motion.

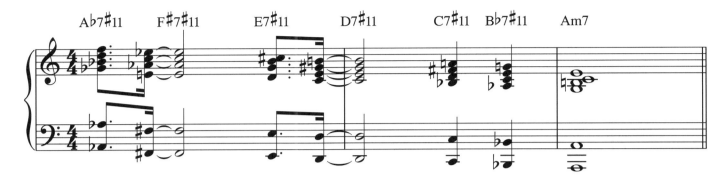

In the above example a melody based on the B whole-tone scale is played over chords derived from the **Bb** whole-tone scale. Notice that this combination of dominant 7#11 chords together with the melody notes creates a parallel series of hybrid or slash chords (Gbmaj7#5/Ab, Emaj7#5/F#, Dmaj7#5/E, etc.), which create a non-functioning harmonic framework over a smoothly-descending stepwise bass line.

The next example typifies short interludes found in some bossa nova tunes, where a chromatically constructed melodic pattern is repeated in various permutations over a harmonic texture featuring constant structures. This particular type of reharmonization is called **independent lead**.

"A Night in Tunisia" provides a similar example in that the basic melodic pattern is repeated and modified slightly while the underlying harmonic support remains constant.

Harmonizing Melodies That Move by Leaps
It is important to realize that every melodic note does not need to be harmonized, with harmonization commonly occurring only on beats 1 and 3 along with their anticipations. However, when a melodic line moves by larger intervals, it may be advantageous either to freely harmonize, or to revoice the previous chord. It is difficult to prescribe formulas in advance. The best approach is to examine the works of significant jazz composers and arrangers in order to develop a feel for how and when to harmonize angular melodic lines.

Some Basic Harmonizations and Reharmonizations

The following examples are representative models for reharmonization of the same or a slightly modified melody.

This example features upper structures with foreign bass notes. Again, it is a new harmonization of the same melody.

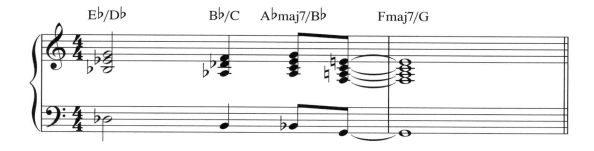

This one is simple but effective.

It is recommended that the following four examples of reharmonization be learned in all twelve keys.

1.

Reharmonization:

2.

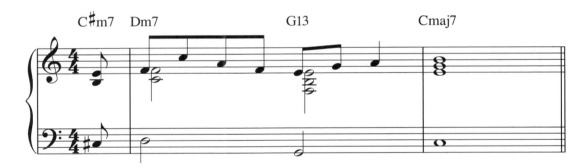

Reharmonization:

3.

Reharmonization:

4.

Reharmonization:

*$\frac{E\flat+}{F\sharp m}$ is a simplified notation for an $E\flat7\sharp9\sharp11\flat13$, which may also be notated as $E\flat7alt$.

Rules for Harmonizing Melodies

- Avoid m2nds or ♭9ths between two notes of a voicing, with the exception of V7♭9 chords. These intervals do work well, however, in modal contexts. (Review for example the voicing for E Phrygian in Chapter 6.)
- Dominant chords (except for V7sus4 chords) should usually include a tritone.
- Shell voicings are sufficient in themselves since they include the essential guide tones: 7th and 3rd.
- Avoid two adjacent thirds when using quartal voicings.
- Avoid small adjacent intervals in the lower register and large adjacent intervals in the upper register.
- The 5th may generally be omitted except in m7♭5 chords.
- Avoid doubling the 7th in the bass if it also occurs in the melody.
- It is common to leave the tritone unresolved. In a V7sus4 chord, a suspended 4th is considered an anticipation of the target chord (I).
- It is common to substitute the 9th for the tonic, and the 13th for the 5th.
- There are endless ways to reharmonize a melody, but this does not mean that every note should be harmonized. When the harmonic rhythm is fast it is very difficult to apply constant chord changes. Even if it were possible to achieve, the result would sound cluttered.
- Harmonizations are most effective when the harmonic rhythm does not appear to force the insertion of new harmonies. The judicious use of pauses and breaks can do much to enhance the overall harmonic effect.

CHAPTER

APPROACHING IMPROVISATION

Some Thoughts on Improvisation

In the broadest sense, the word *improvisation* designates composition in real time. Improvised music is created "on the spot" by a musician who assumes the double role of performer and composer. Improvisation in some form or to some degree has been associated with jazz since its very inception. With the bebop revolution of the 1940s, improvisation became arguably the defining element of jazz.

Jazz improvisation began with a process of embellishment or stylized interpretation of the melody. In ensemble jazz, this took the form of group improvisation, where each instrumentalist exercised a moderate amount of freedom in fulfilling a prescribed melodic or harmonic role. Although occasional breaks and short solos existed in early jazz, the fully developed jazz solo did not appear until Louis Armstrong's work of the mid 1920s. The extended solo provided a useful formula for jazz performance. Successive solos over repeated choruses or sections of the tune allowed suitable length for dancing without all musicians having to play continuously. In the larger ensembles of the swing era, intricate arrangements take the place of continuously repeated solos, as improvisation is reduced to a lesser but still significant role. With the advent of bebop, however, improvisation clearly emerges as the central component of the music. The harmonic structure of the tune assumes more importance than the melody. Whereas many swing musicians had been accustomed to faking solos by ear, the demanding tempos and chord sequences of bebop made it necessary for musicians to learn thoroughly the chords to the tunes they improvised on. This was a major paradigm shift, and it has held sway in most jazz since that time. Jazz musicians before Charlie Parker had the option of simply re-interpreting the melody and making it "hot." Jazz musicians after Charlie Parker were expected to create something new and original from the harmonic structure of the tune.

This chapter will offer some flexible approaches to improvisation, as opposed to prescribing a specific procedure or method. The jazz theory and harmonic vocabulary that have been acquired from this book will provide a firm foundation for improvisation, since there is a concise relationship between the improvised line (melody) and chords (harmony). The ability to outline chords on one's instrument will go a long way toward providing the materials out of which creative and inspired jazz solos are created.

A firm grasp of jazz harmony leads to a clear understanding and appreciation of the devices used regularly by composers and arrangers. Moreover, it also provides the resources necessary to create personal and original melodic lines that are grounded in specific harmonic frameworks. It is but a short step from this point to actual improvisation in real time. This exiting step involves tapping the artistic side of one's nature: one's natural talents, imagination, and creative inclinations. Many musicians are intimidated by the concept of improvisation. The myth persists that it cannot be learned. This is erroneous. Like other musical skills, improvisation can be mastered through practice and diligent study.

This chapter will present a series of improvisational concepts, representative jazz patterns, and solos that should be learned in all twelve keys. The student is also encouraged to construct original solos based on the examples provided. An attempt should be made to base these constructions on what has been studied in this book. At first, students may wish to write down their improvisations as jazz "etudes," but as soon as possible students should attempt to depart from the written music and create their own ideas spontaneously.

Listening is crucial. Jazz is an aural skill, and there is no substitute for having a clear and accurate conception of the sound that one is trying to achieve. Most jazz musicians began by having models and imitating the players who inspired them. There is immense value in transcribing, studying, and learning a jazz solo in order to really understand how the art is practiced. There are countless nuances to be learned, including balance, accents, dynamics, blue notes, inflections, mood, and so forth, that words simply cannot describe. A great solo involves much more than just the notes. It is essential that students of jazz improvisation listen regularly to their favorite players and practice what they hear.

Devices for Improvisation

Harmonic Generalization

Harmonic generalization is the method by which an improviser chooses lines that accommodate two or more chords in succession. The practice is well-established and sanctioned by long use in jazz improvisation. Many pre-bebop musicians with limited knowledge of theory and harmony allowed their ears to dictate note choices, searching for figures that had common tones which would span several chords in a row. Here are typical treatments using single scales to play over entire ii–V–I cadences and turnarounds in both major and minor.

The C major scale is used over this entire chord sequence.

The C harmonic minor scale is used over this entire chord sequence.

Here the C major scale is used over bars 1, 2, and 4. The D major scale aptly addresses bar 3.

In this example the C melodic minor scale is used in bar 1. The G7♭9 in bar 2 suggests C harmonic minor.

Symmetrical Patterning

Symmetrical patterning refers to the construction of lines with constant intervallic content and continuing shape. Usually the same scale or same intervals in series are used throughout, and the rhythm is confined to steady eighth or sixteenth notes. The result is a sense of perpetual motion, as if the line could continue indefinitely.

The C whole-tone pattern used in this example (augmented triads moving by whole steps) shows the scale's naturally symmetric structure. This line is heard in some Thelonious Monk works.

The C diminished half-whole scale is the appropriate choice for C13♭9. The same line would be effective over E♭13♭9, F♯13♭9, and A13♭9.

For the chromatic scale, a device as simple as interlocking descending half steps creates linear interest.

Ascending m3rds move up the chromatic scale to create linear interest.

Here is the same pattern with ascending P4ths.

Melodic Templates

Melodic templates refer to highly recognizable linear elements in jazz improvisation. They allow for the creation of patterns that sound long familiar on first hearing, not because they are quotations but because they employ specific shapes, contours, note combinations, fragments, or simply approaches that have become well known to those who are familiar with the style. In short, they are conventions sanctioned by historical use. Melodic templates provide sources for idiomatic structures that are readily adapted to many contexts, while evoking strong ties with the jazz tradition. They were incorporated in all of the material presented earlier in this chapter. Following are examples of common figures that will be instantly recognized by experienced jazz improvisers.

Dm7 ascending arpeggio

Dm9 descending arpeggio

Dm7 descending arpeggio

Idem, with chromaticism

Dm7

Dm9 ascending and descending arpeggio

Dm7 **G7**

Smooth Alterations: the sound remains the same

Dm7 **G7** **Dm7**

A♭m arpeggio over G7 = Tension *The "Shadow of Your Smile" Template*

Dm7

Dm9 Down-Up arpeggio

G7

G bebop scale ex. 1

G7

G bebop scale ex. 2

G7

G bebop scale ex. 3

G7

G bebop scale ex. 4

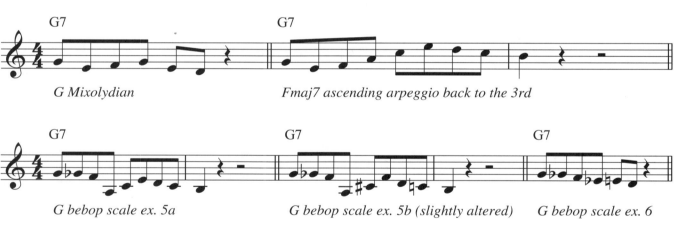

G7

G Mixolydian

G7

Fmaj7 ascending arpeggio back to the 3rd

G7

G bebop scale ex. 5a

G7

G bebop scale ex. 5b (slightly altered)

G7

G bebop scale ex. 6

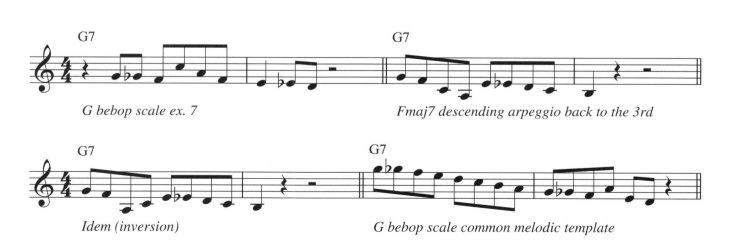

G7

G bebop scale ex. 7

G7

Fmaj7 descending arpeggio back to the 3rd

G7

Idem (inversion)

G7

G bebop scale common melodic template

CESH

In the context of a ii–V cadence, the most common CESH incorporates a moving chromatic line starting from the root of iim7 downward to the 3rd of V7 as shown below.

Descending Chromatic Line

Dm9 arpeggio followed by a CESH

Idem with octave displacement of CESH

Dm smooth arpeggios from the root to the 11th of G7

CESH inner line pattern

CESH line is slightly altered, (#7–root–♭7–3rd) with a chromatic approach note to the root

Idem with a chromatic approach note to the 3rd

Dm arpeggio followed by a CESH

Idem with unresolved 4th, (root–#7–♭7)

Kind of an ascending CESH, (#5–6–♭7–♮7–root)

Ascending chromatic line (rarely used)

Bebop line featuring CESH

Idem with a slight alteration

Pentatonic Scales

Pentatonic scales occur in various musical cultures across the globe and play a significant role in many types of improvisation. Two aspects of the pentatonic scale make it extremely versatile and flexible in jazz improvisation: 1) it does not sound prosaic or trite when stated or spelled directly, and 2) it conveys a clarity of harmonic intention that can hold up under extreme dissonance. Pentatonic scales provide an effective way to make an unambiguous statement. They give the improviser a great deal of control over the degree of dissonance desired in the solo. Following are possible choices of several pentatonic scales over major, minor, subdominant, and dominant chords.

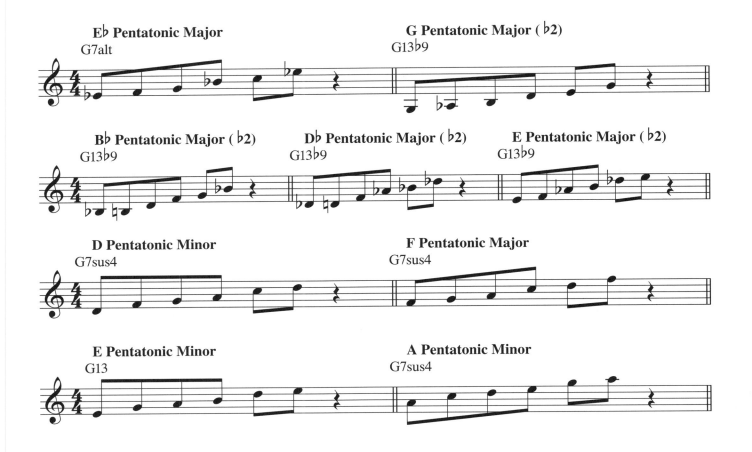

Here is an example of pentatonic melodic continuity, from E pentatonic minor to E♭ pentatonic minor, to D pentatonic minor, to D♭ pentatonic major, then releasing to D pentatonic major.

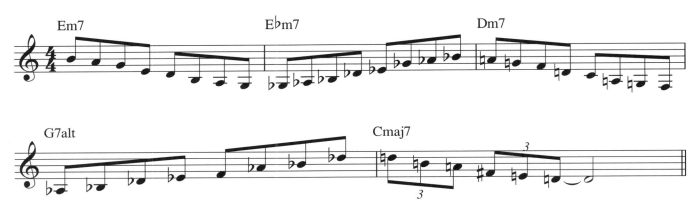

This example shows rapid passages of pentatonic major scales. Notice how they fit with Coltrane changes.

Depending on which note of the chord a pentatonic scale is built on, a player can make a passage sound "inside," "outside," or anywhere in between. This example uses A minor pentatonic over Cmaj7, G major pentatonic over Am7, a Dm7 arpeggio, E♭ major pentatonic, A minor pentatonic over Em7, E♭ major pentatonic over A7, A♭ major pentatonic over Dm7♭5, then D♭ major pentatonic over G7.

This example demonstrates **outside** improvisation through the use of side-stepping. E♭ minor pentatonic over A13♭9 creates an unexpected harmonic tension. D♭ major pentatonic is similarly placed over G7alt.

Chromatic Approach Tones

Non-harmonic notes are sometimes referred to as a **chromatic approach tones**. As the name implies, chromatic approach tones are notes that move chromatically to a member of the chord. Specifically, their function is to approach or lead smoothly into the existing target tones, thus serving to embellish or to smooth out melodic motion between or around chord tones. Non-harmonic tones are notes which are not part of the accompanying harmony. They may be diatonic or chromatic.

A chromatic approach tone is an unprepared dissonance that resolves by half step to a chord tone. Its function is to delay a chord member's arrival, thus adding a sense of expectation and forward momentum to a melodic line. Chromatic approach tones may appear either above or below the chord tone in any metric position, either as upbeats or downbeats.

Non-harmonic tones offer unlimited possibilities for linear constructions. In a sense, the degree of flexibility is nearly overwhelming, since there are very few constraints placed upon the improviser. The only requirement is to make sure the chord is implied by placing essential tones on strong beats.

Here non-harmonic notes are placed on downbeats as chromatic approach tones: C♯ resolves to D, A♯ resolves to B, D♯ resolves to E.

Without CATs the line is acceptable, but bland.

Here the CATs are on upbeats. A♭ resolves to G, E♭ resolves to D, D♭ resolves to C. C over G7 makes a suspended resolution. B is encircled from C to A.

Without CATs, again, the line is acceptable, but bland.

Here are CATs executed in chromatic-run fashion. The final note B is encircled nicely by C and A♯.

This example features CAT encirclements over Dm7. Over G7, each chord tone: root, 3rd, 5th, and 7th, is encircled by half step from above and below.

Diatonic Approach Notes

The next three examples use diatonic approach tones. Over Dm7♭5, B♭ leads diatonically to A♭, G approaches F, and E♭ leads smoothly to D; all are on downbeats. Over G7♭9, the diatonic approach tones are all on upbeats: C approaches D, E♭ approaches F, and B♭ leaps nicely to G.

In this example diatonic approach tones encircle F over Dm7 from G down to E. Over G13♭9, a half-whole diminished scale is played. Notice how chromatic approach tones work over this line. (Of course diminished and diminished half-whole scales may be viewed as already including chromatic approach tones.)

The straightforward use of diatonic approach tones is quite effective in the next example. (Notice the absence of chromatic approach tones!)

Exploring Triadic Structures in Upper Tensions

Some interesting improvisations can be constructed by looking at certain vertical structures as combinations of triads rather than as a single chord. Close scrutiny often reveals that independent upper-structure triads, not the chords built on the harmonic roots, can provide the driving force behind many improvised lines. Triads, whether played directly or woven into linear patterns, are highly recognizable structures, since they provide the basic building blocks for most of the music we encounter throughout our lives. Inserting these fundamental structures into improvised lines can have a powerful effect.

Here are two patterns built upon the 5th, 7th, and 9th of the Dm7 chord. The triadic implications lie above the 5th of the basic harmony.

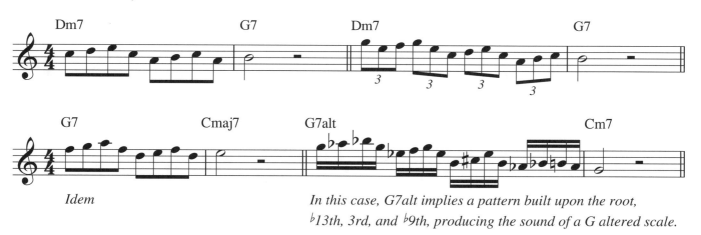

Idem

In this case, G7alt implies a pattern built upon the root, ♭13th, 3rd, and ♭9th, producing the sound of a G altered scale.

This pattern is built on an E♭ triad (E♭–G–B♭), a D♭ triad (D♭–F–A♭), and an A♭m triad (A♭–B–E♭).

Next are two patterns built upon the 5th, 7th, and 9th of Cmaj7. The triadic implications sound like they were built on the 5th of the basic harmony.

Play a major triad arpeggio up a whole step for a coherent Lydian sound over $\frac{6}{9}$ or maj7 chords.

The major triad from the 5th of a maj7 chord produces a major 9th sound.

Two patterns delineating an Am7 but superimposing nicely over Dm7.

Two typical bebop constructions outline Dm(maj7), creating a #11 sound on G7. These two patterns provide the internal logic to palliate the unexpected shock of the dissonant note and reassure the ear.

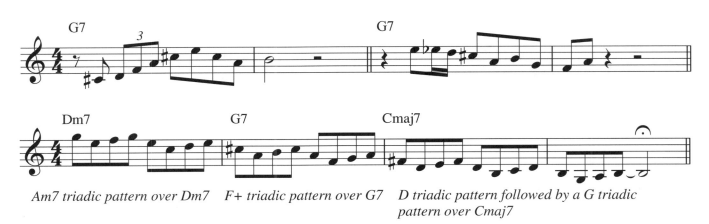

Am7 triadic pattern over Dm7   F+ triadic pattern over G7   D triadic pattern followed by a G triadic pattern over Cmaj7

Am triadic pattern over Dm7   B+ triad followed by E♭7

The same Am melodic pattern over Dm7 is transposed down a half step over G7alt to fit the chord change.

This is another example of the same idea, where a pattern played over Dm7 is transposed up a tritone to fit G7alt.

Building Scales from Superimposed Chords

Another way to look at scales and modes is to think of them as two chords that are either stacked on top of each other (like an extended chord) or side by side (like a bi-tonal chord).

MODE	7th CHORD	DISTANCE TO NEXT CHORD	SUPERIMPOSED CHORD	EXAMPLES	
Major	M7	W	m	Cmaj7	Dm7
Lydian	M7	W	M	Cmaj7	Dmaj7
Lydian Augmented	M7#5	W	M	Cmaj7#5	D7
Mixolydian	7	W	m	C7	Dm7
Lydian Dominant	7	W	M	C7	D7
Super Locrian	m7b5	h	m	Cm7b5	Dbm(maj7)
Dorian	m7	W	m	Cm7	Dm7
Aeolian	m7	W	m7b5	Cm7	Dm7b5
Melodic Minor	m(maj7)	W	M	Cm(maj7)	Dm7
Harmonic Minor	m(maj7)	W	m7b5	Cm(maj7)	Dm7b5
Phrygian	m7	h	M	Cm7	Dbmaj7
Locrian	m7b5	h	M	Cm7b5	Dbmaj7
Locrian #2	m7b5	W	m7b5	Cm7b5	Dm7b5
Diminished	°7	W	°7	C°7	D°7
Half-Whole Diminished	°7	h	°7	C°7	Db°7

The approach shown in the previous table can also be used as an alternative way to view extensions, such as 11th and 13th chords. For many students, working with triads and seventh chords is less intimidating than dealing with the higher intervallic designations associated with chord extensions. Moreover, seeing extended chords as bitonal structures makes the upper structures more accessible and removes confusion as to which extensions are permissible on a given chord. Finally, an alternative approach to extensions is likely to open up new avenues for improvisation and lead to new and different sounds.

Chord-Scale Families

It is useful to group chords and modes into families in order to categorize them and understand their properties. Within each family, characteristic pitches define the essential sound of the chord or mode. Chords and modes within the same family are often interchangeable.

FAMILY	KEY PITCHES	CHORD TYPES	SCALES/MODES
Major	maj3 and maj7	maj7, 6, maj9	Major, Lydian, Lydian Augmented
		as above with ♯11	Lydian, Lydian Augmented
Dominant	maj3 and ♭7	7, 9, 13, 7♭9, 7♯9, 7alt	Mixolydian, Lydian Dominant, Superlocrian
		7♯11	Half-Whole Diminished, Whole Tone
Minor	♭3 and P5	m, m7	Aeolian, Phrygian, Dorian
		m, m6	Dorian, Melodic Minor
		m(maj7)	Melodic Minor, Harmonic Minor
Half-Diminished	♭3 and ♭5	m7♭5	Locrian, Locrian ♯2
Diminished	♭5 and ♭♭7	°7	Diminished
Whole Tone	maj3 and ♯5	7♯5	Whole Tone

For further study on how to improvise on specific chords in specific contexts, see *A Simple and Direct Guide to Jazz Improvisation*, by Robert Rawlins.

Approaching Improvisation

The simplified examples that follow demonstrate how specific melodic lines support the related chords. The suggested approaches to various chords will prove helpful in studying new tunes and in training the ear to hear various chord progressions as represented by the melodic line. More importantly, the student will become accustomed to playing and hearing the jazz language. The goal is to learn to speak this language as fluently as possible.

These exercises should be practiced in various keys—all twelve if possible. The use of a metronome is strongly recommended. An initial tempo of 100 beats per minute is suggested, to be increased gradually to 180 bpm or beyond.

MAJOR CHORD EXERCISE

MINOR CHORD EXERCISE

DIMINISHED CHORD EXERCISE

MINOR ii–V–i CADENCE EXERCISE

MAJOR ii–V–I CADENCE EXERCISE

MODAL EXERCISE

$\quad$ = 126–210

Dm7

Transcribed Solos

Transcribing and learning the solos of the jazz greats is of inestimable value. But a few caveats are in order. Oftentimes our favorite players have technical skills on their instruments that go well beyond the capabilities of the average student (or average mortal, some might say). Moreover, they tend to "push the envelope" as they experiment, try new things, and challenge the traditional methods of approaching their craft. Subsequently, the music they produce may be of the greatest artistic value and yet be of questionable didactic worth. After all, a jazz musician's primary goal is to create, not to teach. They are two different things.

With those thoughts in mind, the following are some original jazz solos specifically constructed for the purpose of teaching. A variety of styles are represented, and chord sequences have been selected that simulate those of actual jazz standards that musicians are likely to encounter. Additionally, analysis and commentary have been provided to help the student understand the improvisational devices that have been incorporated. By thoroughly absorbing the sound of these devices, as well as the theory behind them, the student should attempt to create similar solos on the same chord sequences. The immediate goal is to imitate, while the ultimate goal is to recreate using the same language. Note that some of the textual analyses for the transcribed solos are found following their accompanying notations instead of preceding them in order to facilitate convenient page turns.

F Blues Analysis

Historically, "blues" simply refers to a state of mind, or, more specifically, music that expresses that state of mind. In jazz, blues usually refers to a twelve-bar structure characterized by the occurrence of the tonic, subdominant, and dominant chords in specific places, along with the prominence of blue notes and conventional blues patterns. Substitute chords or reharmonization can be expected in most jazz performances of the blues, but the basic characteristics do not change.

The solo shown typifies the genre. The chord structure contains common bebop progressions, and some change-running does occur, but the emphasis of the linear component clearly points toward the blues. The freedom of the improvised line to deviate from the chord progression in blues contexts cannot be overstated. To a certain extent, as long as the improviser is playing blues lines in the tonic key, it does not matter what chord is in the harmony.

Measures 3 and 4 demonstrate this. The melody emphasizes the ♭3, ♭5, and ♭7 at this point. While it would indeed be possible to explain these notes in terms of extensions of the prevailing harmony, that is not what is going on here. The notes work because they comprise a typical blues pattern, a familiar-sounding figure sanctioned by a hundred years of blues history.

This is not to imply that blue notes cannot interact with the harmony to produce colorful effects. ♭3rds that occur on the tonic chord will strongly suggest I7♯9 chords, while other natural dissonances, such as the ♭5 that occurs on the D7alt in measure 8 can be expected. The expert improviser places these notes carefully so that extended chords tend to occur naturally, as dictated by the line.

Other features of this solo exemplify common blues gestures and devices. Notice the basic and almost reluctant start to the solo—an effective strategy in many jazz contexts. Also, each of the four choruses begins with a direct, blues-oriented statement. Change-running, when it occurs, is reserved for more harmonically active places in the structure. Blues flavor is maintained by the frequent use of ♭3, ♭5, and ♭7, along with thematic development (measures 25–30), repetition of brief figures (measure 9), and rhythmic variety. Effective blues solos incorporate extensive inner dialogue, in which lines interact and play off one another in a manner reminiscent of the vocal artists who invented the genre.

F BLUES

C MINOR BLUES

C Minor Blues Analysis

The concept of a "minor" blues might at first seem paradoxical. After all, a major key is given a blues flavor primarily by flatting the 3rd and 7th of the scale. One might think that would be enough to introduce a minor quality as well, but such is not the case. An examination of the minor blues provided will demonstrate that blues lines constructed over minor chords are distinctly different from those applied to major or dominant chords.

While a collection of blue notes may serve as a blanket scale in major blues—riding over chord changes without changing—such an approach will not work in minor blues. Generally speaking, minor blues improvisations must follow the chord changes more closely, introducing altered pitches that specifically point to the minor key, not just the blues flavor.

Note the careful change-running of the first four bars, an example of how many unexpected ways there are to make the chords "speak." For instance, on beat 3 of measure 2 we see a G♭ on the downbeat of the G7alt chord. This unlikely note actually completes the encirclement gesture begun on the A♭, and any possible ambiguity is eliminated by the direct statement of the triad that follows.

In a more conventional vein, the Cm7 in measure 3 receives two B naturals, and a B♭ does not occur until the anticipation of the next chord. Odd as it may seem, recorded jazz solos make it clear that the major 7th is seen at least as often as the flatted 7th on minor 7th chords. The reason is either encirclement (of the root), or, as occurs here, a suggestion of the chord's V7. In any improvised line we encounter a myriad of surface harmonies that are not reflected in the chord changes to the tune. In this instance, there can be no doubt that a G7 governs the middle part of measure 3. After the Cm7 has been firmly established by the encircling figure that preceded it on beat 4 of measure 2, the ear is more than willing to allow the V7 of Cm7, G7, to stand in for the actual chord.

Following a conventional bebop figure in measure 4, the arrival of the Fm7 signals what is perhaps the most characteristic chord of a minor blues. The ♭3rd and ♭7 of the key are going to occur in all blues, whether in major or minor. But the ♭6 of the key, introducing the minor 3rd of the iv chord, has a distinctly minor flavor.

The treatment of the Fm7 in measure 5 is worthy of close scrutiny. First, notice that a reduction to structural tones leaves a descending F minor triad on the strongest beats. Second, the entire measure can be viewed as one large encircling gesture. The noose tossed by the initial descending 4th on beat 1 of measure 5 is gradually tightened until the root of the chord, F, is reached on the downbeat of the next measure. Finally, note that this large encircling gesture breaks into two nearly symmetrical halves, one encircling the A♭, and one encircling the F. Similar encircling gestures can be found throughout this solo. A good method for finding them is to look for chord tones on strong beats and then identify the approach tones that precede those chord tones.

Many jazz solos are marked by distinct and separate textural areas. In other words, improvisers tend to continue one linear approach for some time, and then move on to another, and so forth. Notice how the relatively angular bebop-like figures of measures 1 through 8 give way to steady eighth notes in measures 9 through 12. Within this section, we see a threefold sequence of a recognizable pattern in measures 11 and 12. Similar textural areas with their own internal logic can be identified in this solo (meas. 18–21, 21–24, 28–29, 35–43). Such areas overlap and cannot be precisely defined. A more fundamental way of viewing this concept is Lester Young's assertion that a jazz solo must "tell a story." A gesture cannot be introduced for no reason at all. It must make sense in terms of what has come before and what will follow. There must be a steady flow of ideas that relate to one another and reveal a logical structure.

"Letter from Bob" Analysis

This chord sequence features ii–V progressions in the major and relative minor key. Few other chords occur. The ♭VImaj7 in measures 4, 12, and 24 is not significant and addressing this chord in the improvised line is an option the soloist may choose to ignore. Similarly, the substitution of A♭maj7 for the anticipated Dm7♭5 in measure 29 is merely to avoid the exact repetition of the preceding chord sequence. It is not absolutely necessary that the soloist address this chord, since the members of the original Dm7♭5 are also found in the A♭maj7 chord, either as chord members or possible extensions. Both chords contain the crucial ♭6 of the key, and as members of the "subdominant minor" category are diatonic substitutions for one another.

This solo takes a straight-ahead bebop approach, yet it would be helpful to take a moment to qualify what we mean by this. This solo is certainly not one that would have been played by Charlie Parker, Dizzy Gillespie, or anyone else working in the mid to late 1940s. The lines and rhythms are too smooth, clean, worked out, and predictable. Clearly, this solo incorporates a "codified" bebop approach—a method of playing that developed in the 1950s after musicians had distilled the devices put forth by Parker and Gillespie and reworked them for their own use.

It is surprising but true that the improvisations of Charlie Parker were far more advanced—in terms of rhythmic manipulation, unpredictability, and deviation from expected norms—than the hard bop recordings that came during the following decade. By the 1950s, "rules" began to develop, even though they were never written down, and musicians tacitly agreed upon a "correct" way of playing the style. John Coltrane's Prestige recordings of the 1950s represent an apotheosis of the post-bop style. His lines are honed to perfection, dissonant enough but faithful to the chord, rhythmically accurate, and harmonically justified. Contrast this with Charlie Parker's sometimes reckless abandon, incorporation of rhythms that defy both notation and the barline, suggestions of substitutions that are neither consistent nor clear, and inclusion of notes that simply cannot be explained. Neither approach is better or displays more artistic merit. But the contrast is worth keeping in mind. It is not at all unusual for a style to develop as an adventurous free-wheeling process of experimentation that is later codified and refined into something that can be understood, learned, and repeated. This is clearly what happened to bebop.

The solo provided is conservative, accurate to the chord changes, and not unlike a typical solo one might encounter on a similar chord sequence in any straight-ahead context. An effort has been made to include recognizable bebop gestures, but always with a bit of a "twist," so that there is something new or fresh about them. For example, the linear construction in bars 5–7 involves standard change- (or mode-) running with guide tones clarifying the harmonic changes. Yet the repeated eighth notes on the downbeat of measure 5, the altered rhythm on the first two beats of measure 6, and the truncated ending on the 6th of the C minor chord in measure 7 all place a subtle but personal stamp on the line. Measure 9 involves a symmetrically patterned ascent of an F melodic minor scale, leading to a possible quotation from "Fools Rush In" in measure 10. A descending bebop major scale begins on beat 3 of measure 11, leading to a classic bebop gesture in measure 12. More standard change-running follows, and the first half of the chorus ends with the "Cry Me a River" lick in measure 15.

A patterned diminished scale begins the bridge, which terminates cleanly by encircling the C minor tonic that occurs in measure 19. Change-running is broken briefly in measure 22 with a blue note. Since the 1920s improvisers have exploited the fact that the $\flat$3rd of the tonic can serve simultaneously as the $\flat$13th of the dominant. When a slightly unexpected substitution occurs in 29, the root and 3rd of the triad are emphasized with quarter notes. Generally speaking, unexpected chords suggest more direct treatment while conventional functions allow for more adventurous lines.

The second chorus receives similar treatment, but a few devices warrant discussion. Notice the alternation of expansive change-running followed by tight change-running in measures 33–34 and 37–38. In other words, following linear motion in which 3rds prevail, the texture changes to chromatic linear motion that does not cover much distance. Note also the long string of eighth notes from measures 37–43 as an example of how to weave in and out of patterns and still have the guide tones land on strong beats. Following this long motor-like passage is a measure of rest, followed by a very strong closing gesture in measures 45–48. The passage ends on the 6th of the Cm chord, a gesture that harks back to measure 7.

A brief piece of a diminished scale starts the phrase beginning in measure 49, and the conspicuous rhythm and shape in measures 51 and 52 practically demand a thematic response in the following measures. The CESH pattern in measures 57 and 58 is standard fare, but is not often heard on a m7$\flat$5 chord. The consequent phrase in measures 59 and 60 is a more familiar sounding pattern. Again, the A$\flat$maj7 receives very direct treatment, leading to an upward leap of a minor 6th on the G7$\flat$9. The rests that follow leave this antecedent phrase very much "open" in anticipation of the consequent phrase in measures 63 and 64. The solo is thus able to close definitively but quietly as well.

LETTER FROM BOB

"Taking 12" Analysis

The solo begins with a simple gesture that emphasizes the major triad but still manages to incorporate a rising minor 6th by moving from the 3rd up to the root. From here on, straight-ahead change-running dominates. B natural has been chosen over B♭ on the downbeat of beat 2, despite the Em7♭5 chord. In this instance, as in most, the principle of enclosure is more important than the actual chord tones associated with the harmony. The crucial C♯ on beat 3, which will drive the harmony toward D minor (the relative minor, an important feature of the harmonic scheme of this tune), is set up and prepared for during the first two beats of measure 2. After all, the expected function of a subdominant chord is to prepare for the arrival of the dominant chord. In many jazz contexts, that preparation is a linear one, which can result in apparent conflict with the prevailing harmony. However, if lines are well constructed, the ear sorts out and rectifies the discrepancies.

Notice how the lines that characterize the change-running in measures 2 through 5 are tight and compact, involving much chromaticism, change of direction, and enclosure. The point to be made is that the term "change-running" does not mean precisely what it says. There are far more possibilities open to the improviser than simply running up and down arpeggios. "Change-running" really means making the harmony manifest in the improvised line itself. It does not mean literally playing the chords. Jazz critics who fail to understand this concept often make disparaging comments regarding change-running, as if it were a formulaic and automatic process. On the contrary, the possibilities are endless.

Measure 5 is a bow to Charlie Parker, who sometimes played this figure on measure 5 of the blues. It is crucial to understand that such references are deliberate efforts by jazz musicians to root their solos in the jazz tradition. Jazz cannot exist in a vacuum. Its spirit and life depend upon referential connections to melodies, figures, and phrases that are stored away in the musical memory. It is appropriate when playing a tune associated with Charlie Parker that some gesture be made to acknowledge him and to show that we have done our homework by studying his solos.

Measure 6 contains a figure that may be a quote from "When Sunny Gets Blue." Oftentimes it is not possible to say if a musical phrase is a quote or not. The improviser may not know. The determining factor is what the listener hears, which cannot always be predicted. What is certain, however, is that jazz solos must contain (and cannot help but contain) passages that will sound familiar to some listeners.

Measures 7, 8, and 9 are loosely sequential and all feature the descending minor seventh arpeggio. Although it is sometimes possible to transpose a figure verbatim through descending chord sequences, it is usually more effective to modify the figure somewhat. Following the third presentation of this figure, in measure 9, the line moves to a standard enclosing gesture aimed at the E of the C7 in measure 10. Next is a classic 3–♭9 gesture that has bebop written all over it. A similar one follows in the turnaround in measure 11. Measure 12 wraps up the first chorus with a memorable melodic gesture that listeners will have heard before, though few will be prepared to say where.

The second chorus begins with a conspicuous motive that may arguably be a reference to "Salt Peanuts." The contour and rhythms found in measures 13 through 16 play off one another, establishing an inner dialogue that lends interest and cohesion to the passage. Measure 17 will be heard by many as a quote from "I Had the Craziest Dream," but the quote is brief and answered by original material in measure 18. The line in measure 19 does not acknowledge the F♯ implied by the D7 chord. There are two reasons for this. First, the expected tonic harmony found in measure 7 of the 12-bar blues form is so firmly established that soloists almost always have the option of returning to it, in spite of prevailing substitutions. Second, the rising scalar passage in measure 19 is setting up a mild surprise in measure 20, and the sense of repose and gradual building of measure 19 would be weakened if the line were to draw attention to itself. The use of C Lydian here would do just that. The figure in measure 20 is highly idiomatic and clearly recognizable as a bebop gesture. It has deliberately been placed to draw attention, since it sounds like nothing that has come before, is prepared by a simple scale, and appears in the upper register. The following measures employ its basic contour as a starting point for standard change-running. Notice how the natural 9th has been chosen on the C7 in this instance, compared with the ♭9, which was the note of choice in measure 10. It is the soloist's prerogative, serving to expand available choices and keep the listener guessing.

TAKING 12

V7–i Latin Solo Analysis

The V7–i Latin solo is highly instructive as an introduction to improvising in minor keys. Among other things, the solo emphasizes the fluid nature of chord movement within the tonic key. From a harmonic viewpoint, V7 and i are diametrically opposed. The dominant chord represents the maximum tension and unrest, while the tonic chord represents resolution and repose. In actuality, however, the build-up and release of tension occur with every note of the melodic line. This is particularly true in minor keys where the 6th and 7th degrees of the scale are active and changeable.

The solo begins with a descending G harmonic minor scale and continues to make use of this construction throughout. The harmonic minor scale may serve as a blanket scale in minor keys. As a pitch collection, it contains the avoid note G on the D7♭9 and the avoid notes C and E♭ on the Gm chord. But its real power lies in the strong voice leading that is built into the scale. The leading tone, 7, along with ♭6, exert strong points of attraction toward the root and 5th of the key respectively. Simply playing the scale implies a miniature V–i chord progression every time these active notes occur.

Note the chromatic passing tones that are inserted in measure 5 in order to ensure that the line lands on B♭ in the next measure. Why B♭? At the local level, B♭ is the ♭13th of the D7♭9 chord, and much more compelling than A, the 5th. But more powerful is the role of this note as the 3rd of the key. This note is in a prominent position (emphasized by register, metric placement, and duration), and represents a brief instant of the tonic within the two bars of dominant function. Beats 3 and 4 of measure 6 swing the harmony back to V7, and resolution occurs expectedly on the Gm of the next measure. Similar instances can be found throughout this solo where the areas of V7 and i implied by the improvised line do not necessarily coincide with the indicated chord changes. This entire solo can in fact be analyzed as an improvisation over a Gm chord, with frequent random suggestions of V7 to add tension to the line.

A case in point is the C natural that is "worked" through measures 19–24. As the background harmony moves through tonic and dominant harmony, the improviser stubbornly returns to this note again and again, exploiting its unusual common-tone status as 11th of the tonic and 7th of the dominant. As a result, the note tends to loom above the harmony as a recurring 4th of the key, independent of chordal movement. This would obviously not be an option in a major key.

A similar strategy is used on the E natural that occurs in measures 35–37, where the preeminence of the linear component becomes irrefutable. The E natural might be justified as the 6th of the Gm chord, but it is certainly not the 9th of D7♭9. Instead, it is part of a rising chromatic line that has dwelled on E for some time before continuing its long ascent up to C, the melodic highpoint of the solo, in measure 41.

V7–i LATIN SOLO

"Nor's Bossa" Analysis

The solo on "Nor's Bossa" displays the characteristic features of bossa nova jazz—subdued melodic figures set to light syncopations over a rich harmonic structure. While soloists are always free to imprint their personal styles on songs they improvise to, generally it is best to incorporate patterns of rhythmic interest in Latin music. Lyricism and melodic interplay are common features. Conventional bebop figures and steady eighth notes are appropriate for textural contrast, but are generally not approaches one would expect to see in music of this type. However, dissonant harmonic implications and change-running are very much a part of the style as long as they maintain the proper mood.

As this solo makes evident, it is possible to construct figures that are melodically fresh and rhythmically inventive that emphasize guide tones and delineate the chords. In other words, bebop-style chord-running is not the only way to "make the changes." In nearly every measure of this improvisation it is possible to hear the chords solely through the improvised line. Yet rarely does an extended series of steady eighth notes occur, and there are few if any figures that qualify as conventional bebop patterns.

One characteristic of mature improvisers is that they are not constricted by the tyranny of the barline. Expert soloists change to the next chord when they are ready, which may be prior to the arrival of the next harmony, or, less often, after the arrival. Many examples of this occur in the "Nor's Bossa" solo. Notice, for example, the C on the "and" of four in measure 9. To object that this is the 13th of E♭m7 is to be oblivious to how jazz lines work. C is a guide tone of A♭7, and will certainly be heard as belonging to the A♭7 no matter how much the listener must adjust its temporal setting to hear it that way. Guide tones are that important.

Measure 15 presents another instance of an anticipated chord. The B and D simply do not function as the major 7th and 9th of the Cm chord, no matter how much they might look like they do on paper. They are in motion, and the B natural in particular, as the leading tone, is aiming for the tonic, C. The delay of its arrival because of the unexpected B♭s in measure 16 only increases anticipation. The B♭s function on two levels. On one hand they are a half step below the leading tone, as if the "spring-loaded" leading tone has been stretched one notch tighter. On another level the B♭s function as the ♯9 of the G7♭9 chord. Temporary resolution to the leading tone finally occurs after four repeated B♭s, followed by a D, which completes the encirclement of the C on the downbeat of measure 17.

Another instance of anticipation occurs on beat 4 of measure 18. Here there is no getting around it. E natural clearly does not belong to the Cm7. Its only possible function is to encircle the F of the following measure. Of course, another way of looking at this is to view the E natural and G as suggesting a surface harmony, C7, which then resolves to Fm7. In either case, the notes clearly "belong" to the following chord.

Several other instances of chord anticipation occur in this solo. Some of the more obvious are found in measures 37–38, 38–39, 56–57, 57–58, 61–62, and 63–64. Examples of the delayed arrival of the approaching chord are less numerous, but measure 54 offers a clear example of that phenomenon.

The treatment of m7♭5 chords warrants some discussion. By rights, this chord should take a natural 9th and not a ♭9th, meaning that the chord scale of choice should be the Locrian natural 2 (the third mode of the melodic minor scale), and not the Locrian mode. When voicing a m7♭5 chord as a vertical entity, Locrian natural 2 (sometimes called Locrian ♯2 because its 2nd is raised in relation to the original) will give the proper group of notes to select from. In a ballad arrangement that includes extended chords played in long notes, this would stand out as the proper choice. But Locrian natural 2 is not the proper scale to play on this chord when improvising. The reason is that the natural 9th happens to be the major 3rd in relation to the minor key. Although this pitch sounds fine as part of the aggregate in a complex chord voicing, it should not be given a prominent position in an improvised line. A glance at the Dm7♭5 chords that occur in this solo will reveal that they invariably receive E♭s in the improvised line. The same observation can be made by studying the countless occurrences of this chord that occur in recorded jazz literature. The conclusion is that individual chords must not be thought of as isolated, self-contained entities that receive specific treatment based on prescribed procedures. Instead, larger tonal areas and the overall key must be taken into consideration. In tonal music, the primary key is omnipresent at some level, continuing to exert its influence on every musical event in the piece.

NOR'S BOSSA

"Across Africa" Analysis

This solo incorporates a series of chords in rapid succession at a very fast tempo. Improvising over a harmonic rhythm that covers two chords per measure presents special challenges. Presumably, each chord will receive four eighth notes. How does one define a chord with four notes? At first the possibilities might seem extremely limited. One can use the digital pattern 1–2–3–5, or its reverse 5–3–2–1. But what then?

Fortunately, the "rules" of change-running loosen at fast tempos involving rapid harmonic rhythms. For one thing, a dominant chord becomes virtually equivalent to a major chord. True, there are a few more options involving the flatted 7th that are not available on major chords, but, on the other hand, dominant chords do not require special treatment at this tempo. Playing directly up the chords, in a manner that would simply not be convincing at slower tempos, is perfectly acceptable here. Examples of this can be seen in measures 6, 17, 21, and 23. Moreover, every chord need not be clearly delineated, since it will pass quickly and the next one, or the next, will give us our bearings. Dominant chords that would be somewhat ambiguous out of context are found in measures 1, 2, 8, 14, 18, 28, 30, and 32.

A basic rule in change-running in this context is to play guide tones and roots wherever possible. There is really no time to deal with extensions, and taboos about playing close to the triad, particularly on dominant chords, are mitigated by the rapidly changing chords. Frequent directional changes are helpful. Notice the large number of measures that contain a clearly arched linear construction within the measure. (Measures 3, 6, 12, 13, 16, 17, 19, 23, 26, and 27 are very lucid examples.) Linear construction in this solo consists mostly of conjunct motion with 3rds. Large skips are not frequent, and are generally followed by rests or scalar passages. This is not an angular solo.

It would be helpful to write out possible patterns for practice. There is an abundant but limited supply of figures that will work in contexts such as this. A good strategy is to begin with some five to ten patterns and practice weaving them into the improvisation. As fluency increases more patterns can be added.

ACROSS AFRICA

"Tiflet's Wind" Analysis

Three one-chorus solos are provided for "Tiflet's Wind." The first was conceived for baritone saxophone, the second for scat vocal, and the third for piano. Each displays a laid-back quality commensurate with the character of the tune. Diatonic patterns prevail, angular lines are infrequent, and rests alternate with rhythmic nuances. Straight-ahead bebop figures are minimal.

The initial solo line sneaks in with the 11th of the A minor chord. This benign upper structure is quite useful on minor chords, adding a "soft" tension to the chord, similar in effect to adding the 9th to a major chord. The internal logic to the contour of the line that covers measures 2 and 3 is apparent, and the space that follows emphasizes the tranquil mood that this opening evokes. Similar lines follow, carefully outlining the chords with smooth directional changes and a minimum of chromaticism. Even the double-time passage of measures 11 and 12 does not stray from the scale of the home key.

A blues flavor is introduced in measure 17. Notice how the blue notes serve as a blanket scale, asserting their autonomy from the changing harmonies. (Of course, in a minor key, what would be a blue 3rd now becomes a blue 5th. The flatted 7th, however, prevails in both major and minor blues contexts.) As an improviser, one must always remember that this option exists—to take the line in a direction that is convincing for internal reasons, independent of the underlying harmony. The blues is by no means the only context in which this is possible. Sometimes the very shape of the line or a quote of a recognizable gesture will be enough to override the harmony.

The second chorus presents an improvisational strategy that might be incorporated by a jazz vocalist. Notice the wide sweep of the linear component of measures 33–36, the smoothness of the directional changes, and the absence of dissonant leaps. Note also how the dominant (E) governs the passage, appearing prominently at the outset, in the descending 7th in measure 35, and the conclusion in measure 36. The plunge to low E in measure 35 is a classic gap-fill configuration, with the ascending A melodic minor scale recouping the space in the beats that follow. An ascending-octave leap in measures 36 and 37 is made inconspicuous by a beat-and-a-half rest. Following is a descending leap from the brief eighth-note E down to B a 4th below. While these leaps are large, they are quite idiomatic to vocal performance, incorporating prominent notes of the home key and avoiding unexpected shifts.

The G♯ on the downbeat of measure 40 warrants discussion. At first the eye is surprised to see what would vertically be construed as a major 7th on a dominant chord. A more realistic interpretation views the G♯ as an accented chromatic passing tone connecting G and A. But in actuality, the concept of harmonic generalization provides the best explanation for this note. Observe how all of the notes heard thus far in this chorus have been members of some form of the A minor scale. Other than the fluctuation of the 6th and 7th degrees of the scale, there has been no chromaticism. The A7 of measure 40 is by no means a structural harmony. Primary chord motion in this tune consists of the alternation of ii–V progressions in either A minor or C major. The A7 in measure 40 serves merely as a secondary dominant to set up the Dm7 that follows. In this instance, the improviser has chosen to ignore this chord. Instead, linear motion in measure 40 simply circles the tonic note A.

Throughout this second chorus especially, we perceive a sense of ambiguity—a refusal to grab on to chord tones that lock us onto the harmony. The improvised line very much plays off the background harmonies, and if the chords were not present it would be impossible to extract them with any certainty from the improvised line. Note, for example, the ii–V progressions found in measures 41–42, 45–46, 50, 52, and 58. Rather than using guide tones to ride the measure-by-measure harmonic changes of the tune, these phrases address the bigger picture, using various devices to achieve melodic independence and autonomy of the improvised line.

The final chorus is meant to present an interpretation that a pianist might create, hence the existence of somewhat more angular lines, increased chromaticism, and pianistic ornaments such as trills and tremolo. Many of the devices discussed thus far in regard to the previous two choruses also occur during this chorus. Matched phrases and inner dialogue are prominent, contour is dictated by melodic choices as opposed to guide-tone requirements, and rhythmic and thematic development play a large part in melodic continuation. This solo is highly instructive as an example of "inside" playing that is true to the changes, yet decidedly not bebop.

TIFLET'S WIND

* Played as even eighth notes.

"Maybe Not" Analysis

"Maybe Not" begins with three measures of CESH over an E♭m chord, but the solo line does not "ride" the obvious line E♭–D–D♭–C. Instead, the opening begins on B♭ and slowly works its way down to E♭ on the downbeat of measure 3. Oftentimes it is wise to avoid the expected, especially at the outset of an improvisation. Rising up through the E♭m/C in measure 3, a gesture appears in measure 4 that may best be understood as convention disguised. Camouflaged beneath the descending chromatic line of measure 4 is the well-known bebop figure sometimes called the "Honeysuckle" lick—here, D♭–C♭–E♭–B♭–A♭, where an eighth rest would ordinarily occur between the C♭ and the E♭. In any case, the chromatic line continues on until the G♭ on the downbeat of measure 5.

The ii–V in measures 5 and 6 is given a fluid treatment. After providing a guide tone on the downbeat of the measure, beats 3 and 4 clearly delineate an undesignated surface harmony (B♭7, the V7/ii) before returning to a direct spelling of the E♭m7, 3rd through 9th, in measure 6. By this time, however, the chord has moved on to A♭7 on the downbeat of measure 6. The point to be emphasized is that an improviser is never tied to the exact chord changes that a ii–V would seem to suggest. When the ii becomes a V is the soloist's prerogative. This was evident in the very first recordings of the beboppers, when the ii–V first began to assert its preeminent position in jazz harmony. A ii–V progression is really a ii–V area. The point of change in the soloist's line is not compelled to coincide with the point of change in the rhythm section. (This is not an excuse for imprecision, of course. A player should still strive to gain exact rhythmic control of chord changes in his improvisations.)

Ambiguity plays a huge role in jazz improvisation. It is extremely effective to introduce passages that clearly function as two things at once. For example, in measure 6 the line directly ascends a G♭maj7 chord, but the chord is A♭7. So, while the ear hears a familiar 7th chord, it also hears the 7th, 9th, 11th, and 13th of the A♭7. This is but one of many ways that improvisers may think of superimposing chords when reaching for upper extensions. Two instances of ambiguity can be found in measure 16. First, the ear will clearly hear that the line moves through a second inversion E♭ triad from the first beat into the second. This is reinforced by the B♭7 harmony that prevails. But, of course, that is not what is really happening at all. These notes are merely part of an encircling gesture that is aiming for the approaching F natural. Why F natural? This is another instance of ambiguity. The F Dorian mode is associated with the related iim7 of the B♭7, but works on another level with the E7 on beats 3 and 4 of measure 16. Here it picks up the ♭9, ♯9, ♯11, and ♭13, in addition to the guide tones. This is an instance of adding dissonance that is grounded in the familiar. Just as dissonant notes in the harmony of a tune are always more compelling when they occur in the melody, so are dissonant notes in an improvisation more compelling when they are part of something that is logical and familiar. They sound as if they are necessary rather than superficial.

Note how measures 17 and 18 hark back to measures 1 and 2. Other figures found in the second half recall motives heard in the first half, without directly restating them. For example, note the "Honeysuckle" lick in measure 24. Finally, as an example of long-range planning, notice the gradually increasing sense of agitation in the solo as is evidenced by the increasing number of sixteenth notes introduced as the solo progresses.

MAYBE NOT

* Played as even eighth notes.

WHEN

"When" Analysis

"When" provides an example of improvisation within a modal context. Modal jazz developed in the 1950s as an alternative to the rapid change-running associated with bebop. With the demands of harmonic rhythm slowed drastically, this style produces an unhurried, meditative aesthetic and suggests abstract, wandering, unpredictable melodic constructions. While the word "modal" might seem to confine the style to the traditional church modes of Western music, such is not the case. Any scale, even major or minor, can form the basis for modal jazz improvisation. Furthermore, modal improvisations are by no means confined to the notes provided by the scale or mode. On the contrary, modal jazz allows for a great deal of departure from the harmony, and in some instances it is difficult to distinguish modal jazz from free jazz.

The solo begins with a clear indication that there is no hurry to get things started. The first sixteen-bar section adheres fairly closely to the Dorian mode, but several chromatic approach tones can be found, including encircling gestures involving the raised 7th (measures 7, 8, and 10). Motivic interplay is apparent with clear relationships between measures 1 and 4, 2 and 5, and 3 and 6. The first three measures are too disjointed to qualify as a phrase, however, and the next three measures, though they echo the first three, hardly serve as a consequent. Symmetrical events, closure, and strong points of articulation are not typical modal gestures and are scarce in this solo. More common are literal repeats or variations of short melodic cells or rhythmic motives.

The shift up one half step to E♭m7sus4 is anticipated by two beats. The right-hand parallel 4ths in measure 17 serve as a precursor to the textural change that occurs later in measures 30 through 35. It will be noticed that D naturals do not occur as part of encircling gestures in either this E♭m7sus4 section (measures 17–24) or the next (measures 43 through 48). As leading tone of the overall tonic key, the C♯ holds a significance throughout the Dm7sus4 sections that the D does not have in the E♭m7sus4 sections. The effect of a particular musical event must be calculated in terms of its perception within the overall key in addition to its position in the local chord or modal area.

The second Dm7sus4 section (measures 25–40) is more chromatic than the first. An instructive instance of multi-stage variance occurs in measures 27–29. As the initial motive A♯–B–F is varied, variations occur on the variations, until the gesture finally evolves into something else entirely. This type of motivic development is common in modal jazz, giving the impression of lines that endlessly spin out of themselves with no clear indication as to where they are going or where they will stop. Yet, all the while, the continuation sounds logical and convincing. Perhaps no one was more masterful at this approach than Miles Davis.

The second E♭m7sus4 section (measures 41–48) has already been discussed in terms of the absence of D natural as an encircling device. In fact, this area adheres very closely to the mode. Accidentals do not occur until measures 47 and 48. In keeping with the tendency for modal areas to become autonomous textural areas in this style, note the preponderance of triplets in this section, a gesture that plays a quite insignificant role in the rest of the solo.

Along these lines, the final Dm7sus4 section (measures 49–64) contains a blues flavor that is first hinted at in measure 50 and continues through measure 59. Measures 52 through 55 adhere very closely to the blues scale. Finally, the solo ends with an area of expansive rising intervals in measures 61 through 64.

Modal jazz is less technically demanding than bebop, but it presents artistic challenges that bebop does not have. In chord sequences with rapid harmonic motion, correct playing over the chord changes will see you through, even when inspiration fails. In contrast, modal improvisation demands that the soloist do something creative. A successful solo in this genre must display an internal logic that is convincing and able to sustain interest. Musical events must not occur at random, but rather should relate to other events in order to form an expressive whole.

"Ok or Not" Analysis

The improvisation on "Ok or Not" is lyrical and song-like throughout. The opening motive sets the stage for the measures to follow. Notice the pairing of phrases in the first eight measures, with two-measure groups answering and playing off one another. The last of these, in measures 7 and 8, introduces a triplet figure that will characterize and dominate the next eight measures.

In measure 17 the tune shifts to the parallel major, a rarity in jazz standards. What kind of gesture would fit this point of demarcation and draw the listener's attention? In this solo it is a double-time figure that is the first bebop-sounding device yet heard. In addition to being highly recognizable and familiar to the ear, the figure holds our attention by soaring into the upper register, covering the distance of two octaves in two measures. Moreover, the line gives us every note in the F major scale at least twice, except for the avoid tone B♭, which is scrupulously avoided. The phrase provides about as clear an assertion of F major as one can get.

The next two measures, 19 and 20, serve as a consequent to the preceding phrase, turning the direction of the line downward and providing an arch-shaped contour to the first four bars of the bridge. In mirror fashion, measures 21 and 22 again provide an ascending phrase, which is answered by a descending one in 23 and 24. Moreover, the content and sound of measures 21 through 24 relate directly to measures 19 through 22, lending a further sense of inner logic to this section of the tune. Such symmetry is by no means a requirement in this or any other style of jazz improvisation, but is rather one of many devices at the improviser's disposal for adding coherence and logic to the improvised structure.

The rest of the solo is marked by pairs of antecedent-consequent phrases, rhythmic interplay of answering passages, and manipulation of contour in a manner similar to that of the opening of the solo.

OK OR NOT

Listening

It has been suggested that we should be suspicious of writers who write more than they read. Substitute the words "play" and "listen" and the caveat is equally true for jazz musicians. There is no more important activity for a jazz musician than listening to the music. When Lester Young spoke to Buddy Tate about replacing Herschel Evans in the Count Basie Band in 1939, the first thing he asked him was, "Have you been listening?" Practice and study are essential, but listening is crucial. Jazz is a communal experience. Ideas are expressed, understood, shared, personalized, and passed back and forth. To participate, one must join the community. One must learn the common language.

Historically, listening has been central to a jazz musician's activities. Musicians have been known to curtail their practice routines after musical maturity, but the best ones never stop listening. Lester Young, Charlie Parker, and Cannonball Adderly were among those known to have practiced ferociously in their early years, but very little in their later years. Yet they never stopped listening. It was said that Lester Young listened to music constantly throughout his life, even going to bed with the radio playing. Charlie Parker was fascinated by 20th-century classical composers during his later years. Cannonball Adderly continued to listen and search for new sounds and idioms throughout his life. In the final analysis, your stature as a jazz musician is determined not by how much you have practiced, but by how well you have listened.

All jazz musicians share one common trait: an indissoluble love for the music. Invariably, this is the starting point. Nearly every jazz musician tells a similar story. At some point in their lives, they heard somebody playing jazz and said, "I want to sound like that." The first step in attaining something is to know what you want: not a general idea or a vague notion of what is desired, but a clear and specific picture. Only through listening can a student of jazz really know what is being sought.

The principles outlined in this chapter have been distilled from the recordings of accomplished jazz musicians. Although the material presented is intended for study and practice, it is also meant to enhance one's ability to listen to jazz. It is only natural that we find some way of categorizing, labelling, and sorting out sensory experiences. We need to understand what we are hearing. By classifying the sounds that we hear and codifying the procedures used to attain those sounds, a theory of jazz results. But it must never be forgotten that the music preceded the theory, and not the other way around.

The devices discussed in this chapter should be studied and practiced so that they become familiar to the ear and comfortable under the fingers. Then, similar devices should be listened for in jazz performances. An excellent approach is to listen with one's instrument handy, playing back passages that catch the ear, and writing them down and memorizing them. The goal is not to collect material as ammunition for firing back in one's own solos, but rather to absorb and understand what is heard. In order to speak a language, one must first learn the vocabulary and understand how phrases and idioms are constructed. Diligent study of the principles outlined in this chapter, supported by attentive and active listening, will go a long way toward developing fluency in the jazz language.

FUNDAMENTALS OF TRADITIONAL JAZZ

For purposes of convenience and clarification, it is useful to divide the history of jazz into two halves: the period that came before bebop and the period that came after. If one had to select a specific year for this point of demarcation, 1944 would be a good choice, since the bebop experiments of the early 1940s had produced a coherent result by this time, and that result was captured on a myriad of recordings that appeared in rapid succession from 1944 onward. The change in the music that occurred at this time was so significant that the period is often referred to as the "bebop revolution." The upheaval it caused in the jazz community was substantial, evoking a war of words between the traditionalists (the "moldy figs") and the modernists (the "reboppers"). Many older jazz musicians either refused or were unable to make the transition to the new style; it was that different. As it turned out, most of the changes brought about by bebop were permanent and have characterized all jazz styles that have appeared since.

The paradox is that a significant part of the history of jazz precedes bebop. Indeed, when bebop appeared it was not at all clear to some people, including its practitioners, that it was really jazz. Jazz was the music of King Oliver, Louis Armstrong, James P. Johnson, Fats Waller, Fletcher Henderson, Duke Ellington, Lester Young, and a host of giants whose recordings attest to the immense contribution they made to the style. Bebop, according to Charlie Parker, seemed to be "something else."

It is inevitable that occasions will arise when jazz musicians will find themselves in the position of performing music with strong ties to traditional jazz. How this should be done is not at all clear. The debate over "period performance practice" in classical music has raged for decades. On the one hand, to play historic music from a modernistic viewpoint with total disregard for how it would have originally sounded is pointless. One has simply borrowed materials from the past to create something new today. On the other hand, to attempt to recreate original performances exactly as they would have sounded in the past is impossible. For a number of reasons, one would need to have lived and worked during that period to sound as the musicians of the time did. It is not possible to re-enter a bygone era several decades later and expect to create authentic music.

The only viable solution is to identify the essential features of the music that are under our control, and perform in a manner that is consistent with the original style. That is essentially what traditional jazz musicians themselves did after the bebop revolution. It is astonishing to consider that many of the pioneers of jazz in the 1920s continued to work professionally well into the 1960s and 70s. Much can be learned from studying the "compromises" these musicians made in recreating their own music. They accepted developments that had occurred over the years that seemed congruent with their music, but rejected others that they considered inappropriate.

This chapter will discuss the basic elements of jazz as it existed prior to bebop. Common tune structures, chord sequences, and approaches to soloing will be examined. The concept of collective improvisation as practiced by New Orleans jazz musicians is beyond the scope of this book, as are the specific roles played by individual members of the rhythm section. The aim of this chapter is to provide enough fundamental material for readers to be able to develop an intelligent approach to the music. Too often, forays into early jazz make a mockery out of the music under the guise of "Dixieland." Wearing striped vests and playing corny licks to "When the Saints Come Marching In" does not qualify as traditional jazz. It is hoped that the principles outlined in this chapter will prepare musicians to approach this music with sincerity and integrity when the occasion arises.

Harmonic Concept

Many of the standard upper structures associated with post bebop jazz are not found in music of the 1920s. But this is not to imply that only triadic structures are present. Impressionistic influences had a significant impact on jazz during the 1920s, especially in written arrangements. Normal chord progressions could be expected to have the 7th on chords with dominant function (more on that below), and possibly a natural 9th or 13th. Major chords could be triads or 6th chords, rarely receiving a 9th, and almost never a major 7th (unless in the melody, as in Louis Armstrong's "Struttin' with Some Barbeque"). A minor chord would most likely be a triad, but might receive and added 6th or 9th. Minor 7th chords were rare. Diminished chords were common, both as triads and 7ths. m7b5 chords were not. Augmented chords were used frequently, as were whole tone scales. These suggestions apply to standard comping in the rhythm section. Soloists were apt to be more adventurous, and arrangers of the time were wont to try anything.

It is revealing to contrast the bebop repertoire with that of traditional jazz. A significant number of early bebop compositions were based on blues or rhythm changes. A few other favorite structures were added to that list, such as "Indiana" changes, "Cherokee" changes, or "Honeysuckle" changes, but it is evident that well over half of all bebop tunes utilized only a handful of chord schemes. This was not true in the 1920s. A seemingly endless number of tunes were available to jazz musicians, and very few, other than the blues, shared the same chord progressions.

That having been said, most chord sequences in early jazz are quite predictable. At the top of the list is the circle of 5ths. The prominence of dominant 7th chords resolving downward to other dominant 7th chords in traditional jazz tunes cannot be overstated. Subdominant chords are not frequent in early jazz chord sequences. It is crucial to observe that the hallmark of bebop harmony, the ii–V progression, is rare in traditional jazz. In the vast majority of chord sequences, dominant 7th chords will either stand alone without preparation, or else be preceded by V of V.

"There'll Be Some Changes Made" (1921) by W. Benton Overstreet and Billy Higgins exemplifies the preference for dominant 7ths in music of this period:

Key: F

```
|| D7  |     |     | G7 |    |    |    ||

|| A7  | D7  | G7  | C7 |    ||

|| D7  |     |     | G7 |    |    |    ||

|| A7  | D7  | G7 | C7 | F | D7 | G7 | C7 | F | F ||
```

As can be seen, the progression wanders incessantly through the circle of fifths, only touching upon the tonic near the end, where it is tagged and finally returns in the penultimate bar. Typically, a progression like this one would be played exactly as indicated, with no upper structures added beyond the 7th.

Many classic jazz standards contain chord progressions whose basic structure will be familiar to present-day jazz musicians. Below are the chords to "Whispering" (1920) by John Schonberger. Adding the related iim7 to each of the dominant chords would produce a set of changes that were often used by bebop musicians.

```
|| C  |    | B7  |    | C  |    | A7  |    ||

|| D7 |    | G7  |    | C  | C  C° | Dm7 G7 | D7 G+ ||

|| C  |    | B7  |    | C  |    | A7  |    ||

|| D7 |    | G7  |    | Dm A7 Dm A7 | Dm Fm6 | C | C ||
```

Notice that more harmonic variety is likely to occur at turnarounds or just prior to the return of the tonic chord.

"Blues My Naughty Sweetie Gives to Me" (1919) by Charles McCarron, Carey Morgan, and Arthur Swanstrom provides an example of an early jazz tune in a minor key (although it ends in major):

```
|| Gm   | Gm D7 | Gm   | G7    | Cm    | Cm G7 | Cm   | Cm    ||

|| D7   | D7    | Gm   | Gm    | A7    |       | D7   |       ||

|| Gm   | Gm D7 | Gm   | G7    | Cm    | Cm    | D7   | D7    ||

|| G7   | G7    | C7   | C7    | F7    | F7    | B♭   | B♭    ||
```

While there is a distinct blues flavor to this song, it is by no means a blues form (even though the first six bars hint at one). Again, dominant chords prevail whenever possible.

Ragtime

Ragtime is not jazz, nor is it a precursor to jazz, but rather is a style that coexisted with jazz during the first two decades of the twentieth century. Nevertheless, the two styles are closely related in significant ways, and many musicians, particularly pianists, were strongly associated with both jazz and ragtime. Jelly Roll Morton, for example, was a pioneer jazz pianist with strong ragtime roots. For the most part, ragtime was a composed instrumental genre, but there is strong evidence that in practice much embellishment and improvisation occurred during performance. It was primarily a piano medium, but ragtime bands were also important, some of them lasting well into the 1920s. James Reese Europe, for example, had one of the successful black orchestras of the 1910s. While his music was on the cutting edge of jazz in rhythmic conception, it is best classified as ragtime. Clearly the two genres were intertwined during the early years of the century, and one style cannot be understood without some knowledge of the other.

Ragtime is characterized by a syncopated melodic component set against a solid march-like accompaniment. Indeed, the primary structure and harmonic materials of ragtime came directly from the march tradition. Ragtime is generally played strictly—the eighth notes do not swing. Although swing interpretations of rags can be heard on early recordings, most ragtime composers clearly wanted their compositions played exactly as written, and most ragtime authorities would frown upon any significant altering of the rhythm. That being said, authentic recordings and piano rolls made directly from ragtime practitioners indicate that subtle alterations of tempo, touch, note length, and rubato were indeed significant elements of ragtime performance. This was by no means "mechanical" music.

Rags were highly structured in form. Although countless variations are possible, all follow something like AAB-BCCAA. Each letter represents an eight-bar strain. Strains are usually repeated literally, but single strains can also occur. The middle section, represented by C here, will usually go to the subdominant, much like the trio of a march. Below are some well-known rags that musicians are likely to encounter in the early jazz repertoire:

"Maple Leaf Rag," Scott Joplin, 1899	AA BB A CC DD
"The Entertainer," Scott Joplin, 1902	Intro AA BB A CC Intro2 DD
"Eccentric," J.Russel Robinson, 1923	AA BB A CC DD
"Twelfth Street Rag," Euday L. Bowman 1914	Intro AA1 Intro2 A2

Ragtime exerted a strong influence on early jazz. Although we now view the two as distinct musical styles, such distinctions were not at all clear during the first three decades of the twentieth century. Many jazz bands used the term "ragtime" to describe their music, commonly incorporating the word into titles of tunes that do not fit our present definition of ragtime form. The confusion is not surprising. "Ragging" was the process of adding syncopation to a melody just as "jazzing" was a process of adding embellishment and rhythmic variation. Moreover, the structure of many early jazz tunes, with their multi-sectional form, contrasting themes, and modulations, derives directly from the ragtime tradition. This will be discussed in more detail in the following section.

Early Jazz Song Forms

Early jazz tunes typically had titles containing words that appear to describe the form (e.g., rag, one-step, blues, cakewalk, or stomp). But that is not quite the case. As we shall see, labels for song forms were very loose at that time. Just because a song was called something does not mean that the structure will necessarily fit into our present conception of what that form is supposed to be. A composer is free to choose any designation for a composition that he or she deems appropriate. There is no requirement to properly label works according to category. This has resulted in confusion about form and structure throughout the entire history of Western music. Moreover, what a term designates at one point in history may not be the same as what it means at another time. This is particularly true of the words "rag" and "blues," terms that had very broad meanings then, but have come to have quite specific implications now.

Blues

The word "blues" designated a much broader collection of song types in the 1910s and 1920s than it does today. Many blues songs from this period are not twelve-bar structures at all. Others that are twelve-bar structures deviate significantly from the basic blues pattern and oftentimes evoke very little blues quality or sentiment. Conventional wisdom has it that the blues started out as a chord sequence involving triads built on I, IV, and V. As musicians experimented with the form, so the story goes, substitute harmonies were gradually added, until, by the end of the bebop era, jazz blues had evolved into a far more complex harmonic structure than it had been several decades earlier. In actuality, however, blues progressions were likely to be loaded with extraneous chords as early as the 1910s, as can be seen in this typical progression:

$$\| \text{E}^\flat \quad | \quad | \quad | \text{E}^\flat 7 \quad | \text{A}^\flat \quad | \text{A}^\circ \quad | \text{B}^\flat \quad | \text{C7} \quad | \text{F7} \quad | \text{B}^\flat 7 \quad | \text{E}^\flat \quad | \quad \|$$

This chord sequence was not at all unusual for an early blues progression. It would appear that many of the reharmonized chords that we now associate with post-bebop jazz were available from the earliest days of jazz recording.

Multi-Part Structures

An examination of several classic jazz standards from this period will give some indication of the forms that improvisers worked from as well as the potentially misleading nature of song titles. Below is the jazz classic "Jazz Me Blues" (1921) by Tom Delaney.

$$\|: \text{E}^\flat \quad | \text{E}^\flat \ \text{B}^\flat 7 \ | \text{E}^\flat \quad | \text{F7} \ \text{B}^\flat 7 \ | \text{E}^\flat \quad | \text{E}^\flat \quad | \text{C}^\circ \ \text{E}^\flat \ | \text{B}^\flat 7 \ \text{E}^\flat :\|$$

$$\| \text{B}^\flat 7 \quad | \text{G}^\circ \quad | \text{B}^\flat 7 \quad | \text{B}^\flat 7 \quad \|$$

$$\|: \text{C7} \quad | \text{C7} \quad | \text{F7} \quad | \text{F7} \quad | \text{B}^\flat 7 \quad | \text{B}^\flat 7 \quad | \text{E}^\flat \quad | \text{E}^\flat \quad :\|$$

$$\|: \text{C7} \quad | \text{C7} \quad | \text{F7} \quad | \text{F7} \ \text{B}^\flat 7 \ | \text{E}^\flat \quad | \text{G7} \quad | \text{Cm} \quad | \text{C7} \quad | \text{F7} \quad | \text{B}^\flat 7 \quad | \text{E}^\flat \quad | \text{E}^\flat \quad :\|$$

Although the multi-part structure follows no prescriptive form, it clearly derives from march and ragtime influences. Solos occur on the second section only, and the entire form is played for the final statement of the tune.

"Royal Garden Blues" (1919) by Spencer Williams and Clarence Williams actually contains a blues enveloped within the larger structure:

```
|| F  C7 | F  C7 | F  C7 | F7      | B♭ A7 | B♭ A7 | B♭ A7 | B♭    | C7    | C7    | F  B♭ | F  C7 ||

|| F  C7 | F  C7 | F  C7 | F7      | B♭ A7 | B♭ A7 | B♭ A7 | B♭    | C7    | C7    | F     | F     ||

|| F7    | F7    | F7    | F7    | B♭    | B♭    | F     | F     | C7    | C7    | F     | F     ||

|| F7    | B♭    | B♭m   | F7    ||

||: B♭   | B♭    | B♭    | B♭7   | E♭    | E♭m   | B♭    | G7    | C7    | F7    | B♭    | B♭    :||
```

The overall structure is AA B Interlude C, where the interlude carries out the modulation to B♭, the subdominant. Solos are over section C. Notice how substitutions are inserted into the basic blues progression that allow for the prominence of dominant 7th chords.

An example of multi-sectional form in a minor key is seen in "That's A Plenty" (1909) by Bert A. Williams.

```
|| Dm  | Dm  | Dm  | Dm  | A7  | A7  | Dm     | A7     ||

|| Dm  | Dm  | Dm  | Dm  | A7  | A7  | Dm A7  | Dm     ||

|| C7  | C7  | F   | F   | C7  | C7  | F      | F      ||

|| C7  | C7  | F   | F7  | B♭  | F D7 | G7 C7 | F  A7 ||

|| Dm  | Dm  | Dm  | Dm  | A7  | A7  | Dm     | Dm     ||

|| Dm  | Dm  | Dm  | Dm  | A7  | A7  | Dm A7  | Dm F7 ||

|| B♭  | B♭  | G7  | G7  | C7  | F7  | B♭     | F7     ||

|| B♭  | B♭  | G7  | G7  | C7  | F7  | B♭     | B♭     ||

|| D   | D   | D   | D   | F   | F   | F   | F   | F7  | F7  | F7  | F7  ||
```

The form requires some explanation. The overall scheme is AA BB AA CC D. Section D functions as a "break strain" or "dogfight," creating tension in anticipation of the return of the C strain. Solos occur over section C. After the last solo is played, a variant of C is played with repeat, followed by the original C strain with repeat as the out chorus. Thus, the overall plan is actually AA BB AA CC D solos D C1C1 CC.

There are scores of multi-sectional jazz classics, and the schematic plans vary widely. The above discussion is merely a brief overview of how these structures are put together. Those interested in pursuing the study of early jazz are urged to listen to the many recordings of these jazz standards that have been accumulating since the early 1920s.

Improvisational Strategy

Certainly the original creators of classic jazz did not have to think about how to improvise to it. Their ears, training, and experiences were all they needed. But for musicians who developed to maturity after the advent of bebop, which is virtually everyone reading this book, the situation is different. In short, our fingers are programmed to play things that are simply inappropriate in classic jazz. Some musicians respond to this by over-reacting—trying to play in a simple and elementary style when playing traditional jazz, avoiding upper structures entirely and mechanically running up and down triads. This is to be avoided. By studying the solos of the jazz masters prior to bebop, it is possible to learn how they approached the art of improvisation. If it is impossible to ever sound like them, we can at least approach their music with integrity and produce viable improvisations of our own that are true to the style.

Listening is essential when studying early jazz. One cannot exaggerate the importance of learning recorded solos. Stories are legion that describe the dedication with which musicians studied the solos of those they admired. Drummer Ray McKinley once told how he met Tommy Dorsey in a restaurant and they regaled each other by singing Louis Armstrong solos from memory. Benny Goodman claimed to have memorized all of Bix Beiderbecke's solos—on the cornet! If those who lived during the same era as the early jazz masters felt the need to learn their recordings, it must be much more important for us to do the same more than a half century later.

Here is a list of guidelines for playing classic jazz:

1. Use care and economy in the selection of notes.
2. Do not become locked into the chord of the moment. Think of broader harmonic areas and the overall tonic key.
3. Generally, it is best to search for common tones rather than guide tones. The jerky effect of riding the changes is generally not appropriate in early jazz.
4. References to the melody are always appropriate.
5. Ignore nonessential harmonies. If a fast harmonic rhythm occurs (such as during a turnaround) do not try to incorporate those chords into the improvised line.
6. Pentatonic scales are quite appropriate.
7. Melodic repetition, alteration, and development are useful. There should be an inner logic to the line.
8. Play with the listener's expectations. Surprises are welcome.
9. Introduce blue notes where appropriate.
10. Use natural 9ths and 13ths freely on major and dominant chords, even in conspicuous places and for extended durations.

This list is, of course, a brief distillation of a colossal body of recorded classic jazz. To show how these principles might play out in actual improvisation, a sample solo is provided on the following page. Readers are encouraged to listen and transcribe original jazz solos from the period. Highly recommended are the Louis Armstrong Hot Five and Hot Seven recordings, as well as any of the recorded solos of Bix Beiderbecke.

TRADITIONAL JAZZ SOLO

CHAPTER 14

PRACTICING— WHY, WHAT & HOW?

Several months before this writing, I asked a colleague how his summer was going, and he replied, "Oh, just trying to find time to practice." Another said, "I've got so much administrative work to do that I hardly have time to practice." But a more fortunate acquaintance mentioned, "I practice in the morning and go to the beach in the afternoon." Lucky him.

It seems you can't talk to a musician without the word "practice" coming up. It's what we do, what we think about. It's what bonds us as few non-musicians would understand. All of us—music students, teachers, and performers alike—recognize and accept the need to practice regularly. Yet we never seem to have the time to practice as much as we want.

With such restrictions on our time, we want to make the most of each practice session. How should we invest these precious blocks of time? Veteran musicians generally have worked out a strategy to deal with restricted practice time. Years of experience have taught the seasoned musician what needs to be practiced in order to keep in shape and to meet upcoming challenges.

But students need to give some thought to the subject. To assert that "my teacher tells me what to practice" does not suffice. You won't always have a teacher. Some teachers work only on specific material at lessons and assume that students are practicing in a well-rounded fashion. Others are there to offer help and guidance, but they allow students to develop according to personal strengths and interests. Clearly, it behooves the student to give some thought to structuring practice time. Deciding what to practice during a given practice session is largely influenced by how long that session will be. It is important to understand what can and cannot be effectively practiced within a given period of time. Trying to cram five or six activities into a thirty-minute session, for example, would be foolish. On the other hand, spending thirty minutes on a single activity will limit overall development and progress. A half hour of scales and arpeggios could be an effective component in an extended practice session, but it would be a wasteful way to spend a complete session. A happy medium must be struck.

Students must learn to pace themselves through longer practice periods. When practice sessions become extended, it is important to make sure they don't turn into hours of drudgery. If something isn't fun, we simply won't do it, at least not for very long. An hour of tonguing exercises or two hours of scales out of a pattern book are not activities that any human being should be subjected to.

The longer a practice session becomes, the more it should resemble actual performance. Drill, isolation, and repetition are essential elements of practice, but you can't do these things all day. Go easy on such activities. Remember, the ultimate goal is to make music.

Charlie Parker is reported to have practiced fifteen hours a day when he was young. Later in life, Parker owned a farm in Pennsylvania where he would relax when he wasn't working. But he still practiced. I once spoke to a man who had lived near Parker, and he told me that Parker would improvise on songs all day—sometimes playing the same song for hours on end. Was he working and concentrating? Yes. Was it hard work and drudgery? Not at all. If I played like Charlie Parker, I'd play all day too.

So let's get to specifics. Assuming that we don't have fifteen hours a day to practice—and we don't play like Charlie Parker—what should we do with our practice time?

A Daily Routine

It's almost impossible not to fall into a daily routine. All of us find a sequence of drills and practice material that appeals to us over time. We learn what works for us and what doesn't. This is a good thing, but we want to be sure that our daily routines develop through thought rather than habit. We also want to keep them flexible enough to accommodate practice sessions of varying lengths.

Long Tones

This is for horn players especially, but guitarists and bassists should not overlook the value of warming up with long notes as a way of making sure they have good tone and a solid connection with the instrument. As a saxophonist, I always begin my practice session with long tones. Some players don't do long tones; others swear by them. I like them. To me they feel like stretching before exercise. It's a way of easing into things. I never fret, worry, strain, or become exasperated about my tone when doing long tones. Instead, I just try to relax and get a big, unrestricted sound. I think about breathing, posture, finger position, and all of the physical elements of performing.

The magic of long tones is that they afford us an opportunity to examine our playing habits at close range. It's our chance to have complete control. How many times have we all tried to correct a bad habit, such as a faulty finger position or poor posture, only to find that we fall back into the same rut when challenged by difficult music? Long tones take the heat off. We can stand in front of a mirror and fine-tune every detail of our performing technique, a big first step toward establishing permanent good habits.

Remember, when you practice, you are reinforcing how you sound and how you feel at that moment. If you don't like how you sound, or if you feel nervous or tense, then stop. Find something else that works for you.

How much time should be spent on long tones? It depends on how much time you have. Some days I spend a couple of minutes on them. Other days I spend five or ten minutes on long tones and then come back to them several hours later if I feel that tension has entered into my playing. Use long tones as a tool when you need them.

Melodies

Playing melodies is a great way to develop tone, intonation, and interpretation. Like long tones, they can be used to reduce tension and focus on the most basic skills involved in playing an instrument. In addition, they embody a central concept.

Sometimes we become so involved in working on scales, technique, pieces, and range, that we forget what our priorities are. Of what use is playing any instrument if you can't play a simple melody and make it sound good? I've known students who could play all their major scales, read well and play difficult pieces accurately, but sounded terrible playing a simple song. Obviously, such students are on the wrong track.

I pause to play a few melodies many times during practice sessions, just for fun. I especially like slow movements by Bach, Verdi arias, and Billy Strayhorn songs. (How's that for mixed company?) Playing from memory is important, as it helps get us past transferring written notes to sound and puts us closer to understanding the song as a whole.

Scales and Arpeggios

Scales and arpeggios prepare us to play patterns we are likely to encounter in real music. No matter how many pieces you practice, you will never cover all of the possibilities that can be included in a simple scale-and-arpeggio routine.

Generally, once all of the major and minor scales are learned along with their associated arpeggios, it's a good idea to turn to one of the many pattern books that are available. These often have titles such as "Daily Studies," "Finger Exercises," and so forth. Since it would be nearly impossible to play through one of these volumes in its entirety each day, most musicians just pick a few favorites or rotate them over the weeks and months.

It is important to understand why we practice scales and arpeggios. I once asked a student if he was working on his scales, and he replied, "I already know them." That's like asking a baseball player if he went to batting practice and getting the reply "I already know how to bat." We do the same exercises over and over again because they are, in fact, exercises. They are never "learned" in the sense that we can put them away and are done with them.

The first step, of course, is to learn the correct notes. Then they must be played evenly, at a reasonable tempo, with proper articulation. But an important benefit of scales and arpeggios that we sometimes forget is that they are tone studies. It's one thing to single out a note and play it with a big expressive tone; it's quite another to get that same tone when passing through it in a series of sixteenth notes. This is a skill that the best instrumentalists work on all their lives.

Etudes

Although *étude* is simply the French word for "study," the designation means something more to a musician. Music that fits this description generally goes beyond the "daily exercise" and qualifies as a musical composition. On the other hand, the purpose of such a work is pedagogical. So we might call an etude an exercise whose purpose is to instruct while sounding as musical as possible.

Since etudes are intended to instruct, it is important to go back to them once they are learned. Review is important. At some point, most musicians find it more advantageous to continue practicing the etudes they already know, rather than learning new ones.

The real value of an etude begins only after the notes have been learned. Then it becomes a valuable instructional tool for future use. It would be folly to work through an entire etude book over a period of several months and then permanently abandon it, placing it on the shelf. Learning should be cumulative.

The musician seeks to create a repertoire of music that has been mastered, not a list of pieces that were learned and then forgotten.

Pieces

Scales, studies, and exercises have one overriding purpose: to teach. Musical pieces, on the other hand, may not have been written for this purpose at all. A musical composition stands as a work of art and is not necessarily intended to be instructional. This calls for a different practice strategy.

Etudes generally include something of educational value in every measure. It is expected that students will practice such exercises in their entirety, often playing them from start to finish without stopping. This is rarely a good approach to learning an extended musical composition, except in the final stages of preparation.

Pieces require much thought and fine tuning. Passages need to be isolated and carefully worked out. Articulations, dynamics, and countless nuances need to be considered. Pieces are essential in the development of interpretation and musicianship, but these skills won't be acquired through sheer repetition. Patience and concentration are required.

Putting It All Together

So what should a typical practice session consist of? This, of course, depends on many factors—the instrument, time available, personal goals, and level of development. For advanced wind players, practicing between one and two hours a day and dividing the practice session into thirds is a common strategy.

For instance, you might begin a two-hour session with forty minutes of basic exercises, including long tones, tonguing or vibrato studies, scales, and arpeggios. The next forty minutes will consist of etudes, with part of that time spent on learning new material and part on review. The final forty-minute segment will be devoted to pieces, orchestral excerpts, improvisation, and sight-reading. This basic plan leaves room for flexibility, includes much variety, and provides a working strategy toward effective use of practice time.

Practice Should Be Fun, But It Must Involve the Mastery of Realistic Goals

How do you get students to practice? In an ideal world, every student would show up for lessons prepared, attentive, and eager to learn. All the teacher would have to do is dispense knowledge and expertise, while the student enthusiastically absorbed the material, eager to hurry home and practice for next week's lesson. I may have had one or two students like this. I may even have been such a student (off and on). Unfortunately, it's not the norm. Many students hate to practice. Some do it anyway; some don't. Without question, motivating students to practice is an essential part of a music teacher's job. One technique that can help teachers to do this is appropriate goal-setting.

A goal is the end toward which an effort is directed. When students practice in order to learn an etude, improve facility in the key of A♭, or make their high notes more resonant, they are involved in goal-directed behavior. They realize that a gap exists between the present situation and the ideal situation. Goal-setting establishes a path between "where students are" and "where they want to be."

Goal-setting improves performance in several ways. First, it directs attention to the task. (If I don't practice this etude, I won't learn it.) Second, goals stimulate the individual to apply effort. (I really want to learn the etude, so I'm going to try hard to learn it.) Third, goals encourage persistence. (I'd really like to do something else today, but I promised myself I'd learn that etude.) Fourth, goals cause students to invent personal strategies for attaining them. (Repeating this etude over and over doesn't seem to be working. Maybe I'll try playing through the difficult sections slowly.)

Goals that are clear and specific, not too difficult, and attainable in the near future tend to be most effective in motivating students. Learning a specific etude is a clear short-term goal. But what about more complex goals, like improving tone? In this case, the goal must be translated into a task that is a proven method of attaining the goal.

For example, a student may assign himself the task of practicing long tones for five minutes each day. But the task must not be confused with the goal. The student must never forget that long tones in themselves will accomplish nothing. If performed conscientiously and carefully, they can serve as an effective tool in developing a fine tone. If they become mindless drudgery, they will not improve one's playing and can actually be harmful. The long-term goal must always be kept in mind, even though it is approached through the application of a daily task.

Set goals that can be reached so that the student will experience a feeling of accomplishment and closure. When I studied flute with Harold Bennett, his procedure was to assign a new etude at each lesson. Occasionally, I arrived at my lesson without having fully prepared the etude. He never asked me to repeat the assignment. Instead, he worked with me as best he could on the ill-prepared etude, advised me to go back to it when I got a chance, then moved on to a new etude. Thus the feeling of momentum—the move toward attainment of a series of short-term goals—was not broken.

In recent years, educational psychologists have reached the conclusion that retention (failing a student for the entire school year) doesn't work. Although this traditional method of ensuring that students are adequately prepared for the next grade makes sense from the school's perspective, the effects on the student run contrary to everything that motivates a human being to learn.

The same is true for music students. Having to repeat an assignment for three or four consecutive lessons ("until you get it right") inflicts a terrible blow to the student's enthusiasm. The student may eventually learn the material, but conclude that practice is no fun at all. And the musician who hates to practice won't be a musician for long.

To better understand the concept of motivation, it is helpful to view its origins as either intrinsic or extrinsic.

Intrinsic motivation stems from internal interest, curiosity, or enjoyment. The intrinsically motivated student does not need threats of punishment or promises of rewards. Such students enjoy the activity itself and the sense of accomplishment that it brings.

Extrinsic motivation depends on external factors, such as rewards, pressures, punishment, or fear of embarrassment. Students do not see the activity itself as rewarding, but focus on the gains that will occur because of it. There is nothing wrong with extrinsic motivation. We use it every time we pay someone for work or give grades. Maximum performance is likely to occur when both internal and external motivation are involved.

Practicing is hard work. Unless the student finds some satisfaction in the activity of practice itself, it is unlikely that external rewards will be sufficient to sustain the individual through long hours of scales and etudes. How do you get students to enjoy practicing?

Part of the solution is to encourage students to become task-involved rather than ego-involved. Task-involved learners are focused on their own activities and not concerned with how they compare with others. They are internally competitive and delight in their own improvement. They enjoy meeting challenges and don't care how they look to others.

Ego-involved learners are preoccupied with themselves. They want to appear to be accomplished and successful, no matter what it takes to convince others. To them it's the performance that counts. They look for shortcuts (sometimes even deceptions) and avoid trying anything that might make them appear incompetent in front of others.

Acclaimed flutist Geoffrey Gilbert, teacher of James Galway, cautioned against practicing for specific events and performances. "To progress, practice regularly... with no goal except to improve," he advised. Practicing is the musician's laboratory. It's where the real work is done. Teachers must not give young musicians the impression that practicing is a necessary evil, a painful procedure to be endured for the results it will bring. This is a prescription for frustration and failure.

It is important that students receive assignments that are of an appropriate level of difficulty. Students should feel challenged, but not frustrated. This range tends to be narrower with beginning students than with more advanced ones.

Advanced students know how to assess a piece of music and approach it effectively. If a piece is too difficult, they slow it down, remove articulations, or work on small portions at a time. If a piece presents no particular technical difficulties, mature students can make it challenging by focusing on attacks, articulation, tone, and pitch. In short, they understand that they are striving for improvement above all else, and they have learned how to adapt the assignment to their needs.

Young students cannot do this. All they know is that they must learn the music, and they do this using the limited repertoire of strategies they know. Once a beginner has mastered a piece that is too easy, the student will likely keep repeating the piece indefinitely, with no particular purpose in mind. Since the ear has not yet developed to the point where the student can critically address fine points of tone and articulation, the student has derived most of the benefit the piece had to offer and is now just putting in time.

On the other hand, if the piece is too difficult, the student won't know how to approach it. For some reason, young students resist playing passages very slowly, even if that is the only way they have a chance of getting the notes. It seems they want music to sound like music at all times, which is not a bad thing. For the same reason, they resist segmenting music into small chunks that can be mastered one at a time. In short, the techniques that allow advanced students to tackle a wide variety of pieces are simply not available to beginners. Therefore, it is crucial that their assignments lie within, but at the verge of, their capabilities.

Practicing should be fun. Some teachers and publishers think this means that assignments should include popular music and relevant themes. Maybe they should. Band activities and preparation for concerts can also serve as incentives to practice. But practicing will be fun only when it involves a sense of mastery and accomplishment, no matter what kind of music is played. The student who loves to practice is the one who feels he or she is making steady progress and who enjoys the satisfaction that comes from meeting and overcoming challenges.

If Practice Makes Perfect, Structure Practice Time to Deliver Maximum Effect

When I was a boy, my parents took me to New York to experience a real jazz club. I was awestruck as I sat and watched from our front-row table. It seemed so strange to see and hear adults playing the same band instruments that my classmates and I played, and I marveled at their effortless facility.

After the performance, I was taken backstage where I met, among others, the legendary trumpeter Bobby Hackett. He gave me an autographed picture, which I still have to this day, that contains one word of advice: Practice!

Surely "practice" is the guiding watchword of music teachers and students alike. Almost any question involving correction, improvement, or progress will elicit the same reply: How can I get better high notes? How can I improve my tone? How can I improve my sight-reading? Practice!

If there's one aspect of practice that all music educators agree on, it's that there should be more of it. But beyond this common desire, perhaps there is more we can do to ensure that students make the most of the time they already devote to practice.

While some students have restrictions on when and where they can practice, most have a variety of options available to them. Should they practice every day? Is it okay to take a day off? Two days? Is it best to practice the same amount each day or to designate certain days as heavy or light practice days?

Scheduling time within the practice session itself is another concern. How should time be divided between scales, lesson material, pieces, sight-reading, band music, and so on? Should each practice session be the same? Should you keep playing scales once you know them? Should band or recital music be practiced to the exclusion of everything else as the performance approaches? These are all questions that do not have a universal answer, but nevertheless should be given careful consideration.

When you're serious about a task, you make a plan. This doesn't mean that you have to be restricted by your plan; plans are meant to be changed. But having one will ensure that things are not done in a haphazard, offhand manner.

Teachers and students should discuss long-term goals. Students should ask themselves, "Where do I want to be several years from now, and what will it take to get there?" Goals do not have to be lofty or far-reaching. They can be as modest as wanting to participate in the school band or as ambitious as hoping to become a professional performer.

In between are many possibilities. Some students want to be competent performers but have no interest in pursuing a career in music. Others want to be music teachers. Many simply want to participate in school music activities and have no interest in continuing with their instruments after high school or college. These are all viable goals for high-school musicians.

Students must understand what it will take to reach their goals, and I don't simply mean admonitions such as "if you expect to be a professional musician, you should be practicing three hours a day," and so forth. Beyond the amount of practice time spent, the kind of practice needed will depend on long-term goals.

Many high-school students simply play through their band music occasionally and then practice intensely a few days before the concert (much the same as they prepare for examinations in other subjects). Others have a weekly lesson, which may be devoted primarily to band music. More serious students will have significant pieces to prepare for their weekly lessons and upcoming competitions or auditions.

But truly dedicated students must get past the "preparing-for-the-event" mentality. Even an important competition or recital must not make a significant interruption in a student's practice habits. It must never be forgotten that the fundamental purpose of practice is to improve.

It might be possible to cram for a history test and get an A, but over-practicing one or two pieces of music for a single event to the exclusion of everything else is not a wise approach to practice. The proper attitude should not be "I've got to learn this by Saturday," but rather, "I'm simply working to improve, so that I will become the best musician I can be."

I recall a conversation with a student during which we discussed which etudes and pieces he was working on. When I asked why his teacher didn't require scales, he replied, "Well, she thinks I do them, but she doesn't ask for them at lessons." This student was obviously caught up in the "prepare-for-the-event" mentality—in this case, the event being his weekly lesson.

If this student were looking at the big picture, he would not shortchange himself this way. He should have been asking himself, "How much and what kind of practice must I engage in over the months and years ahead to become the kind of performer I expect to be?"

The Weekly Picture

Before considering what a wise distribution of weekly practice time might look like, let me outline an unfortunate scenario that some students tend to fall into. Let's imagine that a hypothetical student has a lesson on Wednesday and keeps a practice log for the week. It might look something like this:

Wednesday: I got through my lesson somehow. Now I need to relax and relieve the stress. No practice for me tonight.

Thursday: I've certainly earned a day off from practice after yesterday's lesson. I'll practice tomorrow.

Friday: I think just a short practice session will be adequate for today. After all, my lesson isn't until next week and I want to go out tonight. Now let me see—what did my teacher tell me about these pieces? It's hard to remember.

Saturday and Sunday: Gee, it's hard to practice over the weekend. I don't go to school during the weekend, so why do I have to practice?

Monday: My lesson is in two days. I'd better practice. I know my teacher told me things to work on with these pieces, but I can't remember what they were.

Tuesday: I'm going to practice all night. I've got to get this lesson prepared for tomorrow.

So the student comes into the lesson with a sore lip from too much practice the day before and has neglected to apply most of the advice that was given at last week's lesson. Somehow, he gets through the harrowing experience, ready to repeat the same mistake the following week. How can this cycle be broken?

The first step is to put an end to the "day-before" syndrome. I think taking one day a week off from practice is a grand idea. But I would recommend taking off the day before a lesson. For one thing, the student will conserve strength and be able to come into the lesson with improved tone and endurance. For another, taking off the day before will eliminate any chance of postponing practice until the last minute. Ideally, practice time should be distributed evenly throughout the week. Marathon practice sessions are not a good idea. But if some days are to be heavier practice days than others, those days should be early in the practice week.

First, the pressure of having to cram is removed. Second, there is a psychological boost in getting a jump start on the week's practice. Perhaps most important, it is easier to remember the teacher's advice shortly after the lesson.

Letting a day or two go by without considering a teacher's comments and applying the advice is a big mistake. During my more conscientious periods, I recall sitting down outside my teacher's office after lessons and jotting down everything I could remember about the lesson while it was still fresh in my mind.

The Daily Routine

Daily routines will vary depending upon the instrument, length of the practice session, level of achievement, and a host of other particulars. There is no single specific routine that's right for everyone. But the importance of having a daily routine cannot be overstressed. Unfortunately, many students do not follow a routine, but simply work through their practice sessions in a random, disorganized fashion. This should be discouraged.

A reasonable approach is to begin with scales, followed by lesson material, and then band music. Even students with moderate ambitions need to follow a plan similar to this one.

Many high-school instrumentalists play in the band but do not receive weekly lessons. To think that their practice sessions should consist entirely of band music is folly. A more reasonable approach would be to begin with some scales, then play methodically through some previous lesson material, and then move on to band music. Even if only ten minutes are spent on scales and review, at least some effort should be made to practice the instrument in a logical and thorough manner.

Students with more ambitious goals should, of course, adopt a more rigorous routine. A sequence consisting of studies, then etudes, then pieces, then other music, is a good one.

By studies, I refer to scale and chord studies contained in method books. Serious students should not simply play scales and arpeggios off the top of the head, but should choose one of the many method books that are available. To an extent, it doesn't matter which one is used, as long as the student selects one and sticks with it. This initial, unchanging part of the daily routine is perhaps the most important. I know working professionals who have no time to learn new music but find it necessary to practice daily exercises from a favorite method book.

There are probably as many opinions on how and what to practice as there are teachers of music. A healthy response to this sea of options is to adopt one and see it through. As with various endeavors in many disciplines, any system will work—if you work the system.

The one thing that all systems have in common is that they promote organization and avoid chaos. Adopting an organized approach toward practice that fits a student's goals will ensure that time and energy are spent as wisely as possible.

APPENDIX

Jazz Standards

Jazz musicians routinely turn to fake books as a source for jazz standards. Typically, these collections present tunes in a concise format including only the melody, chord changes, and sometimes the lyrics. Unlike collections of sheet music that include formulaic, simplified arrangements, fake books allow for stylistic diversity and creative freedom. High-quality fake books from reputable publishers (such as the Hal Leonard *Real Book*) are essential to any jazz musician's library.

A

A Sleepin' Bee—Robin
Afternoon in Paris—Lewis
Ah-Leu-Cha—Parker
Ain't Misbehavin'—Waller/Brooks/Razaf
Airegin—Rollins
Alfie—Bacharach/David
Alice in Wonderland—Hillard/Fain
All Blues—Davis
All God's Chillun (Got Rhythm)—Jurmann/Kaper/Kahn
All of Me—Simons/Marks
All of You—Porter
All the Things You Are—Kern/Hammerstein
Alone Together—Schwartz/Dietz
Along Came Betty—Golson
Ana Maria—Shorter
Angel Eyes—Dennis/Brent
Anthropology—Parker
April in Paris—Duke/Harburg
Ask Me Now—Monk
Au Privave—Parker
Autumn in New York—Duke
Autumn Leaves—Kosma/Mercer

B

Bag's Groove—Jackson
Barbados—Parker
Baubles, Bangles, and Beads—Wright/Forrest
Beatrice—Rivers
Beautiful Love—Gillespie/Young/King/Van Alstyne
Bemsha Swing—Monk
Bernie's Tune—Miller
Bessie's Blues—Coltrane
Best Thing for You, The—Berlin
Billie's Bounce—Parker
Birk's Works—Gillespie
Black Narcissus—J. Henderson
Black Nile—Shorter
Black Orpheus/Day in the Life of a Fool—Bonfa
Blame It on My Mouth—Jarrett
Blue Bossa—Dorham
Blue Daniel—Rosolino

Blue in Green—Davis
Blue Monk—Monk
Blue Seven—Rollins
Blue Train—Coltrane
Blues for Alice—Parker
Blues on the Corner—Tyner
Blues Walk, The—Brown
Bluesette—Thieleman
Body and Soul—Green/Heyman/Sour/Eyton
Bolivia—Walton
Born to Be Blue—Wells/Torme
Bouncin' with Bud—Powell
Boy Next Door, The—Blane/Martin
But Beautiful—Van Heusen/Burke
But Not for Me—G. Gershwin/I. Gershwin
Bye Bye Blackbird—R. Henderson/Dixon
Byrdlike—Hubbard

C

C Jam Blues—Ellington
Call Me (Come Back Home)—Green/Jackson, Jr.
Cantaloupe Island—Hancock
Captain Marvel—Corea
Caravan—Ellington/Tizol/Mills
Carnival—Evans
Ceora—Morgan
Chega De Saudade—Jobim
Chelsea Bridge—Strayhorn
Cherokee—Noble
Cheryl—Parker
Child Is Born, A—Jones
Children of the Night—Shorter
Come Rain or Shine—Arlen/Mercer
Come Sunday—Ellington
Con Alma—Gillespie
Confirmation—Parker
Coral—Jarrett
Coral Keys—Bishop, Jr.
Countdown—Coltrane
Cousin Mary—Coltrane
Crisis—Hubbard
Crystal Silence—Corea
CTA—Heath

D

Daahoud—Brown
Dancing on the Ceiling—Rodgers/Hart
Darn That Dream—Van Heusen/De Lange
Dat Dere—Timmons
Day by Day—Cahn/Stordhal/Weston
Days of Wine and Roses—Mancini/Mercer
Dearly Beloved—Kern/Mercer
Desafinado—Jobim/Mendonca
Dig—Davis
Dindi—Gilbert/Jobim/Oliveria
Dolphin Dance—Hancock
Don't You Know I Care—Ellington
Donna Lee—Parker
Doxy—Rollins

E

Easy Living—Robin/Rainger
Easy to Love—Porter
Eighty-One—Davis/Carter
Elsa—Zindars
Embraceable You—G.Gershwin/I. Gershwin
Emily—Mercer/Mandel
End of a Love Affair—Redding
Epistrophy—Clarke/Monk
Equinox—Coltrane
ESP—Davis
Evidence—Monk

F

Fall—Shorter
Falling Grace—Swallow
Falling in Love with Love—Rodgers/Hart
Fee-Fi-Fo-Fum—Shorter
Feel Like Making Love—McDaniels
Five Hundred Miles High—Corea
Fly Me to the Moon—Howard
A Foggy Day—G. Gershwin/I. Gershwin
Footprints—Shorter
Forest Flower—Lloyd
Fortune Smiles—Jarrett
Four—Davis
Four Brothers—Guiffre
Freddie Freeloader—Davis
Freedom Jazz Dance—Harris
Funkarello—Evans

G

Georgia on My Mind—Carmichael/Gorrell
Giant Steps—Coltrane
Gingerbread Boy—Heath/Imbel/De Moraes
Girl from Ipanema—Jobim

Gloria's Step—Lafaro
God Bless the Child—Holiday/Herzog
Golden Earrings—Young/Livingston/Evans
Gone with the Wind—Magidson/Wrubel
Good Bait—Dameron
Good Morning Heartache—Fisher/Higginbotham/Drake
Grand Central—Coltrane
Green Dolphin Street—Keper/Washington
Gregory Is Here—Silver
Groovin' High—Gillespie

H

Hackensack—Monk
Half Nelson—Davis
Hallucinations—Powell
Have You Met Miss Jones—Rodgers/Hart
Hello Young Lovers—Rodgers/Hammerstein
Here's That Rainy Day—Van Heusen/Burke
Hi-Fly—Weston
Hot House—Dameron
How High the Moon—Lewis
How Insensitive—Jobim
Hummin'—Adderly

I

I Can't Get Started—Duke/I. Gershwin
I Could Write a Book—Rodgers/Hart
I Didn't Know What Time It Was—Hart/Rodgers
I'd Like to Get You on a Slow Boat to China—Loesser
I Get a Kick out of You—Porter
I Got It Bad and That Ain't Good—Ellington/Webster
I Hear a Rhapsody—Frajos/Baker/Gasparre
I Let a Song Go out of My Heart—
    Ellington/Mills/Nemo/Redmond
I Love Lucy—Daniel/Adamson
I Love You—Porter
I Mean You—Monk/Hawkins
I Remember Clifford—Golson
I Remember You—Schertzinger/Mercer
I Should Care—Cahn/Stordahl/Weston
I Thought about You—Mercer/Van Heusen
I Want to Talk about You—Eckstine
I Won't Dance—
    Kern/Fields/Hammerstein II/McHugh/Harbach
I'll Remember April—Raye/Depaul/Johnston
I'm All Smiles—Martin/Leonard
I'm Getting Sentimental over You—Bassman/Washington
I'm Old Fashioned—Kern/Mercer
I've Got a Crush on You—G. Gershwin/I. Gershwin
I Got Rhythm—G. Gershwin/I. Gershwin
I've Got the World on a String—Arlen/Koehler
If I Should Lose You—Robin/Rainger
If I Were a Bell—Loesser
If You Could See Me Now—Dameron
Impressions—Coltrane
In a Mellow Tone—Ellington

In a Sentimental Mood—Ellington/Mills/Kurtz
In Love in Vain—Kern/Robin
In Walked Bud—Monk
In Your Own Quiet Place—Jarrett
In Your Own Sweet Way—Brubeck
(Back Home Again in) Indiana—Hanley/Macdonald
Infant Eyes—Shorter
Inner Urge—J. Henderson
Invitation—Kaper/Webster
Isotope —J. Henderson
Israel—Carisi
It Could Happen to You—Van Heusen/Burke
It Had to Be You—Jones/Kahn
It Might as Well Be Spring—Rodgers/Hammerstein II
It's You or No One—Styne/Cahn

J

Jeannine—Newell/Conway
The Jitterbug Waltz—Waller
Jordu—Jordan
Joshua—Feldman
Joy Spring—Brown
Juju—Shorter
Just Friends—Lewis/Kelmmer
Just in Time—Styne/Comden/Green
Just One of Those Things—Porter
Just the Way You Are—Joel

K

Katrina Ballerina—Shaw
Killer Joe—Golson
Killing Me Softly with His Song—Fox/Gimbel

L

La Fiesta—Corea
Oh, Lady Be Good—G. Gershwin/I. Gershwin
Ladybird—Dameron
Lament—J.J. Johnson
Laura—Raskin/Mercer
Lazy Bird—Coltrane
Let's Fall in Love—Arlen/Koehler
Like Someone in Love—Van Heusen/Burke
Limelight—Mulligan
Line for Lyons—Mulligan
Little Sunflower—Hubbard
Long Ago and Far Away—Kern/I. Gershwin
Loop, The—Corea
Love For Sale—Porter
Our Love Is Here to Stay—G. Gershwin/I. Gershwin
Lover—Rodgers/Hart
Lover Come Back to Me—Romberg/Hammerstein II
Lover Man—Davis/Ramirez/Sherman
Lucky Southern—Jarrett
Lullaby of Birdland—Shearing/Weiss
Lush Life—Strayhorn

M

Mack the Knife—Weil/Brecht
Mahjong—Shorter
Maiden Voyage—Hancock
Man I Love—G. Gershwin/I. Gershwin
Manteca—Gillespie/Fuller
The Masquerade Is Over—Magidson/Wrubel
Mean to Me—Waller
Meditation—Jobim
Memories of Tomorrow—Jarrett
Mercy, Mercy, Mercy—Zawinul
Midnight Sun—Burke/Mercer
Milestones—Davis
Minority—Jarrett
Misterioso—Monk
Misty—Garner/Burke
Molten Glass—Farrell
Moment's Notice—Coltrane
Monk's Mood—Monk
Mood Indigo—Ellington
Moon Child—Jarrett
Moon Rays—Silver
Moon River—Mancini/Mercer
Moonglow—Hudson/Delange/Mills
Moonlight in Vermont—Suessdorf/Blackburn
Moose the Mooch—Parker
More I See You—Warren/Gordon
More than You Know—Youmans/Rose/Eliscu
Mr. Clean—Hubbard
Mr. P.C.—Coltrane
My Cherie Amour—Cosby/Moy/Wonder
My Favorite Things—Rodgers/Hammerstein II
My Foolish Heart—Young/Washington
My Funny Valentine—Rodger/Hart
My Old Flame—Coslow/Johnston
My One and Only Love—Wood/Mellin
My Romance—Rodgers/Hart
My Shining Hour—Arlen/Mercer

N

Naima—Coltrane
Nardis—Evans
Nature Boy—Ahbez
Nearness of You—Carmichael/Washington
Nefertiti—Shorter
Nica's Dream—Silver
Nice Work if You Can Get It—G. Gershwin/I. Gershwin
Night and Day—Porter
Night Dreamer—Shorter
Night Has a Thousand Eyes, The—
    Weisman/Garrett/Wayne
Night in Tunisia—Gillespie
No More Blues (Chega De Saudade)—Jobim/De Moraes
Now's the Time—Paker
Nutville—Silver

O

Old Devil Moon—Lane/Harburg
Old Folks—Brel/Blau/Shuman
Oleo—Rollins
On a Clear Day (You Can See Forever)—Layne/Lerner
Once I Loved—Jobim
Once In a While—Edwards/Green
One Note Samba—Jobim
Ornithology—Parker
Our Delight—Dameron
Our Love Is Here to Stay—G. Gershwin/I. Gershwin
(You Came from) Out of Nowhere—Green/Heyman
Over the Rainbow—Arlen/Harburg

P

Parisian Thoroughfare—Powell
Passion Dance—Tyner
Peace—Silver
Pensitiva—Fischer
Pent Up House—Rollins
People—Styne/Merrill
Perdido—Tizol, Drake/Langsfeller
Polka Dots and Moonbeams—Van Heusen/Burke
Prelude to a Kiss—Ellington/Gordon/Mills

Q

Quiet Nights (of) Quiet Stars (Corcovado)—Jobim
Quiet Now—Zeitlin

R

Recordame (No Me Esqueca)—J. Henderson
Robbin's Nest—Thompson/Jacquet
Room 608—Silver
'Round Midnight—Monk/Williams
Ruby My Dear—Monk
Rhythm-A-Ning—Monk

S

Salt Peanuts—Gillespie
Samba De Orfeu—Bonfa
Sandu—Brown
Satin Doll—Mercer/Strayhorn/Ellington
Save Your Love for Me—Johnson
Scotch and Soda—Guard
Scrapple from the Apple—Parker
Search for Peace—Tyner
Secret Love—Fain/Webster
Serenade to a Bus Seat—Terry
Serenata—Anderson/ Parish
Serenity—J. Henderson
Seven Steps to Heaven—Feldman

Shades of Light—Lewis
Shadow of Your Smile, The—Mandel/Webster
Shiny Stockings—Foster/Fitzgerald
Sister Sadie—Silver
Skylark—Carmichael/ Mercer
Smoke Gets in Your Eyes—Kern/ Harbach
So Nice (Summer Samba)—Valle/Valle
So Tender—Jarrett
So What—Davis
Softy as in a Morning Sunrise—Romberg
Solar—Davis
Some Other Blues—Coltrane
Some Other Time—Bernstein/Comden//Green
Someday My Prince Will Come—Churchill/Morey
Someone to Watch over Me—G. Gershwin/I. Gershwin
Song for My Father—Silver
Song Is You, The—Kern/Hammerstein II
Sonnymoon for Two—Rollins
Sophisticated Lady—Ellington/Mills/Parish
Soul Eyes—Waldron
Spain—Jones/Kahn
Speak Low—Weil/Nash
Speak No Evil—Shorter
Spring Is Here—Rodgers/Hart
St. Thomas—Rollins
Stablemates—Golson
Star Dust—Carmichael/Parish
Star Eyes—Depaul/Raye
Stars Fell on Alabama—Perkins/Parish
Stella by Starlight—Young/Washington
Stompin' at the Savoy—
          Sampson/Webb/Goodman/Razaf
Stormy Weather—Arlen/Koehler
Straight Life—Hubbard
Straight No Chaser—Monk
Strollin'—Silver
Sugar—Pinkard/Mitchell
Summer Knows, The—
          Legrand/A. Bergman/M. Bergman
Summertime—G. Gershwin/Heyward
Sunny—Kern/Hammerstein II
(On the) Sunny Side of the Street—McHugh/Fields
Sweet Dulcinea—Evans
Sweet Georgia Brown—Pinkard/Casey

T

Take the "A" Train—Strayhorn
Tangerine—Schertzinger/Mercer
Tenderly—Gross/Lawrence
Tenor Madness—Rollins
That's All—Brandt/Haymes
Theme for Ernie—Lacy
Theme from "Gabriela"—Jobim
Theme, The—Davis
There Is No Greater Love—Jones/Symes
There Will Never Be Another You—Warren/Gordon

Things Ain't What They Used to Be—Ellington
Think on Me—Cables
Three Little Words—Kalmar/Ruby
Thrivin' on a Riff—Parker
Time after Time—Styne/Cahn
Touch of Your Lips—Noble
Triste—Jobim
Tune Up—Vinson

U

Unit Seven—Jones
Up Jumped Spring—Hubbard
Up with the Lark—Kern/Robin
Upper Manhattan Medical Group—Strayhorn

V

Valse Hot—Rollins
Very Early—Evans
Virgo—Shorter

W

Wailbait—Jones
Walkin'—Carpenter
Waltz for Debbie—Evans
Watch What Happens—LeGrand/Gimbel
Wave—Jobim
Way You Look Tonight, The—Kern/Fields
We'll Be Together Again—Fischer/Laine
Weaver of Dreams—Young
Well, You Needn't—Monk
West Coast Blues—Montgomery
What a Difference a Day Made—Grever
What Are You Doing the Rest of Your Life—
        LeGrand/A. Bergman/M. Bergman
What Is This Thing Called Love?—Porter
What Was—Corea
What's New—Haggart
When I Fall in Love—Heyman/Young
When Lights Are Low—Kahn/ Koehler/Fiorito
When Sunny Gets Blue—Fisher/Segal
Whisper Not—Golson
Who Can I Turn To?—Bricusse/Newly
Wild Flower—Stothart/Harbach/Hammerstein II
Willow Weep For Me—Ronell
Windows—Corea
Witch Hunt—Shorter
Without a Song—Youmans/Rose/Elisco
Woody 'n' You—Gillespie
Work Song—Adderly

Y

Yardbird Suite—Parker
Yes or No—Shorter
Yesterdays—Kern/Harbach
You and the Night and the Music—Dietz/Schwartz
You Are the Sunshine of My Life—Wonder
You Don't Know What Love Is—Raye/Depaul
You Say You Care—Robin/Styne
You Stepped out of a Dream—Brown/Kahn
You'd Be So Nice to Come Home To—Porter
You're My Everything—Warren/Dixon/Young
You've Changed—Fischer/Carey

MINOR ii–V–i 3-NOTE VOICINGS FOR LEFT HAND

Type A

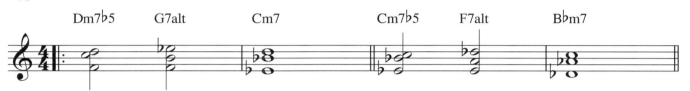

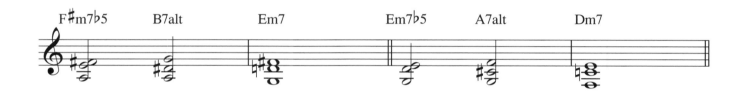

Type B

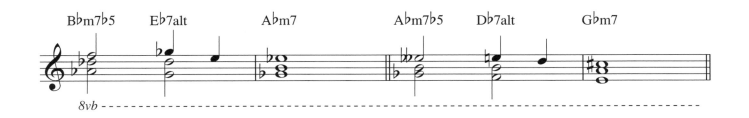

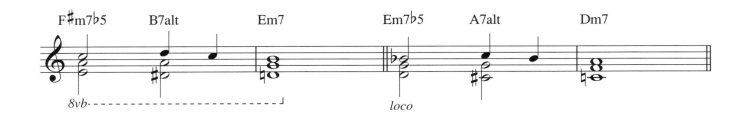

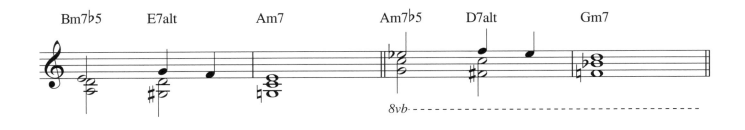

MAJOR ii–V–I 3-NOTE VOICINGS FOR LEFT HAND

Type A

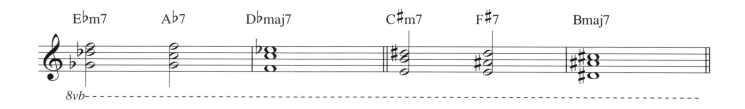

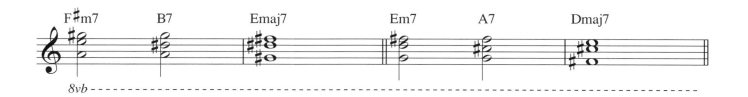

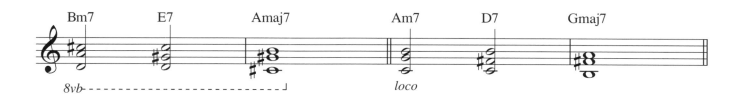

Type B

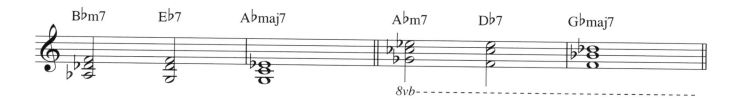

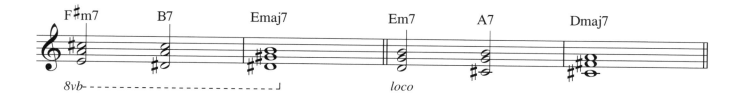

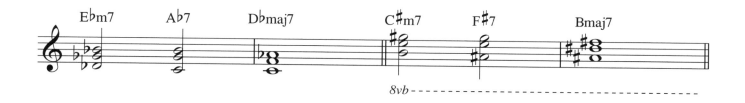

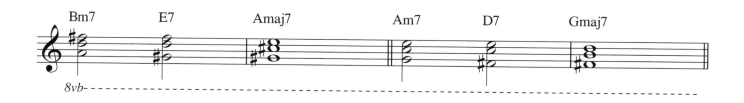

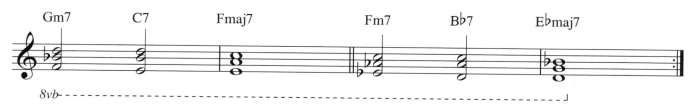

MINOR ii–V–i 4-NOTE VOICINGS FOR LEFT HAND

Type A

Type B

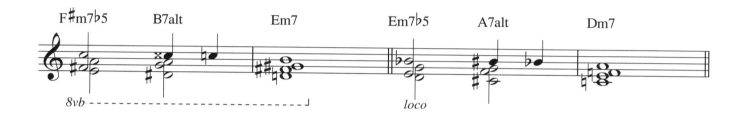

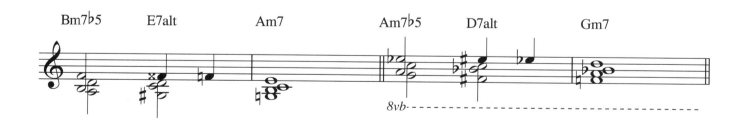

MAJOR ii–V–I 4-NOTE VOICINGS FOR LEFT HAND

Type A

Type B

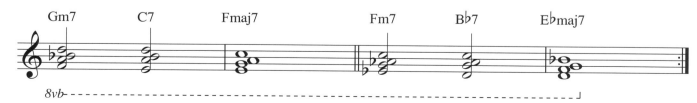

MAJOR ii–V–I CADENCE USING 3/7 GUIDE TONES

Type A

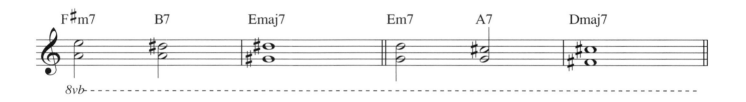

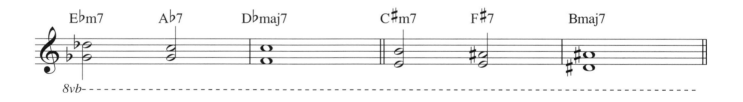

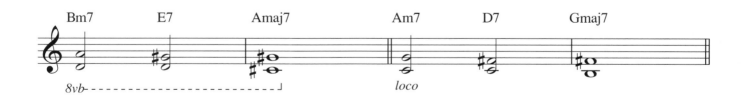

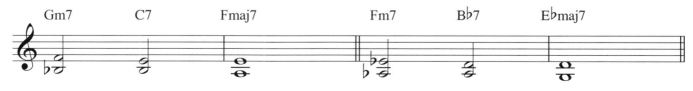

Type B

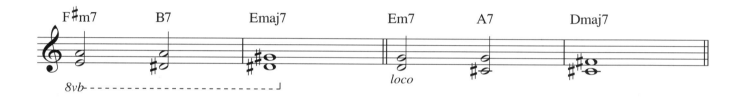

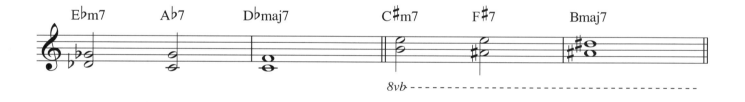

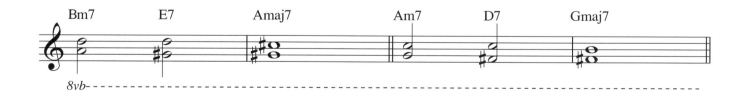

MAJOR ii–V–I CADENCE USING SHELLS

Root–7th

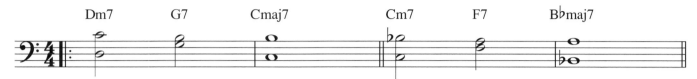

Root–3rd

F BLUES USING 3/7 GUIDE TONES

Type A

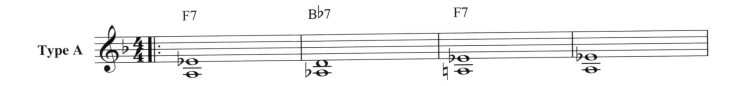

Type B

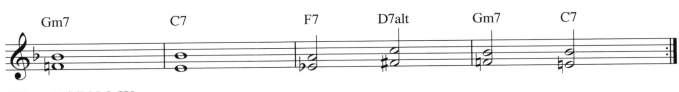

F BLUES 3-NOTE VOICINGS

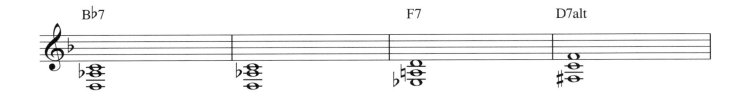

F BLUES 4-NOTE VOICINGS

Type A

Type B

ANSWER KEY

Chapter 1 Exercises

1. Identify the following intervals.

M3   P5   M2   m2

m3   M6   °5   P1

+5   m3   +1   M9

m10   +6   P8   M13

2. Provide the following intervals above the given pitch.

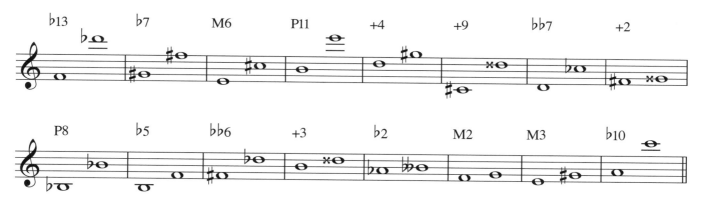

♭13   ♭7   M6   P11   +4   +9   ♭♭7   +2

P8   ♭5   ♭♭6   +3   ♭2   M2   M3   ♭10

3. Write the following intervals (from any pitch).

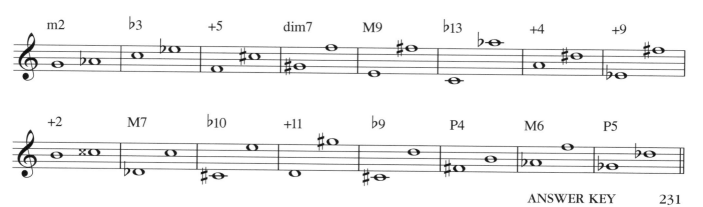

m2   ♭3   +5   dim7   M9   ♭13   +4   +9

+2   M7   ♭10   +11   ♭9   P4   M6   P5

4. Write the following intervals above the given note.

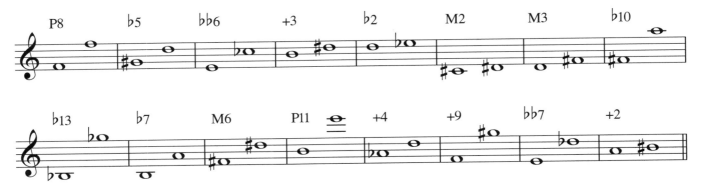

5. Identify each interval as either consonant or dissonant by writing "con" or "diss" below.

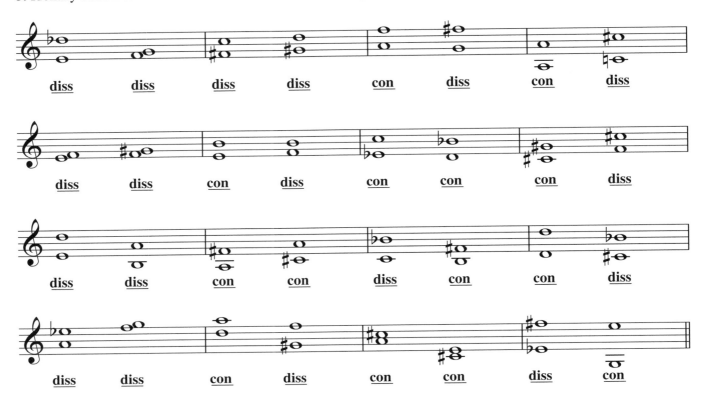

diss diss diss diss con diss con diss

diss diss con diss con con con diss

diss diss con con diss con con diss

diss diss con diss con con diss con

Chapter 2 Exercises

1. Identify the following chords, labeling inversions as 1st inv., 2nd inv., or 3rd inv.

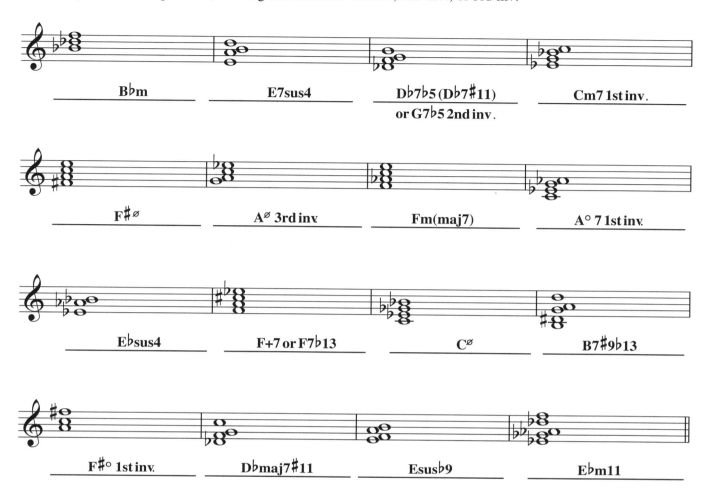

Bbm

E7sus4

Db7b5 (Db7#11)
or G7b5 2nd inv.

Cm7 1st inv.

F#ø

Aø 3rd inv

Fm(maj7)

A° 7 1st inv.

Ebsus4

F+7 or F7b13

Cø

B7#9b13

F#° 1st inv.

Dbmaj7#11

Esusb9

Ebm11

2. Build the following chords in root position.

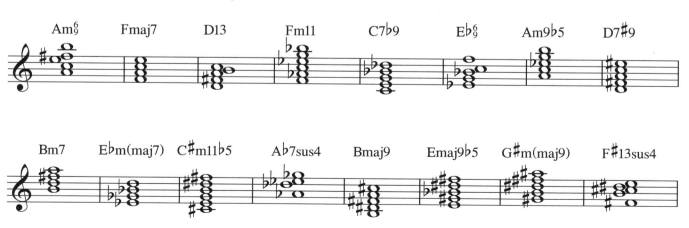

Am6/9   Fmaj7   D13   Fm11   C7b9   Eb6/9   Am9b5   D7#9

Bm7   Ebm(maj7)   C#m11b5   Ab7sus4   Bmaj9   Emaj9b5   G#m(maj9)   F#13sus4

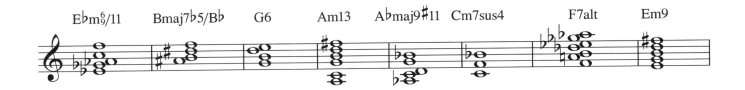

E♭m⁶/11   Bmaj7♭5/B♭   G6   Am13   A♭maj9♯11   Cm7sus4   F7alt   Em9

B°7   Bm7♭5   Dm6   F+7   G9♯11   F♯m(maj7)   Bmaj13   F°7

3. Write the tritone interval(s) found in each of the following chords.

C♯7   Em⁶/9   F9♯11   B♭maj7♭5   E♭m7♭5   D13   A♭7   F♯m⁶/9

C♯°7   E♭9♯5   Gm11♭5   B7♭9♯11   Fmaj13   A♭m9♭5   C7sus4♭9   G7alt
                                              NONE

4. Write the 3rd and the 7th of the following chords. (Dominant 11th or sus4 chords have a P4th instead of a 3rd.)

Am7   D7   Emaj7   B♭m7♭5   G°7   F♯m11   A♭maj9   G13♭9

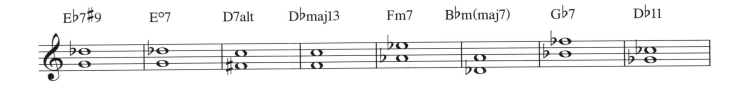

E♭7♯9   E°7   D7alt   D♭maj13   Fm7   B♭m(maj7)   G♭7   D♭11

Am(maj7♭5)   G9sus4   Em7♭5   Am9   D°7   E7♭5♯9   F♯°7   E♭7sus4

5. Identify each chord and specify whether it is best understood as an upper structure (US), hybrid (Hyb), or slash chord (Sl). Some structures are subject to multiple interpretations.

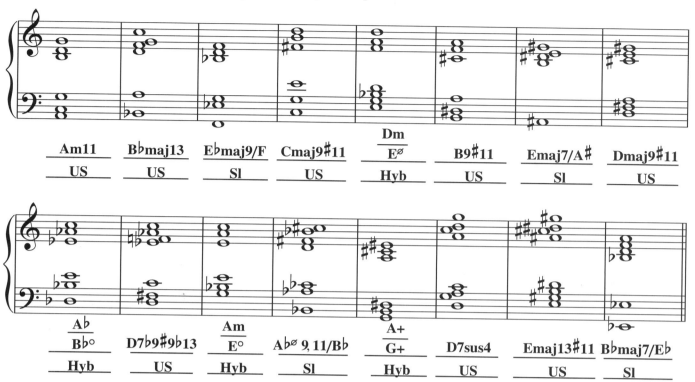

Am11	B♭maj13	E♭maj9/F	Cmaj9#11	Dm / E∅	B9#11	Emaj7/A#	Dmaj9#11
US	US	Sl	US	Hyb	US	Sl	US

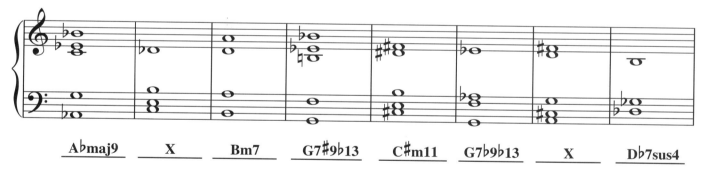

A♭ / B♭○	D7♭9#9♭13	Am / E○	A♭∅ 9,11/B♭	A+ / G+	D7sus4	Emaj13#11	B♭maj7/E♭
Hyb	US	Hyb	Sl	Hyb	US	US	Sl

6. Identify each chord. All chords are in root position. If it contains wrong notes or inappropriate upper structures, place an "x" beneath the chord.

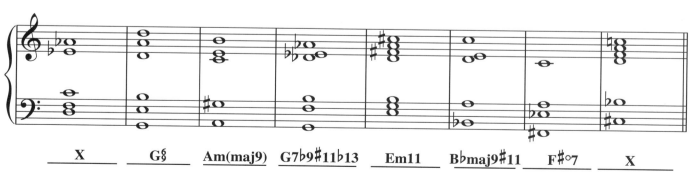

A♭maj9	X	Bm7	G7#9♭13	C#m11	G7♭9♭13	X	D♭7sus4

X	G⁶/₉	Am(maj9)	G7♭9#11♭13	Em11	B♭maj9#11	F#○7	X

Chapter 3 Exercises

1. Write the following major scales. Write the name below.

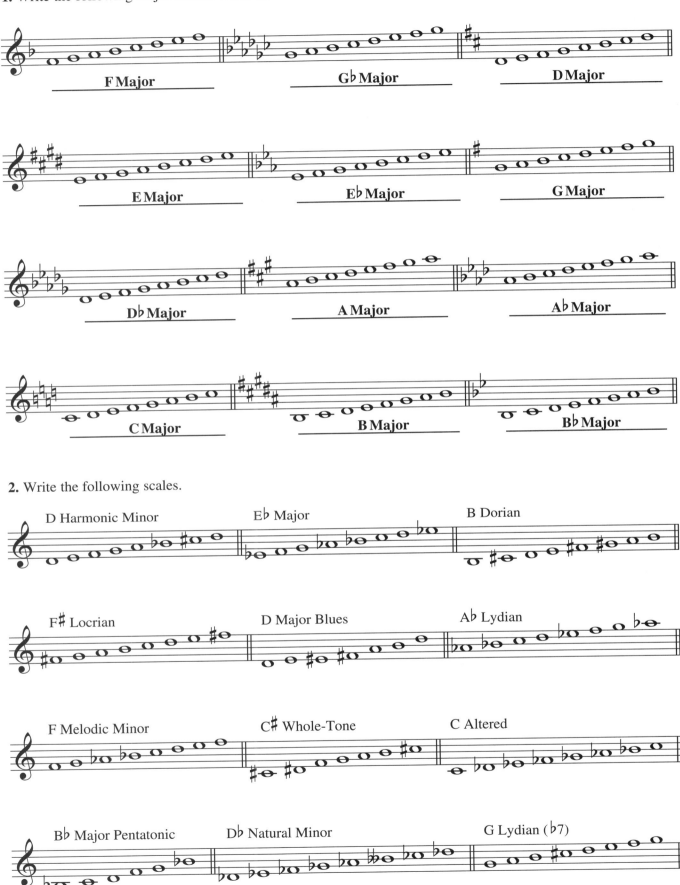

F Major   G♭ Major   D Major

E Major   E♭ Major   G Major

D♭ Major   A Major   A♭ Major

C Major   B Major   B♭ Major

2. Write the following scales.

D Harmonic Minor   E♭ Major   B Dorian

F♯ Locrian   D Major Blues   A♭ Lydian

F Melodic Minor   C♯ Whole-Tone   C Altered

B♭ Major Pentatonic   D♭ Natural Minor   G Lydian (♭7)

E Whole-Half Diminished   A Minor Pentatonic   E Kumoi

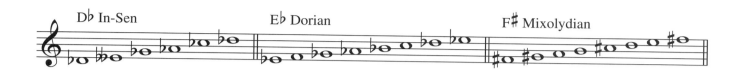

D♭ In-Sen   E♭ Dorian   F# Mixolydian

G Harmonic Minor   E♭ Locrian (#2)   B Mixolydian (♭9,♭13)

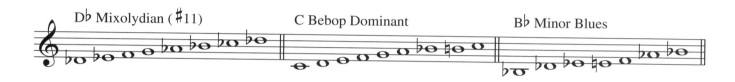

D♭ Mixolydian (#11)   C Bebop Dominant   B♭ Minor Blues

3. Write the following scales with the appropriate key signature. In the space below, indicate the relative major or minor.

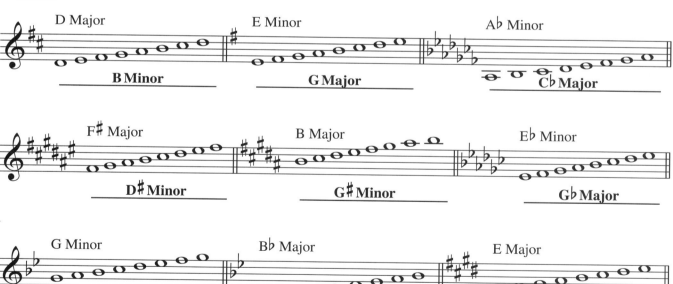

D Major   E Minor   A♭ Minor

B Minor   **G Major**   **C♭ Major**

F# Major   B Major   E♭ Minor

D# Minor   **G# Minor**   **G♭ Major**

G Minor   B♭ Major   E Major

B♭ Major   **G Minor**   **C# Minor**

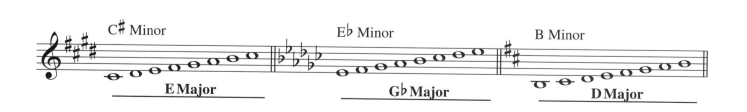

C# Minor   E♭ Minor   B Minor

E Major   **G♭ Major**   **D Major**

4. Add flats or sharps to form the correct scale.

F Phrygian

F# Mixolydian

E Harmonic Minor

A Lydian

F Locrian

E Dorian

B Melodic Minor

Eb Major

G# Harmonic Minor

B Lydian

5. Write an appropriate scale for the following chords. Give the correct name.

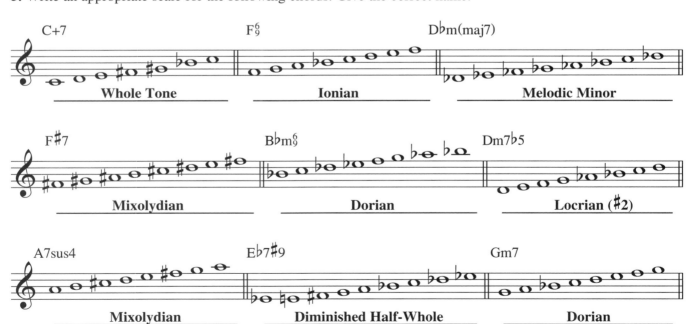

C+7   **Whole Tone**

F$^6_9$ **Ionian**

Dbm(maj7)   **Melodic Minor**

F#7   **Mixolydian**

Bbm$^6_9$ **Dorian**

Dm7b5   **Locrian (#2)**

A7sus4   **Mixolydian**

Eb7#9   **Diminished Half-Whole**

Gm7   **Dorian**

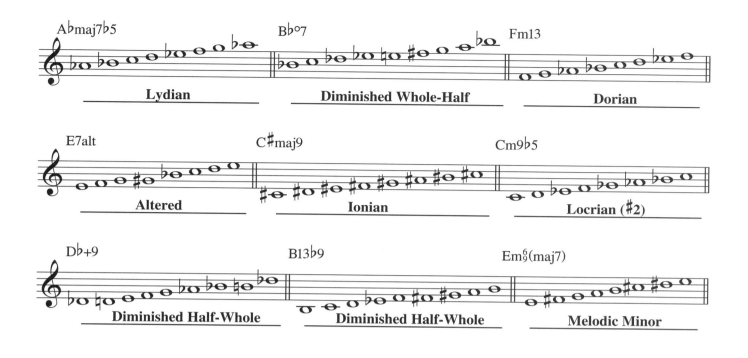

Lydian — Ab maj7b5

Diminished Whole-Half — Bb°7

Dorian — Fm13

Altered — E7alt

Ionian — C#maj9

Locrian (#2) — Cm9b5

Diminished Half-Whole — Db+9

Diminished Half-Whole — B13b9

Melodic Minor — Em⁶/₉(maj7)

6. [NO ANSWERS PROVIDED]

7. [NO ANSWERS PROVIDED]

8. What are the functions of each of these chords in the following given scales?

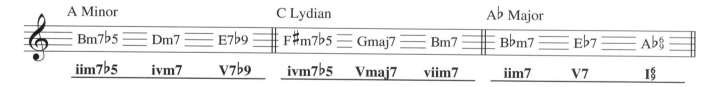

A Minor

Bm7b5	Dm7	E7b9
iim7b5	ivm7	V7b9

C Lydian

F#m7b5	Gmaj7	Bm7
ivm7b5	Vmaj7	viim7

Ab Major

Bbm7	Eb7	Ab⁶/₉
iim7	V7	I⁶/₉

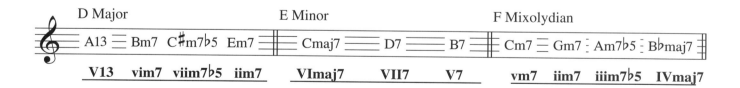

D Major

A13	Bm7	C#m7b5	Em7
V13	vim7	viim7b5	iim7

E Minor

Cmaj7	D7	B7
VImaj7	VII7	V7

F Mixolydian

Cm7	Gm7	Am7b5	Bbmaj7
vm7	iim7	iiim7b5	IVmaj7

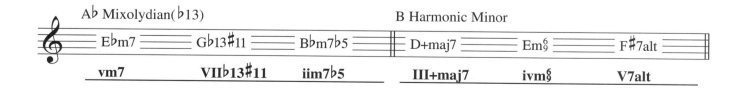

Ab Mixolydian(b13)

Ebm7	Gb13#11	Bbm7b5
vm7	VIIb13#11	iim7b5

B Harmonic Minor

D+maj7	Em⁶	F#7alt
III+maj7	ivm⁶	V7alt

9. Identify the key in which the following chords will have the function indicated.

Bm7 is vim7 in the key of: **D Major**

A♭m7 is iiim7 in the key of: **F Minor**

G#m7♭5 is iim7♭5 in the key of: **F# Minor**

A♭maj7 is ♭VImaj7 in the key of: **C Minor**

Dm7♭5 is iim7♭5 in the key of: **C Minor**

D♭maj7 is ♭IIImaj7 in the key of: **B♭ Minor**

A♭m7 is vim7 in the key of: **C♭ Major**

F#maj7 is IVmaj7 in the key of: **C# Major**

D♭7maj7 is IVmaj7 in the key of: **A♭ Major**

Cm7 is vim7 in the key of: **E♭ Major**

10. Notate the following.

The two maj7 chords in Cm. **E♭maj7, A♭maj7**

The three m7 chords in E♭. **Fm7, Gm7, Cm7**

The three m7 chords in A♭. **B♭m7, Cm7, Fm7**

The two maj7 chords in C#. **C#maj7, F#maj7**

The two maj7 chords in G#m. **Bmaj7, Emaj7**

The three m7 chords in C♭. **D♭m7, E♭m7, A♭m7**

The three m7 chords in B. **C#m7, D#m7, G♭m7**

The two maj7 chords in A♭. **A♭maj7, D♭maj7**

The two maj7 chords in D♭. **D♭maj7, G♭maj7**

The two maj7 chords in Bm. **Dmaj7, Gmaj7**

The three m7 chords in F#. **G#m7, A#m7, D#m7**

The three m7 chords in A. **Bm7, C#m7, F#m7**

The two maj7 chords in E. **Emaj7, Amaj7**

The two maj7 chords in G♭. **G♭maj7, C♭maj7**

The three m7 chords in D. **Em7, F#m7, Bm7**

The three m7 chords in B♭. **Cm7, Dm7, Gm7**

The two maj7 chords in Em. **Gmaj7, Cmaj7**

The two maj7 chords in F#m. **Amaj7, Dmaj7**

The three m7 chords in F. **Gm7, Am7, Dm7**

The two maj7 chords in A♭m. **C♭maj7, F♭maj7**

The two maj7 chords in C#m. **Emaj7, Amaj7**

The three m7 chords in D♭. **E♭m7, Fm7, B♭m7**

11. Write the following scales, with their modes on another sheet of staff paper.

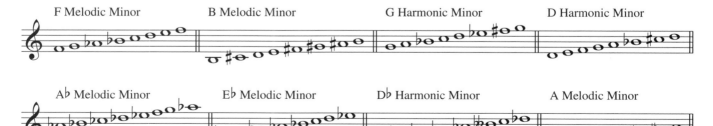

F Melodic Minor   B Melodic Minor   G Harmonic Minor   D Harmonic Minor

A♭ Melodic Minor   E♭ Melodic Minor   D♭ Harmonic Minor   A Melodic Minor

12. Write the chord-scale relationship (in other words, harmonize the scale with 7th chords) for these scales and modes. Show harmonic functions.

G Ionian

Gmaj7	Am7	Bm7	Cmaj7	D7	Em7	F#m7♭5	Gmaj7
Imaj7	iim7	iiim7	IVmaj7	V7	vim7	vii°7	Imaj7

F# Phrygian

F#m7	Gmaj7	A7	Bm7	C#m7♭5	Dmaj7	Em7	F#m7
im7	IImaj7	III7	ivm7	v°7	VImaj7	viim7	im7

F Lydian

Fmaj7	G7	Am7	Bm7♭5	Cmaj7	Dm7	Em7	Fmaj7
Imaj7	II7	iiim7	iii°7	IVmaj7	vm7	vim7	Imaj7

G Melodic Minor

Gm(maj7)	Am7	B♭maj7	C7	D7	Em7♭5	F#m7♭5	Gm(maj7)
im(maj7)	iim7	IIImaj7	IV7	V7	vi°7	vii°7	im(maj7)

F Aeolian

Fm7	Gm7♭5	A♭maj7	B♭m7	Cm7	D♭maj7	E♭7	Fm7
im7	ii°7	IIImaj7	ivm7	vm7	VImaj7	VII7	im7

B Dorian

Bm7	C#m7	Dmaj7	E7	F#m7	G#m7♭5	Amaj7	Bm7
im7	iim7	IIImaj7	IV7	vm7	vi°7	VIImaj7	im7

G Mixolydian (♭9, ♭13)

G7	A♭maj7	B°7	Cm(maj7)	Dm7♭5	E♭maj7#5	Fm7	G7
I7	IImaj7	iii°7	ivm(maj7)	v°7	VImaj7#5	viim7	I7

B Locrian

Bm7♭5	Cmaj7	Dm7	Em7	Fmaj7	G7	Am7	Bm7♭5
i°7	IImaj7	iiim7	ivm7	Vmaj7	VI7	viim7	i°7

B Major

Bmaj7	C#m7	D#m7	Emaj7	F#7	G#m7	A#m7♭5	Bmaj7
Imaj7	iim7	iiim7	IVmaj7	V7	vim7	vii°	Imaj7

E Harmonic Minor

Em(maj7)	F#m7♭5	Gmaj7#5	Am7	B7	Cmaj7	D#°7	Em(maj7)
im(maj7)	ii°7	IIImaj7#5	ivm7	V7	VImaj7	vii°7	im(maj7)

B♭ Lydian

B♭maj7	C7	Dm7	Em7♭5	Fmaj7	Gm7	Am7	B♭maj7
Imaj7	II7	iiim7	iv°	Vmaj7	vim7	viim7	Imaj7

B Altered

Bm7♭5	Cm(maj7)	Dm7	E♭maj7#5	F7	G7	Am7♭5	Bm7♭5
i°7	iim(maj7)	iiim7	IVmaj7#5	V7	VI7	vii°7	i°7

13.–15. [NO ANSWERS PROVIDED]

Chapter 4 Exercises

1. Write major and minor ii–V–I cadences in the following keys.

Example

2. Complete the following ii–V–I cadences.

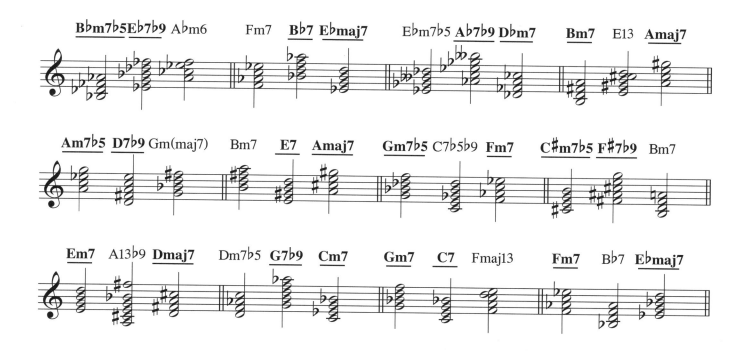

3. Write turnarounds in the following keys. Answers may vary.

Example

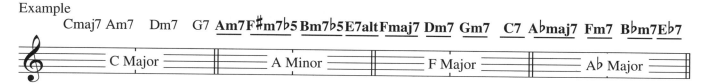

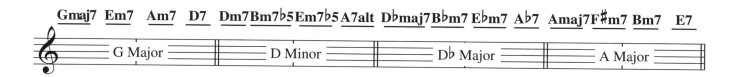

4. Create ii–V chains moving upward by a M3rd, then downward by a M3rd from the original.

Example

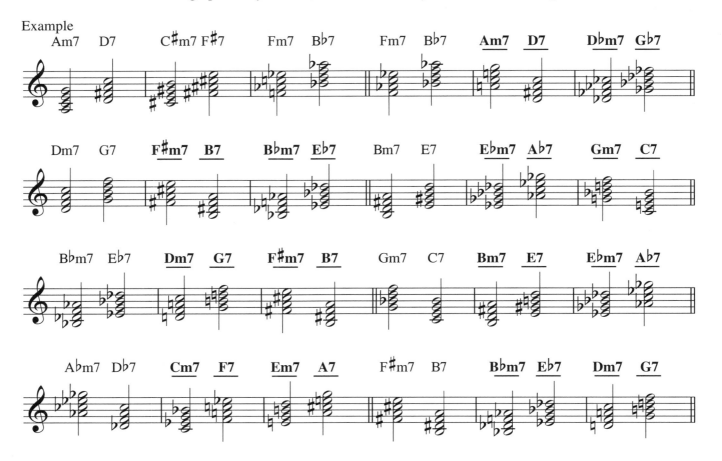

5. Create ii–V chains moving upward by a M2nd, then downward by a M2nd from the original.

Example

6. Create ii–V chains moving up and down chromatically.

Example

Chapter 5 Exercises

1. a. Show major and relative minor II–V–I cadences using the following key signatures and analyze using brackets and arrows.
   b. List all possible secondary dominants in these keys on another sheet.
   c. Identify the harmonic function of each secondary dominant.

Example

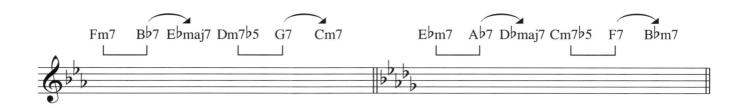

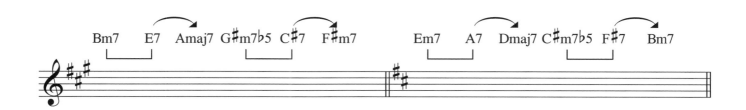

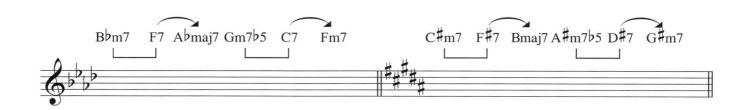

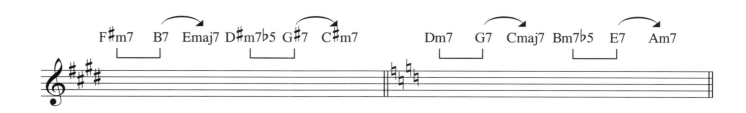

2. a. Complete the following and fill in the blanks.
   b. What kind of dominant chords are these?
   c. Find all possible secondary dominants in these keys.

Example

3. Complete the following chord progressions and add harmonic analyses.

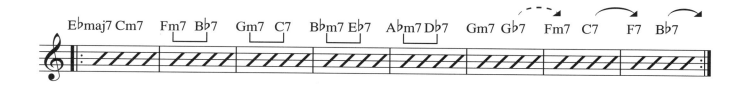

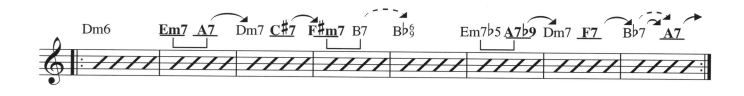

4. Identify the key in which the following chords will have the function indicated. Use enharmonic equivalents where convenient.

G7 is V7/V in the key of: **F Major**
D♭7 is V7/IV in the key of: **D♭ Major**
F♯7 is V7/ii in the key of: **A Major**
E7 is V7/IV in the key of: **E Major**
B°7 is vii°7/V in the key of: **F Major**
C♯7 is V7/V in the key of: **B Major**
B♭7 is V7/vi in the key of: **G♭ Major**
D♯°7 is vii°7/iii in the key of: **C Major**
F♯°7 is vii°7/iii in the key of: **E♭ Major**
E♭7 is V7/V in the key of: **D♭ Major**
D7 is V7/vi in the key of: **B♭ Major**

5. Analyze the following progressions indicating chord function, considering harmonic structure.

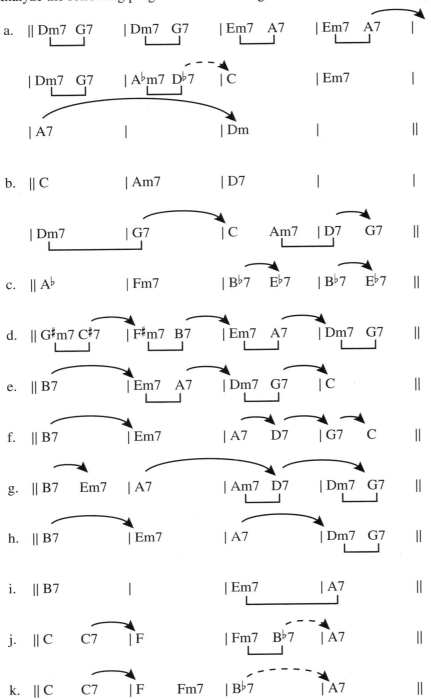

a. ‖ Dm7 G7 | Dm7 G7 | Em7 A7 | Em7 A7 |

| Dm7 G7 | A♭m7 D♭7 | C | Em7 |

| A7 | | Dm | ‖

b. ‖ C | Am7 | D7 | |

| Dm7 | G7 | C Am7 | D7 G7 ‖

c. ‖ A♭ | Fm7 | B♭7 E♭7 | B♭7 E♭7 ‖

d. ‖ G♯m7 C♯7 | F♯m7 B7 | Em7 A7 | Dm7 G7 ‖

e. ‖ B7 | Em7 A7 | Dm7 G7 | C ‖

f. ‖ B7 | Em7 | A7 D7 | G7 C ‖

g. ‖ B7 Em7 | A7 | Am7 D7 | Dm7 G7 ‖

h. ‖ B7 | Em7 | A7 | Dm7 G7 ‖

i. ‖ B7 | | Em7 | A7 ‖

j. ‖ C C7 | F | Fm7 B♭7 | A7 ‖

k. ‖ C C7 | F Fm7 | B♭7 | A7 ‖

6. [NO ANSWERS PROVIDED]

Chapter 6 Exercises

1. Voice the following chords using 3rd and 7th guide tones with 3-note voicings, 4-note voicings, drop 2, and drop 2–4. For the purposes of these exercises suggested range limits may be exceeded.

Example

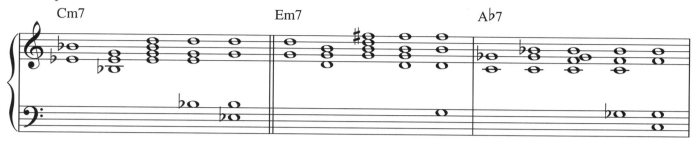

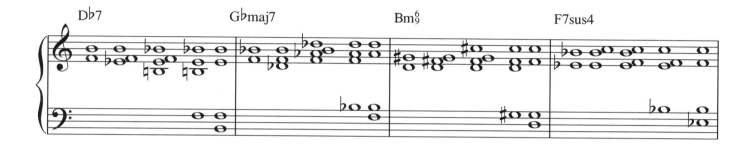

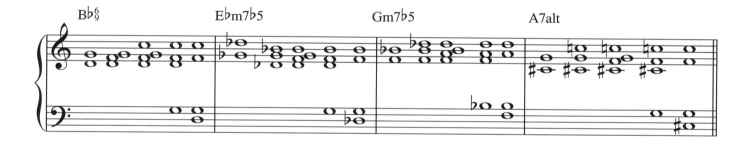

2. Voice the following three turnarounds with 3rd and 7th guide tones, then again on separate staff paper with 3-note voicings, 4-note voicings, drop 2, and drop 2–4. Use both inversions, types A and B.

3. [NO ANSWERS PROVIDED]

Chapter 7 Exercises

1. Identify tonicization and modulation in the following.

a.

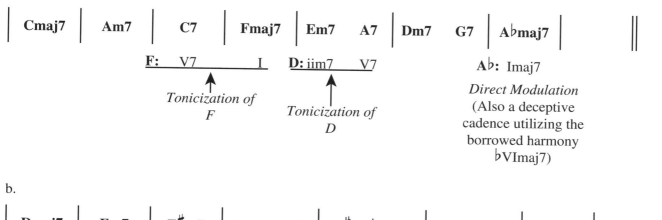

b.

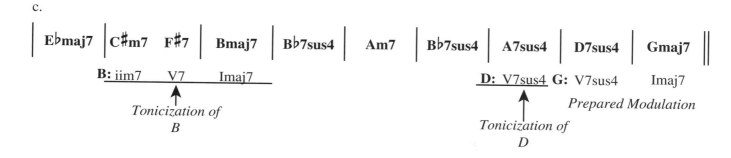

c.

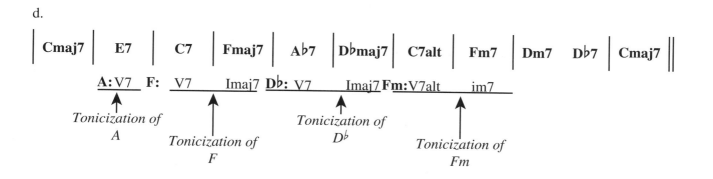

d.

2.–6. [NO ANSWERS PROVIDED]

7. Name the parallel major and minor keys that contain the respective chord functions shown below. Assume enharmonic equivalents when necessary.

Example

	Cm7		**Emaj7**
A♭:	iiim7	**A♭m:**	♭VImaj7

	C♯m7		Fmaj7			Dm7		G♭maj7
A:	iiim7	**Am:**	♭VImaj7		**B♭:**	iiim7	**B♭m:**	VImaj7

	Cmaj7		G♯m7			G♯m7		Cmaj7
Em:	VImaj7	**E:**	iiim7		**E:**	iiim7	**Em:**	VImaj7

	D♭maj7		Cm7			C♯m7		Dm7
B♭m:	♭IIImaj7	**B♭:**	iim7		**A:**	iiim7	**Am:**	ivm7

	Gmaj7		B♭maj7			Cm7		C♯m7
D:	IVmaj7	**Dm:**	♭VImaj7		**A♭:**	iiim7	**A♭m:**	ivm7

	Fm7		G♭m7			D♭maj7		Emaj7
D♭:	iiim7	**D♭m:**	ivm7		**A♭:**	IVmaj7	**A♭m:**	VImaj7

	Bmaj7		Dmaj7			Amaj7		F♯maj7
F♯:	IVmaj7	**F♯m:**	♭VImaj7		**C♯m:**	VImaj7	**C♯:**	IVmaj7

	Am7		B♭m7			Amaj7		Cmaj7
F:	iiim7	**Fm:**	ivm7		**E:**	IVmaj7	**Em:**	VImaj7

	E♭maj7		G♭maj7			Amaj7		Fm7
B♭:	IVmaj7	**B♭m:**	♭VImaj7		**C♯m:**	VImaj7	**C♯:**	iiim7

	F♯m7		Gm7			Gm7		Bmaj7
D:	iiim7	**Dm:**	ivm7		**E♭:**	iiim7	**E♭m:**	VImaj7

	A♭maj7		Bmaj7			Dmaj7		Cmaj7
E♭:	IVmaj7	**E♭m:**	♭VImaj7		**A:**	IVmaj7	**Am:**	IIImaj7

	D♯m7		Gm7			Dmaj7		Emaj7
B♭m:	ivm7	**B♭:**	vim7		**Bm:**	IIImaj7	**B:**	IVmaj7

	Cmaj7		E♭maj7
G:	IVmaj7	**Gm:**	♭VImaj7

	Cm7		Bm7
Gm:	ivm7	**G:**	iiim7

	Em7		A♭maj7
C:	iiim7	**Cm:**	♭VImaj7

	B♭m7		Bm7
F♯:	iiim7	**F♯m:**	ivm7

	B♭m7		Dmaj7
F♯:	iiim7	**F♯m:**	VImaj7

8. [NO ANSWERS PROVIDED]

Chapter 8 Exercises

1. Each pair of chords below derives from the chord scale indicated. Show one applicable substitute chord for each chord listed. Remember that function does not apply in modal contexts.

Fm7 and B♭7 (F Dorian)	**A♭maj7**	**D⌀7**
Gmaj7 and D7 (G Ionian)	**Bm7**	**F♯⌀**
Am7♭5 and E♭maj7 (E♭ Lydian)	**F7**	**Cm7**
C♯m7 and G♯m7♭5 (A Major)	**Amaj7**	**E7**
Cm7 and B♭maj7 (D Phrygian)	**E♭maj7**	**Gm7**
Fm7♭5 and A♭m⁶ (A♭ Mel. Min.)	**G7alt**	**B♭7sus♭9**
Gmaj7 and A7 (D Major)	**Em7**	**C♯⌀**
Cm(maj7) and B°7 (C Harm. Min.)	**E♭maj7♯5**	**D°7**
B7alt and F13(♯11) (B Altered)	**Cm⁶**	**D7sus♭9**
F♯m7♭5 and Cmaj7(♭5) (F♯ Locrian)	**D7**	**Am⁶**
Fm7♭5 and E♭7 (D♭ Lydian ♭7)	**D♭7**	**B♭m6**
Em7 and Am7 (E Minor)	**Gmaj7**	**Cmaj7**
G♭maj7 and A♭7 (B♭ Minor)	**E♭m7**	**C⌀**
Fmaj7 and G7 (F Lydian)	**Dm7**	**B⌀**

2. Provide tritone substitutes for the following dominant chords.

A♭7	D7	B7	E♭7	G7	C♯7	F7	B♭7	A7	C7	E7
D7	**A♭7**	**F7**	**A7**	**D♭7**	**G7**	**B7**	**E7**	**E♭7**	**F♯7**	**B♭7**

3. Provide tritone substitutions for the following chord progression. Show harmonic analysis.

Gm7	A⌀ A♭(13♯11)	Gm7 G♭7	Fm7 E7	E♭maj7	E⌀ E♭(13♯11)

Gm: im7   ii⌀ SV13♯11 **F:** iim7 SV7 **E♭:**iim7 SV7   Imaj7 **Dm:** ii⌀ SV13♯11

D⌀ D♭(13♯11)	Cm7 C♯(13)	F♯m7 B7	E7 E♭7	D7 A♭(13♯11)	Gm(maj7)

Cm:ii⌀ SV13♯11   im7   **Gm:**<u>V7/ii SV7/V V7   SV13♯11</u> im(maj7)

               B♭:iim7 V13/♭vi ♭vim7   <u>SV7</u> ⟵   *Sequential Dominants*

4. a. Provide chord quality change substitutions for the above chord progression (exercise 3) with harmonic analysis.

| Gm7 | Am7 D13♭9 | G^ø C7alt | F^ø B♭7alt | E♭m§ | Em7 A13 |

Gm: im7 · iim7 · V13♭9 · **F:** ii^ø · V7alt **E♭:** ii^ø · V7alt · im§ **Dm:** iim7 · V13

| Dm7 G13 | C^ø G7alt | Cmaj7 Fmaj7 | B♭maj7 A7 | A♭maj7 D13♭9 | G§ ‖

Cm: iim7 · V13 **B♭:** ii^ø · V7alt/ii · IImaj7 Vmaj7 · Imaj7 **G:**V7/I · ♭IImaj7 V13♭9 · I§

b. Compose a chord progression for F minor blues that includes these chord quality changes: major for minor, dominant for major.

c. Analyze each new chord progression.

Original Fm Blues

‖: Fm | G^ø C7♭9 | Fm | C^ø F7alt |

| B♭m7 | G^ø C7 | Fm7 | D^ø |

| G^ø | C7alt | Fm7 D^ø | G^ø C7alt :‖

Fm Blues with chord quality change: Major for Minor

‖: Fmaj7 | Gm7 C7 | Fmaj7 | Cm7 F7 |

Imaj7 · iim7 V7 · Imaj7 **B♭:** iim7 V7

| B♭maj7 | Gm7 C7 | Am7 | D7 |

Imaj7 **F:** iim7 V7 · iiim7 · V7/ii

| Gm7 | C7alt | Fmaj7 D7 | Gm7 C7alt :‖

iim7 · V7alt · Imaj7 V7/ii · iim7 V7alt

Fm Blues with chord quality change: Dominant for Major

‖: F7 | Gm7 C7 | F7 | Cm7 F7 |

I7 · iim7 V7 · I7 **B♭:** iim7 V7

254 JAZZOLOGY

| Bb7 | Gm7   C7 | Aø | D7alt |

I7   F: iim7   V7   iiiø   V7alt/ii

| Gm7 | C7alt | F7   D7 | Gm7   C7alt :‖

iim7   V7alt   I7   V7/ii   iim7   V7alt

d. Make new chord progressions from the above by using diatonic and tritone substitutions.

Fm Blues with diatonic and tritone substitutions
Chord Progression #1

‖: Fmaj7 | Gm7   Gb7 | Fmaj7 | F#m7   B7 |

| Bbmaj7 | Dbm7   Gb7 | Fmaj7   Gm7 | Am7   Ab7 |

| Dbm7 | Gb(13) | Fmaj7   Ab7 | Db7   Gb7 :‖

Chord Progression #2

‖: Fmaj7 | Bbmaj7   Gb7 | Aø   D7 | Amaj7   B7 |

| Bb7 | Dbm7   C7 | Aø   Gm7 | F7   Ab7 |

| Emaj7 | Bbø | Aø   Cø | Gø   Gb7 :‖

5. Apply diminished 7th chords over the progression given in exercise 3.

| Gm7 | F#°7 | Gm7   C7 | Fm7   Bb7 | Ebmaj7 | C#°7 |

| B°7 | Cm7   G7b9 | C7   F7 | Bb7   A7 | Ab7   D7alt | Gm(maj7) ‖

6. Make diminished substitutions over the progression given in exercise 3.

| Gm7 | Aø   B7b9 | Gm7   Eb7b9 | Fm7   Db7b9 | Ebmaj7 | Eø   Eb7b9 |

| Dø   E7b9 | Cm7   Bb7b9 | A7b9   D7b9 | E7b9   F#7b9 | Ab7   B7b9 | Gm(maj7) ‖

7. Add ii–V's to the following chord progressions and provide harmonic analyses.

a.

Gm7	A$^{\varnothing}$	D7	Gm7	C7	Fm7	B♭7

Gm: i m7   ii$^{\varnothing}$ V7   **F:** iim7   V7   **E♭:** iim7   V7

E♭maj7	D$^{\varnothing}$	G7	Cm7	A♭m7	D♭7

Imaj7 **Cm:** ii$^{\varnothing}$7   V7   im7   ♭vim7   SV7

Cm7	F7	Em7	A7	D7alt	Gmaj7

B♭: iim7   V7   **D:** iim7   V7   **Gm:** V7alt   Imaj7

b.

Fmaj7	E$^{\varnothing}$7	A7	D$^{\varnothing}$7	G7	Cm7	F7

F: Imaj7 **Dm:** ii$^{\varnothing}$7   V7 **Cm:** ii$^{\varnothing}$7   V7 **B♭:** iim7   V7

B♭maj7	B♭m7	E♭7	A♭maj7	Gm7	C7	Fmaj7

Imaj7 **A♭:** iim7   V7   Imaj7 **F:** iim7   V7   Imaj7

c.

Gmaj7	Fm7	B♭7	E♭maj7	C#m7	F#7

G: Imaj7 **E♭:** iim7   V7   Imaj7 **B:** iim7   V7

Bmaj7	B♭$^{\varnothing}$7	E♭7	A♭m6	G$^{\varnothing}$7	C7

Imaj7 **A♭m:** ii$^{\varnothing}$7   V7   im6 **Fm:** ii$^{\varnothing}$7   V7

Fm6	E$^{\varnothing}$7	A7	Dm6	Cm7	F7

im6 **Dm:** ii$^{\varnothing}$7   V7   im6 **B♭:** iim7   V7

B♭maj7	A$^{\varnothing}$7	D7	Gm6

Imaj7 **Gm:** ii$^{\varnothing}$7   V7   im6

8.–10. [NO ANSWERS PROVIDED]

GENERAL BIBLIOGRAPHY

Aebersold, Jamey, and Ken Slone, transcribers and editors. The Charlie Parker *Omnibook*. Atlantic Music Corp., 1978.

—. *Transcribed Piano Voicings, Vol. 1, Jazz: How to Play Jazz and Improvise.* New Albany: Jamey Aebersold, 1992.

—. *The II–V7–I Progression, Vol 3.* New Albany: Jamey Aebersold, 1976.

Acuña, Alex. *Alex Acuña.* Kansas City: Music Source International, 1989.

Armstrong, Louis. *Louis Armstrong's 44 Trumpet Solos and 125 Jazz Breaks.* New York: Edwin H. Morris & Co., 1951.

Adolfo, Antonio. *Brazilian Music Workshop.* Rottenburg: Advance Music, 1993.

Aiken, Jim. "The Blues Scale." *Contemporary Keyboard* 8 (1982): 28–29.

Baker, David. *A Creative Approach to Practicing Jazz: New and Exciting Strategies for Unlocking Your Creative Potential.* New Albany: Jamey Aebersold Jazz, Inc., 1994.

—. *Advanced Ear Training for Jazz Musicians.* Lebanon: Studio P/R, 1977.

—. *Jazz Improvisation. A Comprehensive Method for all Players.* Rev. ed. Bloomington: Frangipani Press, 1983.

—. *Advanced Improvisation.* Chicago: Maher Publications, 1983.

—. *Jazz Pedagogy: A Comprehensive Method of Jazz Education for Teacher and Student.* Chicago: Maher Publications, 1979.

—. "Two Classic Louis Armstrong Solos." Downbeat 1971.

Banacos, Charlie. *Pentatonic Scale Improvisation.* Dracut: Charles Banacos Music, 1972.

Barr, Walter. "The Salsa Rhythm Section." *NAJE Educator* 12 (1970/1980): 15–18; 48–50.

Barron, William. "Improvisation and Related Concepts in Aesthetic Education." Diss. U of Massachusetts, 1975.

Benedetti, Vince. *Melody in Jazz Improvisation.* Publishing information unavailable.

Bergonzi, Jerry. *Melodic Structure.* Rottenburg: Advance Music, 1992.

—. *Pentatonics.* Rottenburg: Advance Music, 1994.

—. *Jazz Line.* Rottenburg: Advance Music, 1996.

Berliner, Paul. *Thinking in Jazz: the Infinite Art of Improvisation.* Chicago: U of Chicago P, 1994.

Bicket, Fiona. "Improvisation: How Barry Harris Teaches Bebop." *Piano Stylist* Oct./Nov. 1998: 4–5.

Bishop, Walter. *A Study in Fourths.* New York: Caldon Publishing, 1976.

Blake, John. *Beginning to Improvise.* Westford: JIME Publications, 1993.

Blake, Ran. "The Monk Piano Style." *Keyboard Magazine* July 1982: 26–30.

Blanq, Charles Clement. "Melodic Improvisation in American Jazz; the Style of Theodore 'Sonny' Rollins, 1951–1962." Diss. Tulane U, 1997.

Boling, Mark. *The Jazz Theory Workbook.* Rottenburg: Advance Music, 1990.

Brandt, Carl, and Clinton Roemer. *Standardized Chord Symbol Notation.* Sherman Oaks: Roerick Music, 1976.

Buhles, Gunter. "Atonalität und Jazz." *HiFi Sterophonie* 18 (1979): 1732–1738.

—. "Thelonious Monk: Jazz Composer." *Jazz Podium* 27 (1978): 21–22.

Coker, Jerry, Bob Knapp, and Larry Vincent. *Hearing the Changes.* Rottenburg: Advance Music, 1996.

—. *Complete Method for Improvisation.* Miami, FL: Warner Bros., 1997.

—. *The Teaching of Jazz.* Rottenburg: Advance Music, 1989.

—. *Elements of the Jazz Language for the Developing Improviser.* CPP/Belwin, 1991.

—. *Improvising Jazz.* Englewood Cliffs: Prentice-Hall, 1964.

Coltrane, John. *The Music of John Coltrane.* Milwaukee: Hal Leonard, 1991.

Coltrane, John, and Don DeMichael. "Coltrane on Coltrane." *Downbeat* 27, no.20 (9/29/60): 26–27.

Combs, Ronald, and Robert Bowker. *Learning to Sing Non-Classical Music.* Englewood Cliffs: Prentice-Hall, 1995.

Crook, Hal. *How to Improvise.* Rottenburg: Advance Music, 1991.

—. *How to Comp.* Rottenburg: Advance Music, 1995.

Davis, Miles, and Quincy Troupe. *Miles: the Autobiography.* New York: Simon and Schuster, 1989.

Delp, Ron. "Contemporary Harmony: Guide Tones in Improvisation." *Musician, Player & Listener* 19 (1979): 70.

—. "Contemporary Harmony: Progression – Guide Tones." *ibid.,* 17 (1979):72.

—. "Contemporary Harmony: More on Guide Tones." *ibid.,* 18 (1979):72.

—. "Contemporary Harmony: Arranging, Harmonizing a Melody." *ibid.,* 22–27 (1980): 82, 90, 96, 110.

Demsey, Dave. "Chromatic Third Relations in the Music of John Coltrane." *Annual Review of Jazz Studies* (1991): 145–180.

DeGreg, Phil. *Jazz Keyboard Harmony.* New Albany: Jamey Aebersold, 1994.

DeVeaux, Scott. "Bebop and the Recording Industry. The 1942 AFM Recording Ban Reconsidered." *Journal of the American Musicology Society* 41, No.1 (1988): 126–65.

—. *The Birth of Bebop.* Berkeley: Univ. of California Press, 1997.

Dial, Gary. "Harmony: the Harmonic Minor." *Piano Stylist,* Oct./Nov. 1989: 20.

DiBlasio, Denis. *A Survival Guide for Scat Vocalists.* New Albany: Jamey Aebersold Jazz, 2000.

—. *Jazz Figures for Individual and Group Performance.* Lebanon: Houston Publishing, Inc., 1998.

—. *Basic Workout Drills for Creative Jazz Improvisation.* Lebanon: Houston Publishing, Inc., 1993.

—. *DiBlasio's Bop Shop: Getting Started in Improvisation.* Delevan: Kendor Music, 1986.

Dobbins, Bill. *A Creative Approach to Jazz Piano Harmony.* Rottenburg: Advance Music, 1991.

—. *Jazz Arranging and Composing: A Linear Approach.* Rottenburg: Advance Music, 1991.

—. *The Contemporary Jazz Pianist.* 4 vols. New York: Charles Colin, 1984.

—. Transcriber. *Herbie Hancock: Classic Compositions and Piano Solos.* Rottenburg: Advance Music, 1992.

—. Transcriber. *Chick Corea: Now He Sings, Now He Sobs.* Rottenburg: Advance Music, 1992.

Doershuck, Bob. "Thelonious Monk." *Keyboard Magazine* July 1982: 11–16.

Dunbar, Ted. *A System of Tonal Convergence for Improvisers, Composers, and Arrangers.* Kendall Park: Dunte Pub. Co., 1975.

Earnshaw, Mickey. *The Essence of Rhythm.* Hal Leonard, 1994.

Fujioka, Yasuhiro, Lewis Porter, and Yoh-ichi Hamada. *John Coltrane. A Discography and Musical Biography.* Lanham: Scarecrow Press, 1995.

Garcia, Russell. *The Professional Arranger Composer.* Criterion: 1954.

Genna, George. *George Genna's Jazz Stylings.* West Trenton: Musicians Publications, 2004.

Gillespie, Luke. *Stylistic II–V–I Voicings for Keyboardists.* Jamey Aebersold, 2000.

Goldberg, Norbert. "South of the Border: the Mambo." *Modern Drummer* 3 (1979): 36–37.

Goldstein, Gil. *The Jazz Composer's Companion.* Rev. ed. Rottenburg: Advance Music, 1993.

Gridley, Mark. *Jazz Styles.* Englewood Cliffs: Prentice-Hall, 1985.

Grove, Dick. *Basic Harmony and Theory as Applied to Improvisation.* Studio City: Dick Grove Publications, 1971.

Haerle, Dan. *Scales for Improvisation.* Studio P/R, 1975.

—. *The Jazz Language.* Miami, FL: Warner Bros., 1982.

—. *Jazz Piano Voicing Skills.* New Albany: Jamey Aebersold, 1994.

—. *The Jazz Sound.* Milwaukee: Hal Leonard, 1989.

Handy, William Christopher, ed. *Blues: An Anthology.* New York: A. & C. Boni, 1926.

Haywood, Mark. "The Harmonic Role of Melody in Vertical and Horizontal Jazz." *Annual Review of Jazz Studies.* 1991: 111–120.

Hodier, Andre. *Jazz: Its Evolution and Essence.* Da Capo, 1975.

Honshuku, Hiroaki. *Jazz Theory I & II.* Cambridge, Mass.: A-NO-NE Music, 1997.

Incencio, Rivera. *The Bass Player's Guide for Modern Latin Rhythms.* Boston: Reno Music, 1979.

Jaffe, Andrew. *Jazz Harmony.* Rottenburg: Advance Music, 1996.

—. *Jazz Theory.* Dubuque: W.C. Brown, 1983.

Jones, Arthur. *Morris Studies in African Music.* 2 vols. New York: Oxford UP, 1959.

Keller, Gary. *Sonny Stitt's Greatest Transcribed Solos.* Lebanon: Houston Publishing, 1990.

Kernfield, Barry, ed. *New Grove Dictionary of Jazz.* 2 Vols. London: Macmillian, 1988.

—. "Two Coltranes." *Annual Review of Jazz Studies* 1983: 7–66.

Koch, Lawrence. "Ornithology, a Study of Charlie Parker's Music, Part 1." *Journal of Jazz Studies* 2 (1974): 61–87.

—. "Ornithology, a Study of Charlie Parker's Music, Part 2." *Journal of Jazz Studies* 2 (1975): 61–85.

—. "Harmonic Approaches to the Twelve-Bar Blues Form." *Annual Review of Jazz Studies* 1982: 59–71.

—. "Thelonious Monk: Compositional Techniques." *Annual Review of Jazz Studies* 1983: 67–80.

Kofsky, Frank. "Elvin Jones, Part 1: Rhythmic Innovator." *Journal of Jazz Studies* 4 (1976): 3–24.

—. "Elvin Jones, Part 2: Rhythmic Displacement in the Art of Elvin Jones". *ibid.,* 4 (1977): 11–32.

Kunkel, Jeffrey. "Jazz Piano Workshop: A Hyper Database for Jazz Piano Pedagogy (MacIntosh)." Diss. Pennsylvania State U, 1995.

Kuzmich, John. "Survey of Teaching Materials for Jazz Improvisation." Manhattan: IAJE Publications, 1990.

LaBarbera, Pat. "Diatonic 7th Chords and Modes." *Canadian Musician* 2 (1980): 64.

—. "Playing on Changes." *ibid.,* 67.

—. "Extensions & Alterations on ii-7, V7, IMaj 7." *ibid.,* 64.

Lateef, Yusef. *Repository of Scales and Melodic Patterns.* Amherst: Fana Music, 1981.

Laverne, Andy. "Bill Evans' 'Twelve-Tone Tune' for Solo Piano." *Jazz & Keyboard Workshop,* Nov. 87: 1, 27.

Lawn, Richard, and Jeffrey Helmer. *Jazz Theory and Practice.* Belmont: Wadsworth Publishing, 1993.

Lax, Roger, and Frederick Smith. *The Great Song Thesaurus.* 2nd ed. New York: Oxford UP, 1989.

Levine, Mark. *The Jazz Piano Book.* Petaluma: Sher Music Co., 1989.

—. *The Jazz Theory Book.* Petaluma: Sher Music Co., 1995.

Leymarie, Isabelle. "Rhythm: Montunos & Mambos – More Latin Rhythmic Devices." *Jazz Keyboard Workshop* Vol. 1, #5, 1986: 8–9.

Ligon, Bert. *Connecting Chords with Linear Harmony.* Milwaukee: Hal Leonard, 1999.

Lord, Tom. "The Jazz Discography." Vols. 1–7. West Vancouver: Lord Music Reference Inc., 1992–94.

Markewich, Reese. *The New Expanded Bibliography of Jazz Compositions Based on the Chord Progressions of Standard Tunes.* Plesantville: Markewich, 1974.

—. *Inside Out: Substitute Harmony in Jazz and Pop Music.* New York: n.p. 1967.

Martin, Henry. "Jazz Harmony: A Syntactic Background." *Annual Review of Jazz Studies* 1988: 9–30.

—. *Charlie Parker and Thematic Improvisation.* Paper. Fifty-Eighth Annual Meeting of the AMS, Pittsburgh, 1992.

Mauleon, Rebeca. *The Complete Salsa Guidebook.* Petaluma: Sher Music Co., 1993.

Meadows, Eddie. "Improvising Jazz: A Beginner's Guide." *Music Educator's Journal* Dec. 1991: 41–44.

—. *Prolegomenon to the Music of Horace Silver.* Jazzforschung/Jazz Research 18 (1986): 123–32.

Miedama, Harry. *Jazz Styles and Analysis: Alto Sax.* Chicago: Maher Publications, 1975.

Mehegan, John. *Jazz Improvisations.* 4 vols. Watson-Guptill Publications, 1962–77.

Metzger, David. *Finale and Jazz Arranging for the Macintosh.* Salem: David Metzger, 1993.

Miller, Lloyd. "African and Turkish Roots of Jazz – Roots of the Blues." *IAJE Research Papers* 1990: 61–74.

Miller, Ron. *Modal Jazz Compositions and Harmony, Vol. 1.* Rottenburg: Advance Music, 1992.

—. *Modal Jazz Compositions and Harmony, Vol. 2.* Rottenburg: Advance Music, 1997.

Nelson, Oliver. *Patterns for Improvisation.* New Lebanon: Jamey Aebersold, 1996.

Nestico, Sammy. *The Complete Arranger.* Delevan: Kendor Music, 1993.

Nettles, Barrie, and Richard Graf. *The Chord Scale Theory and Jazz Harmony.* Rottenburg: Advance Music, 1997.

Novello, John. "Improvisation: Getting Acquainted with Giant Steps." *Jazz & Keyboard Workshop* April/May 1987: 10–11.

Owens, Thomas. "Charlie Parker Techniques of Improvisation." Diss. UCLA, 1974.

Parrish, Avery. Transcribed by Roy Blakeman. "After Hours." *Piano Stylist.* Oct/Nov. 1989: 26–28.

Pass, Joe. *Chord Encounters of Guitar, Book I: Blues, Chords and Substitutions.* Los Angeles: Charles Hansen, II, Music and Books of California, 1979.

Porter, Lewis. "John Coltrane's Music of 1960–67: Jazz Improvisation as Composition." Diss. Brandeis U, 1983.

Rawlins, Robert. *A Simple and Direct Guide to Jazz Improvisation.* Milwaukee: Hal Leonard, 1995.

Reeves, Scott. *Creative Jazz Improvisation.* Englewood Cliffs: Prentice-Hall, 1989.

Ricker, Ramon. *The Ramon Ricker Improvisation Series, Vol. 1: The Beginner Improviser.* Rottenburg: Advance Music, 1996.

—. *The Ramon Ricker Improvisation Series, Vol. 2: Blues.* Rottenburg: Advance Music, 1996.

—. *The Ramon Ricker Improvisation Series, Vol. 3: The II–V–I Progression, Rhythm Changes, and Standard Tunes.* Rottenburg: Advance Music, 1996.

—. *Pentatonic Scales for Jazz Improvisation.* Hialeah: Studio P/R, 1976.

Rinzler, Paul. *Jazz Arranging and Performance Practice.* Lanham: Scarecrow Press, 1989.

—. "McCoy Tyner: Style and Syntax." *Annual Review of Jazz Studies* 1983: 109–49.

Roberts, Howard, and Jerry Hagberg. *Guitar Compendium, Vol. 1–3.* Rottenburg: Advance Music, 1989.

Robbins, James. Review. "Themes Composed by Jazz Musicians of the Bebop Era: A Study of Harmony, Rhythm, and Melody." *Bulletin of the Council for Research in Music Education* 1987: 65–73.

Russell, Ross, ed. Martin Williams. *Bebop in the Art of Jazz: Essays on the Nature and Development of Jazz Education.* New York: Oxford UP: 1959, 187–214.

Russo, William. *Jazz Composition and Orchestration.* Chicago: U of Chicago P, 1961.

—. *Composing for the Jazz Orchestra.* Chicago: U of Chicago P, 1961.

Sauls, Noreen. "Turning Modes into Melodies." *Piano Stylist* April/May 1989: 10–11.

Schuller, Gunther. *Early Jazz: Its Roots and Musical Development.* New York: Oxford P, 1968.

—. "Sonny Rollins and the Challenge of Thematic Improvisation" in: *Musings, The Musical World of Gunther Schuller.* New York: Oxford UP, 1986: 8–97.

Shanaphy, Edward. "Harmony: The New Chord Symbols." *Jazz & Keyboard Workshop, Vol.1, #1* 1986: 1–5.

—. "Tricks of the Trade: Count Basie Blues Riffs." *Jazz & Keyboard Workshop, Vol.1, #3,* 15–16.

Shaw, Woody. "My Approach to the Trumpet and Jazz." *Crescendo International* 15 (1976/77): 14–15.

Sher, Chuck. *The New Real Book.* Petaluma: Sher Music Company, 1991.

Shipton, Alyn. *A New History of Jazz.* London and N.Y.: Continuum Books, 2001.

Slonimsky, Nicholas. *Thesaurus of Scales and Melodic Patterns.* New York: Scribners, 1947.

Smallwood, Richard. "Gospel and Blues Improvisation." *Music Educators Journal* 66 (1980): 100–104.

Steinel, Mike. *Building a Jazz Vocabulary.* Milwaukee: Hal Leonard, 1995.

—. *Essential Elements for Jazz Ensemble.* Milwaukee: Hal Leonard, 2000.

Stewart, Milton Lee. "Structural Development in the Jazz Improvisational Technique of Clifford Brown." Diss. U of Michigan, 1973.

—. "Some Characteristics of Clifford Brown's Improvisational Style." *Jazzforschung/Jazz Research* 11 (1979): 135–64.

Strunk, Steven. "Bebop Melodic Lines." *Annual Review of Jazz Studies* 1985: 97–120.

—. "The Harmony of Early Bop: A Layered Approach." *Journal of Jazz Studies* 6 (1979): 4–53.

Sturm, Fred. *Changes over Time: The Evolution of Jazz Arranging*. Rottenburg, Advance Music, 1995.

Taylor, Billy. "Jazz Improvisation: Melodic Invention." *Contemporary Keyboard* 6 (1980): 82.

—. "Jazz Improvisation: Learning to Improvise, Part 1: Introductions." *ibid.*, 68.

—. "Jazz Improvisation, Part 2: Harmonic Resources." *ibid.*, 53.

—. "Jazz Improvisation, Part 3: Rhythmic Devices." *ibid.*, 67.

—. "Jazz Improvisation: Bebop, Part 1." *Contemporary Keyboard* 6 (1980): 74.

—. "Chord Substitutions." *ibid.*, 56.

—. "Jazz Improvisation: the Clave." *Contemporary Keyboard* 5 (1979): 63.

—. "Jazz Improvisation: Blues Piano." *ibid.*, 72.

—. *Jazz Piano: a Jazz History*. W. C. Brown, 1983.

Thomas, J.C.. *Chasin' the Trane: The Music and Mystique of John Coltrane*. Doubleday, 1975.

Tirro, Frank. *Jazz: A History*. New York: W.W. Norton, 1977.

Ulahla, Ludmila. *Contemporary Harmony: Romanticism Through the Twelve-Tone Row*. Rottenburg: Advance Music, 1995.

Voigt, Jon, Randall Kane. *Jazz Music in Print and Jazz Books in Print*. Winthrop, 1982.

Wang, Richard. "Jazz Circa 1945: A Confluence of Style." *Musical Quarterly* 59, #4: 531–46.

White, Andrew. *The Works of John Coltrane*. 10 vols. Washington: Andrew's Music, 1973–8.

Wolking, Henry. "Jazz Theory and Functional Harmony." *NAJE Educator* 11 (1979): 82–83.

Woods, Phil. *Jazz Tutor. Vol. 1*. Ridgewood: MasterClass Productions, 1994.

Wright, Rayburn. *Inside the Score*. Delevan: Kendor Music Co., 1982.

ABOUT THE AUTHORS

Nor Eddine Bahha
Composer; Arranger; Jazz, African, and Arabic Music Researcher

This book is the fruit of my own practice and research in jazz music over the past ten years. Never having had any institutional training in harmony and theory, but with a deep desire to learn and understand, I attempted to acquire and organize all of the information I could find about this subject. Two overriding questions intrigued me from the outset: how does jazz harmony work and how do jazz musicians and arrangers acquire and develop their skills? Perhaps the real answer to the second question is life-long practice.

It took me three years of continuous work to complete this project. I hope the material contained in this book will be useful to all jazz enthusiasts seeking to improve their knowledge and skills. Moreover, I hope that the theoretical knowledge provided will assist all musicians in making the artistic choices necessary for improvising, composing, and arranging in the jazz idiom. Finally, it is my sincere desire that the information contained in this book will encourage readers to continue to study and learn all they can about this music. *Jazzology* includes a wealth of material on jazz theory, common skills associated with jazz musicians, useful terms, and a myriad of techniques for speaking the jazz language effectively. It is intended both as a compendium of information on jazz and as a springboard for further study and exploration.

I dedicate this work to the memory of my father and to my musical family; my mother, brothers, and sisters, my faithful friends: Hassan Attifi, Rachid El Hachimi, and Abdelkrim El Hattab. Also, I give my sincere and deep acknowledgements to Hanks Tresser, Hiroaki Honshuku, and Mike Nelson, for their kind permission in allowing the use of their material. I'm so grateful to Jamey Aebersold, Chuck Sher, David Liebman, Dominic Alldis, Mark Levine, Phil DeGreg, Ralph Patt, Richard J. Lawn, Scott Reeves, Richard Graf, and Vince Benedetti.

I must also thank my very good friends Andy Jaffe and Armin Keil for their very kind guidance and support, and my faithful friend Robert Rawlins, who worked closely with me throughout the writing of this book. It was a successful collaboration and I thank him for his support. To all those who contributed directly or indirectly to this book, "I can't thank you enough!"

On a personal note, I would like to acknowledge my brother-in-law Erwan Le Pape and his wife, Khadija Le Pape Bahha for their very kind encouragement and support.

Peace.
Nor Eddine Bahha
Jazz Keyboard Composer, Copyist,
Researcher, Member, and Teacher
at Karawen Music School, Morocco

Robert Rawlins

Robert Rawlins grew up in New Jersey where he began playing the saxophone at the age of 11. This was the beginning of a long and exciting musical journey that would result in a wide variety of musical experiences. During his high school years he played in a traditional jazz band that modeled themselves on the Austin High Gang of the 1920s, adopting the name "The New Chicago Rhythm Kings." His college years were marked by an absolute fascination with the music of Charlie Parker, during which time he transcribed literally hundreds of Parker's solos.

College was followed by serious study of the other woodwind instruments—clarinet with Harold Karabell of Philadelphia and flute with Adeline Tomasone of Philadelphia and Harold Bennett of New York. After a few years of big-band freelancing, during which time he worked with leaders such as Sammy Kaye, Bob Crosby, Ray McKinley, and Les Elgart, Rawlins then embarked on a 20-year stint as a full-time musician working the showrooms and theaters of Atlantic City and Philadelphia. Rawlins's varied musical experiences over this period also included jobs as a classical flutist, a jazz saxophonist, a Dixieland clarinetist, and frequent performances with the Philly Pops.

During his years as a professional musician, Rawlins continued his formal education, completing three master's degrees and a Ph.D. in Musicology. He began teaching at Rowan University in 1997 and became department chairman in 2003.

Rawlins has written numerous articles and books on various aspects of music theory, history, and performance. His current research interests are jazz theory and jazz history. He can be reached at rawlinsr@rowan.edu.

Personal Note:
When Nor Eddine first contacted me three years ago to discuss jazz theory issues, I had no idea that our email exchanges would culminate in a full-length book, but that is precisely what happened. The collaboration was fruitful from the beginning. As a Moroccan keyboard player with a deep knowledge of his region's music and culture, Nor was able to provide me with an entirely new perspective on the music I thought I knew so well. Conversely, my training in traditional European music theory coupled with my university teaching experience provided Nor with insights that were previously less available to him. As I recall, it was I who suggested at some point, "Why don't we write a book?" Nor took the initiative immediately and began work on the project. Our email conversations eventually turned into large file transfers and ultimately the completed work. I enjoyed our collaboration immensely and am greatly indebted to Nor for his expertise, commitment, and hard work.

I would like to gratefully dedicate this book to my wife, Nancy, for her assistance in preparing and editing the manuscript as well as her patience and understanding throughout this project. Additionally, I would like to acknowledge my colleague Denis DiBlasio, my ever-ready jazz consultant, who is always willing to share his great gift for reducing the most abstract concepts down to their most lucid terms.

Robert Rawlins

The authors would like to thank Jeff Brent for contributing to the accuracy of this book.